LAURA RIDING & ROBERT GRAVES

Essays from *Epilogue*

LAURA (RIDING) JACKSON (1901–1991) is among the most influential yet misread writers of the twentieth century. She renounced poetry after her *Collected Poems* appeared in 1938 and after she had written a body of work which left its mark upon Auden, Ashbery and many others. Her collaborations and her own essays, stories and poems are central to the creative and critical debate surrounding twentieth-century English and American literature. A great deal of her work is still being published.

ROBERT GRAVES (1895–1985) was a major lyric poet and – as the monumental three-volume *Complete Poems* (1995–9) demonstrates – an enormously prolific one. He was also an unusually versatile writer of prose: his works include historical novels, reworkings of mythology, the celebrated autobiography *Goodbye to All That* and *The White Goddess* (subtitled 'A Grammar of Poetic Myth'), as well as a wide range of literary criticism, some of which originated in these *Epilogue* essays.

MARK JACOBS, born in 1941, attended the Universities of York and Leicester, writing his doctoral thesis on Laura (Riding) Jackson and corresponding with her from 1971 to her death. He is a member of the Laura (Riding) Jackson Literary Board and has previously published three works on her poetry. He has been a poet and joint editor of *Omens*.

LAURA RIDING AND ROBERT GRAVES

Essays from 'Epilogue' 1935–1937

Edited by Mark Jacobs

CARCANET

First published in *Epilogue* 1935–1937
This edition published in Great Britain in 2001 by
Carcanet Press Limited
4th Floor, Conavon Court
12–16 Blackfriars Street
Manchester M3 5BQ

A CIP catalogue record for this book
is available from the British Library
ISBN 1 85754 516 4

The publisher acknowledges financial
assistance from the Arts Council of England

Set in Ehrhardt by XL Publishing Services, Tiverton
Printed and bound in England by SRP Ltd, Exeter

Contents

Introduction by Mark Jacobs   vii

Preliminaries *by Laura Riding*   1
The Idea of God *by Thomas Matthews and Laura Riding*   5
    Supplementary Argument *by Laura Riding and Thomas Matthews*   29
Nietzsche *by Madeleine Vara*   38
Poems and Poets *by Laura Riding with questions and comments*
    by Robert Graves   48
Coleridge and Wordsworth *by Robert Graves*   58
Keats and Shelley *by Robert Graves*   66
A Note on the Pastoral *by Robert Graves*   72
Homiletic Studies *by Laura Riding*   78
    Stealing *by Robert Graves*   80
    In Defence of Anger *by Laura Riding*   88
The Exercise of English *by Laura Riding and Robert Graves*   101
The Bull-Fight *by Laura Riding*   120
Lucretius and Jeans *by Robert Graves*   130
The Literary Intelligence *by Laura Riding*   141
Neo-Georgian Eternity *by Robert Graves*   149
George Sand *by Madeleine Vara*   158
From a Private Correspondence on Reality *by Laura Riding*
    and Robert Graves   164

Notes   181
Appendix   189
Index of Names   193

Dedicated to
Hazel and Asche
for their help,
for their patience...

Introduction

THE THREE VOLUMES of the now quite rare *Epilogue* – represented here – were edited by Laura Riding, with Robert Graves described as 'Assistant Editor' on the title-page of the first volume but as 'Associate Editor' on its cover, and as 'Associate Editor' in both places on the next two. Laura Riding's written contribution was, in quantity, roughly twice that of Robert Graves. Other contributors included John Cullen, James Reeves, Honor Wyatt, Len Lye, Thomas Matthews, John Aldridge, Ward Hutchinson, Norman Cameron, Kenneth Allott, Alan Hodge, Sally Graves and Jacob Bronowski, all of whom later became widely known and respected for their work in their various fields.

Epilogue was a handsome octavo hard-back periodical, which had a John Aldridge engraving of a stage with figures imprinted on the front board (in the style of those he executed for Laura Riding's poem, 'The Life of the Dead'); each volume is about 250 pages in length. It was published jointly by Riding and Graves's Seizin Press and Constable. Three volumes appeared (1935, 1936, 1937), and the fourth was presented as a book, *The World and Ourselves* (1938), described as a 'Symposium on State of World, Edited with Commentaries, by Laura Riding'.

The principles, vision and editorial scope of *Epilogue* were Laura Riding's, as the editor. However, as she was keen to make clear in the prefatorial 'Preliminaries' of Volume I, everything that appeared was to be the result of 'collaborative arrangement' between editors and contributors. Thus, all the essays are either collaborations between two or more authors, or have footnotes and endnotes by other contributors. Even the 'primary material' of the poems, stories, photographs and art has some collaborative element, whether of direct comment or arrangement.

The level of interest in the work of both Laura Riding and Robert Graves, as witnessed by the number of their books currently being reprinted, republished or newly published, is high, and this selection of essays from *Epilogue*, focusing exclusively on work by the two authors, reflects that interest; most of these essays have not been republished until now. *Epilogue*, however, is unique in several respects. Unlike other collaborative work published by the two, such as *A Survey of Modernist Poetry*

(1927), *A Pamphlet against Anthologies* (1928) or their translation of George Schwarz's *Almost Forgotten Germany* (1936), which are almost seamlessly collaborative, what may be observed here is some of the behind-the-scenes working-practice of Laura Riding and Robert Graves which underpinned their almost legendary partnership between 1926, when they first met, and 1939, when they parted. It stimulates some interesting questions, too, not just on the work of that period but on what followed, in the very different directions both authors took in their subsequent writings. Thus, the first essay here, 'The Idea of God', which is also the opening essay of *Epilogue I*, exemplifies Laura Riding's intellectually rich view of not just God but woman; it contradicts the mythologising of a number of Gravesian commentators in their frequently overstated – in this light – views of Laura Riding; and it illuminates Graves's later theorising in *The White Goddess* (1948). Similarly, the essay 'The Exercise of English' by both authors points us towards Riding's concentration upon language, particularly after 1940, and towards her and Schuyler Jackson's book *Rational Meaning* (1997); it also contains the germ of such books as Graves's and Alan Hodge's *The Reader Over Your Shoulder* (1943), as well as later work of Graves, where he focuses closely on the contextual meaning of words, as in his Cambridge and Oxford lectures.

It is, as a matter of fact, extraordinary that critics and commentators on the work of Riding and Graves have failed to study the *Epilogue* volumes for the light they throw on the two authors. In Riding's case, in the two books which have been published on her work (by Joyce Wexler, 1979, and Barbara Adams, 1990, respectively, both of which books she discountenanced), mention of *Epilogue* is less than perfunctory. In Graves's case, critical and biographical books have multiplied over recent decades, but *Epilogue*, with the rarest exception, although it might be cited, is nowhere critically examined or discussed as a possible source of his later work.

Epilogue represents a crucial stage of development in both its editors' work. For Laura (Riding) Jackson, it signals her increasing preoccupation with language and with words as the pivotal centre of the advancement of the human mind to fullness and completeness of utterance (expression) and thus to understanding of the human position in the universe, looking towards such subsequent major books of hers as *The Telling* (1972) and her and her husband's *Rational Meaning*. For Robert Graves, it became a seed-bed for his ensuing books, from *The Reader Over Your Shoulder* and *The White Goddess*, to *King Jesus* (1946), his and Joshua Podro's *The Nazarene Gospels Restored* (1953), and the better part of his later critical work on poetry, much of which takes its impetus and its distinctiveness from the *Epilogue* volumes.

The essays in *Epilogue* are rigorous, tough, complex. They make no concessions to literary flourish, and are written in plain, jargon-free English. The complexity is that of deliberate hard thinking. In a note of

1974 on *Epilogue* (in the Berg Collection), Laura Jackson writes:

> 'The Work' was how I called the complex of activities of study and treatment in critical unity that I conceived as a rallying ground for the association of writers in a new modern coherence of purpose; my conception involved devotion to an objective of introducing a new order of truth into literature – truth as the general end of literature, humanly and linguistically, not as a moral by-product of literary art. This vision of mine of a practical spiritual rehabilitation that became pressingly obvious in the first half of the 'thirties' at first resolved itself into an idea of a continuous work of co-ordinated writing-activity that I thought of as a Critical Vulgate; indeed, before the project took on a final, definite form as a literary project I called it, loosely, the 'Vulgate'... privately and informally referred to by myself, and jointly so with me by my associates in it, as 'The Work'.

The aim, as 'Preliminaries' makes clear, is no less than to lay to final rest those unanswered, although much speculated on, questions about human life still lying clutteringly about, moving from the uncertainties of the nature of God, to language, poetry, politics, the anxiety over Germany as it presented itself in the 1930s, the nature and meaning of 'reality', and such personal concerns as honesty, anger, bull-fighting, and literature in general. (Essays not presented in this selection include those on drama, philosophy, films, photography, crime, humour and advertising.) Just thirteen essays are reprinted here (or fourteen if 'Preliminaries' is counted), and they have been selected to represent as wide a range as possible in terms of subject-matter and style of the two editors. One of these, that on Nietzsche, is signed 'M.V.', as are a number of the footnotes. This is 'Madeleine Vara'. Just as arguments have arisen over the question of who-wrote-what in the two authors' earlier collaborations, *A Survey of Modernist Poetry* (1927) and *A Pamphlet against Anthologies* (1928), in *Epilogue*, one controversy among others has been over the pseudonym 'Madeleine Vara', which appears throughout the volumes as an author. Robert Graves first implicitly claimed the 'Madeleine Vara' essay, 'Nietzsche', from *Epilogue I*, by republishing it in his *The Common Asphodel* (1949), and later in the USA and Penguin editions (1956; 1959) of *The Crowning Privilege*: in each of these books it is included among the 'Essays From *Epilogue*' without mention of its original signature. In 1966, Graves's bibliographer F.H. Higginson first claimed 'Madeleine Vara' as a Seizin/*Epilogue* 'house pseudonym'. Commentating on this eight years later – 1974, cited in Higginson's second edition, 1987 – Laura (Riding) Jackson stated unequivocally that the name was her pseudonym alone, for all work that appeared under it. While several Gravesian critics and commentators have accepted Higginson's original account, they do not seem to have asked why the Nietzsche essay should have remained (as it has) the sole Vara item claimed for Graves, nor to have taken account of the existence of *Convalescent Conversations*, the book-length story by 'Madeleine Vara' published in 1936 (the year after the Nietzsche essay) with the authorial name certainly used there specifically as a pseudonym for Laura Riding. It is not my intention to pursue this controversy further, but I have included the essay 'Nietzsche' by 'Madeleine Vara', so that readers can make up their own minds as to whether the author is Robert Graves or Laura Riding.

I have kept in general to the layout and format of the original *Epilogue* volumes, in terms of the authors' order of names, the use of authors' initials rather than full names at the end of essays, separate parts of the essays and in the notes; and the numbering of sections of essays as they fall into parts. The notes, however, I have now placed as endnotes, in keeping with modern practice, and not footnotes, as in the original essays. I have also kept to *Epilogue*'s spelling, which is not much different from contemporary usage except in minor points, for instance, the use of 'z' instead of 's' in such words as 'criticized', 'moralized', etc.

There are a number of essays I should have liked to have included, such as the extraordinary one on 'Crime', which sweeps from Chandler and Hammett to Hamlet, Greek theatre, Faulkner and Hemingway; and 'Drama', from the classic to the contemporary; 'Politics', which sums up the whole left-right problem – and others. They are as pertinent and fresh now as then. But space forbids.

MARK JACOBS

PRELIMINARIES

Laura Riding

Now time has reached the flurrying curtain-fall
That wakens thought from historied reverie
And gives the word to uninfected discourse.

CRITICAL EXAMINATION, WHATEVER the subject, must begin where there is most confusion; and with the simplest possible object – precision. Our general subject is thought, and the most chaotic elements of thought are ideas; we begin at ideas. And our object is first of all a statistical one: to survey ideas in their numerical abundance. Ideas are emotional interpretations of truth. People whose thought is not emotionally determined do not 'have ideas' – interpret – behave; they have wisdom rather than ideas. Wisdom consists of what we may call 'recognitions' – recognitions of truth. Such recognitions are the most homogeneous elements of thought; wisdom is the equivalence of thought with truth, which is unity. Wisdom has unity, as truth is unity.

An idea is a short-cut in thought motivated by historical ends; however reasonable it may seem, it obscures truth because it expresses only that part of it which it is at the moment convenient to know. Ideas, though elements of thought, whose function it is to discover truth, pervert truth in expressing it; the sum of ideas is not wisdom but confusion. Ideas can be only historically true, by their subservience to historical ends. We must be aware of these ends in defining ideas, for it is as agents of history, not of truth, that they have reality: as agents of truth they have an equivocal reality. Thus we can clarify a standard of reality – by making thought seek its level in the range from historical to absolute reality.

*

In the sense that we shall explore the historical entirety of thought as conscientiously as a newspaper travels its world for news, we ought to have for the reader who is interested in 'everything' something of the attraction that a newspaper has, in its unstinted expansiveness. Nor shall the reader be presumed to be a particular kind of reader: either a heavy or a light reader; or yet the reader who is not so much interested in news itself as in the way in which it is reported – the 'literary' reader. Nor shall we give merely the most recent news, with yesterday's or last year's background left irritatingly to the chance of memory or scholarly enterprise. We plan to give all the news, and in the tranquillity of knowing that there is no new news to come, and the leisure to open the files at any day, at any subject. All the Chinese bandits having chopped off all the foreign ears, we have time to consider not only the subject *Atrocity*, but the subject *Bandits*, and the subject *Missionaries*, and the subject *Foreigners*, and the subject *Chinese*. All the politicians who are going to be elected have been elected; and all the artificial excitement in events which no one really regards as either very important or very interesting has been exhausted. All the historical events have happened. And we shall report them without calculating whether the reader is interested in this as against that; one more interested in Finance than in Religion, or another more interested in Poetry than in Science, or another more in Politics than in Art.

*

We do not mean to create or anticipate particular kinds of reactions to our findings; and in this we imitate the mood of a court of justice rather than of a newspaper. A court has an extensive patience with all the minutiæ of evidence and argument, and assumes in those present no different mood from its own. The mood of a court is a coherent attention to the case before it. We mean to maintain the mood of a court, in the matter of style; and a newspaper-like energy in the matter of content. That the ideas with which we deal are varied and numerous represents a journalistic rather than an encyclopædic method, since we do not attach any intrinsic significance to the historical quantity of thought. Truth is not an encyclopaedic accumulation. It is a compound of completeness and order, and there is no instinct of completeness or order in ideas, the thought-units into which consciousness resolves itself in time. History is a casual synthesising; it proceeds without any presumption of finality. For the notion of finality it substitutes the notion of quantity.

Truth is not to be construed from the historical records. There is a missing factor of truth which these records, as a self-sufficient aggregate, suppress. And in our examining them, therefore, the particular idea, or historical item, can have for us only a journalistic value, since the encyclopædic sum of ideas has no validity as truth. The particular idea may indeed be relatively true – may somehow survive its own topicalness; but if it does, this is by a historically erratic intuition of the missing factor, not by its historical standing as one idea among others. In all ideas, then, we have, first of all, an equally energetic journalistic interest. But beyond this we have a judicial compulsion to identify and define the missing factor as value, and a corollary compulsion to reveal truth as a compound of completeness and order – a universe of values.

*

It is awkward to appear in periodical form: people tend to read periodicals in a tentative frame of mind, especially what they feel to be a 'literary' periodical. A periodical suggests some impermanent digression from the ordinary frame of mind and the ordinary material of everyday experience. In the case of a literary periodical, people have a sense of arbitrary community with other experimentally interested readers, and with the experimentally communicative contributors; which inevitably ends in a reaction of disinterest. But EPILOGUE represents a sustained, consecutive work, a publicising of work already done rather than a precipitation on the public of accidental pieces of writing: it is not a literary trying-out ground. Its contributors must be students of this work before they are contributors. And our appeal is to readers with a sustained interest in a work of this kind; to readers who will not disappear from us between the successive numbers. Our purpose and function are not to be a serial performance for the benefit of a spasmodic curiosity to 'see' something different on the stage of letters. We do not want to be seen but read; and we do not present something different, but something *more*.

*

No one should merely 'submit' material to us: we are not interested in writing which is sent to us because its author would like to see it in print. Contributions must be the result of collaborative arrangement. Our activity is collaborative, and there can be no collaboration without an adjustment of interest to a central theme. Our central theme is a time-surviving truth, and a final unity of values in this truth. We welcome contributors who will take pleasure in thus adjusting their interests, which is to say their work, to a governing standard: who feel the need of stabilising their work in accordance with a standard whose finality is verified by its applicability to other work, other interests, other subjects as well.

We shall publish, besides critical material, a certain amount of 'direct' material – poems, stories, photographs of paintings, etc. The appropriateness of all such direct material will depend on whether or not it exemplifies a sense of finality as the characteristic trait of consciousness of its author. All direct work, in whatever medium, is an exemplification of consciousness; and we are critically concerned with all degrees of consciousness. But no work has dramatic pertinence for us which does not exemplify consciousness of a final degree: which has not an aftertime quality, which is not a fitting epilogue of its kind. For we understand the immediate moment to be a summary moment, and the truly contemporary mind to be finally, rather than historically, alive. So our decision regarding direct material will rest not on a judgement of its goodness or badness based on a confidence in our selective taste, but on the dramatic impression of finality it makes on us – on the power of contemporaneousness it displays. And by contemporaneousness we do not mean an ill-tempered, propagandist reaction to past degrees of consciousness, but a natural acceptance and pursuance of the responsibilities of *this* immediacy – as not merely the temporal sequel to preceding instalments of life, but the concentrated essence of life. It is this that we shall look for: a simplicity which is essentiality, and a strength which is concentratedness.

*

We do not expound opinions but report, besides what has happened (been thought), the single event possible after everything has happened: a determination of values. And we are not 'literary' except in that we regard words as the most authoritative indexes of value, since they are at once the most specific and the most sensitive instruments of thought; we have no professional prejudice in favour of words as an æsthetic medium. In deciding on any text offered to us we shall be concerned not with its 'literary' merits but with its active sensitiveness to value. What is value? We do not say that this or that is value; we do not hold an opinion about value. An opinion is a special view defensively held against other special views. We have no special view. We affirm only the existence of value. We affirm a necessary final law of relation; and in saying that we affirm it we mean that it is a law in immediate effect rather than a law we should like to be brought into effect. We affirm a consciousness of the immediate effectiveness of value, as the consciousness of an event. And our purpose is to create in others a cognizance, if not a consciousness, of this event; to release it to all its implications, and thus to achieve what has never yet been achieved and could not be achieved until now – a vivid reality of thought.

L.R.

THE IDEA OF GOD

Thomas Matthews and Laura Riding

1. Does God exist? In what sense?
2. Who and what is God (omnipotent, omniscient, infinite, indivisible, anthropomorphic, tribal)?
3. What is God's relation to Space? To Time?
4. What is God's relation to Man? Is God on our side? Has God a 'side'? (From the human point of view, is God good, bad, or indifferent?)
5. Has God sons (Buddha, Christ, etc.)? Daughters? What is their relation to God? Are they only a part of God, or is God only a part of them? (How does God show himself to Man?)
6. Does the Devil exist? Who is he? What is his relation to God? To Man?
7. Where does the female principle come into God's world?
8. When men say they 'know' God, 'see' God, 'serve' God, what do they mean?

T.M.

1

'GOD' IS THE NAME given to the most 'important' human idea. In English, as in other languages, the original sense of the word is obscure. But the character of the name is the same in all languages: it is a question. 'God' is the question 'Is there something more important than, something besides, man?' Man would like to feel self-sufficient, yet he feels dependent. 'God' states the discrepancy between what man would like to feel about himself and what he actually feels; but equally it represents his attempt to make a compromise between what he would like to feel and what he actually feels. In 'God' he chooses those meanings for the 'something else' which interfere least with what he would like to feel about himself. Man says to himself: 'I like feeling the lord of my world, and yet I cannot help feeling that it is not altogether my world.' He feels that there is something else, but he does not *know* it. To know something one must identify one-self with it; and the result of identifying oneself with it is the discovery of one's precise relation to it. Man has a repugnance toward knowing what he cannot possess. He cannot possess the something else; therefore he does not know it. He places the something else at a distance where it cannot offend his feelings. He does not try to know it, only to understand it – to know it with his feelings. But in making this removal a sense of guilt remains. Perhaps he has done something untrue – something which will ultimately be held against him?

Woman is something other than man. She is the contradictory being by whom man attempts both to identify himself with the something else, and to exorcize it; and she apparently yields to the contradiction. But she is not in herself contradictory; she is the answer to man's contradictory behaviour toward the something else, which is both insulting and propitiatory. She is the answer to the question 'Does God exist?'

'God' as the most important human idea is only the idea of a something else competing in man's consciousness with his idea of his own importance. 'God' represents man's attempt to stand the something else outside his consciousness – not to think about it. 'Faith' is man's way of not thinking about it, hoping to be left alone; as irreligiousness is thinking about it hostilely and aggressively – trying to force it to leave him alone. Woman is the immediate answer which the something else makes to man's behaviour toward it; and his behaviour toward her is his immediate behaviour toward it. Man does not willingly think about woman; when he does, the result is either obscene (irreverent) or sentimental (guilty). He interprets her behaviour either as endearingly submissive complaisance or as devilishly inhuman caprice. But man's most constant conclusion about woman is that she is something not to be understood.

The more ambitious man became, the more boldly he denied the existence of a something else as an immediate reality – the further he removed it from himself. By removing it he cleared a time-line of progress for his consciousness. When he reaches the end of the time-line, the dead-end of consciousness at which his strength fails, he regards himself as having achieved complete existence because he can achieve no more. In distinguishing between himself and a something else he felt a sense of weakness and insufficiency. As he became stronger, the something else, which began as a sense of what he was not, became a sense of what he might be; it became a mere symbol of human progress. And now that he is all that he can be he declares himself all that is; even as he has more and more counted himself not merely man, but woman also.

Thus modernistic literature, dead-end literature, abounds in womanisms. It is as ununderstandable as woman is traditionally supposed to be.

It is shamelessly coy, and shamelessly perverse; and, for all that, extremely virile – to show that it is man-made. In some instances, it is woman-made. But women, in identifying themselves with a male state of mind and behaving like men, are not merely prostituting their identity; they are approving the state of mind and the behaviour as the Church approves wickedness and sin in assisting in its confession. Women see to it that nothing is suppressed. If there is any danger of suppression they become tempters. If man feels any timidity in doing what it is in his will to do, they do the thing along with him, to put the matter on record. And since man now wills to be so comprehensively man-like and woman-like, woman, going along with him, is his abettor. In the process many women are necessarily sacrificed, as priests fall in love with wickedness and sin in the conscientious fulfilment of their confessionary office. And it does not matter that many women are sacrificed, individually – as it has never mattered. Woman herself remains intact in the same way that truth remains intact while being also criticism: in criticizing, truth must temporarily succumb to the hypnotism of the criticized state of mind and behaviour. It does not matter; what matters is for everything to be put on record.[1]

Gertrude Stein's ununderstandability is to be explained, however, in another way; it is, indeed, in Old Testament rather than modernistic mood. She is woman representing the something else, against which man has now immediately come, as a blank scene where it is as inaccessible to man as at the beginning of time. She represents the blind impact of the human consciousness upon the something else; which returns to man a precise but meaningless record of his failure to sustain himself in the scene. The meaning of her record is only the failure of the human consciousness to go beyond itself. The ununderstandability of Gertrude Stein is the stupidity of man himself, offered to him as a sedative for the acute pangs of vanity he suffers when his consciousness fails. Instead of assuming mysterious airs because, impudently treading on mysterious ground, he is unwilling to admit that the mystery is something apart from himself, he can, with Gertrude Stein's medicine, protect himself from the spiritual delusions of consciousness: consciousness becomes his disease, stupidity his doctor.

The effect of ununderstandability which much modernistic writing is designed to give is often enhanced by the use of what is thought to be 'primitive' technique; and many modernist writers like to fancy themselves primitives. But primitive man was no writer, and no writer can be a primitive. Primitiveness is basic simplicity of mind; the literary consciousness must be complex, in its function of ordering complexities. Literary naïveté is really shiftless confusion of thought – not wholesome elementariness. And the emotional bisexuality characteristic of so much modernistic writing does not derive from any primitive instinct of simplification, but from disorderly experimentalism. Although the primitive mind recognized few morphological distinctions, it ordered itself strictly by these distinctions.

A primitive was 'feminine' in that he imitated the something else; but imitation meant ritualistic sympathy, not experimentalism. He recognized woman as the ritualistic manifestation of the something else, and his spiritual sensibilities were therefore sexual sensibilities. That taboos had mostly to do with his relations with women did not mean, however, that woman was controlled by man; it was a recognition of control through woman. In woman the unknown was implicitly present; she represented the mysterious source of personal existence. Primitive man did not say 'God'; he said 'origin', training his mind myopically on the given situation, clinging to it because it constituted life. Mystery lay all around him, something not himself, something that overshadowed the little clearing he made himself in it. But he did not dare to divorce himself from mystery; it was the indispensable other factor of his being. In saying 'God' man put mystery away from him; he enlarged his little clearing. And when he can enlarge it no further he naturally concludes that he has conquered mystery. And from this conclusion there naturally follows the sentimental deduction that he himself is the mystery.

In dealing with your first question, I have also dealt with your seventh ('*Where does the female principle come into God's world?*'), and partially with your eighth ('*When men say they "know" God, "see" God, "serve" God, what do they mean?*'). To 'know' God is to understand the something else as a final value whose finality is that it justifies human values. Here also comes my answer to *b* of your fourth question ('*Is God on our side?*'). To 'know' God is to argue the subservience of the final value to human values ('our side'). If man cannot persuade himself that the final value is an amenable value, then God is not 'known': the final value is not 'God', but fate, the intractable. Fate is the something else as indifferent to human values: a value to which to be indifferent, a value to ignore, a value whose operation may disastrously affect some while leaving others alone – the certain possibility of the escape of *some* being called 'luck'. In this understanding the something else is a capricious alien force, sometimes standing off from the human world, sometimes plunging suddenly into it to show its power, but never to be reckoned with in human behaviour – for which human values are absolute except for the possible arbitrary intrusion of this force. Triumph over fate, by concentration on human values alone and the building up of a shock-proof human resistance, is luck, as ambition of such triumph is hope.

With 'God' there is confidence instead of hope – confidence in the amenability of the final value: Man argues with himself that God is 'good', on his side. God as on the human side is the something else as having only one side. It is a loose, passive force capable of being ultimately identified with and included in the human world, completely energized with human will: as a thing in itself it is merely a sort of unharnessed overflow from the human world, representing, if harnessed, just so many new fields of endeavour. And instead of luck there is a sense of virtue: the human consciousness, proud of its confidence, dispenses virtue to itself as the reward of confidence. The reward of hope is luck, and luck is not dispensed by the consciousness; it must 'happen'. When man doubts himself and yet remains ambitious, he dispenses with both 'God' and his consciousness and stubbornly bides his time, waiting for luck. Hope and luck have pulled man through the discouraging stages of history. In his prosperous periods man avails himself of his consciousness and of 'God'; he is confident and virtuous, not merely hopeful and lucky.

Atheistic realism, in denouncing the idea 'God', is denouncing the idealistic consciousness into which men organize their emotions. Thus the present-day Russian hate of God is a criticism of the Christian conscious-ness, as dispensing a kind of happiness – the enjoyment of a sense of virtue – which satisfies only the vanity of the spiritually pretentious; and also of the social system sustained by Christian ideology. The present-day Russian mind rejects the Christian gospel as prejudicial to the humbler human needs: as an instrument with which the prosperous few may bully the less fortunate members of society into silence, by making it seem shameful to complain of the lack of material happiness when Spiritual happiness is universally available. And certainly the Russians can feel justified in hating 'God' when a modern pope consoles a delegation of unemployed with the happy thought that God has denied them substance in order that when they have it they will appreciate it better: that is, that when they have employment again, they will not so easily yield to vulgar social discontent. The Russians assert, therefore, a more ascetic consciousness, from which the 'higher' needs are excluded, and another kind of pride – that of not playing the ambitious fool before an uncom-promising fate. In hating God they are despising spiritual vanity, trying to save human dignity by urging the common-sense human mass to disown the follies of individual idealists. All of which contains my answer to *c* of your fourth question: '*Has God a "side"?*' (*From the human point of view, is God good, bad, or indifferent?*).

'*What is God's relation to Man?*' (*a* of your fourth question) is also contained in your eighth question. I have explained 'knowing' God as an intellectual fiction: human values synthesized into a final value. To 'see' God means, under the stimulus of intellectual confidence, to let the emotions enjoy what has been intellectually defined. The intellectual structure 'God' has been created by stretching the emotions to the farthest conceivable point from the immediate emotional centre and forming them into a favourable figure of human achievement. To 'see' this figure is to bring it back along the track of intellectual translation to the immediate emotional centre. The enjoyment is in the contrast between the crude natural emotions and their elevation and refinement in the figure; 'base' perceives the 'lofty' in the ecstatic awareness that the lofty is also the base. This is the nature of all mystical experience. Which contains also my answer to your question about 'serving' God. The base seems to serve the lofty, but it is actually the lofty serving the sensual gratification of the base. So do men flatter themselves that they 'serve' women (compare the phrase 'the stallion serves the mare'). Which returns us to the sexual meanings suppressed in the word 'God': in the dualistic hypothesis 'man and God' sexual significance is evaded. Sexual differentiation is really odious to man, as the existence of 'something else' is odious. He deals with 'difference' not by trying to discover how he may be compatible with the different thing in a monistic order, but by trying to conquer difference – to adjust the principle to the variant instead of adjusting the variant to the principle; he puts the burden of difference on the something else, though he is the phenomenon. 'God' is the ideal of a successfully masculinized (humanized) something else.

There can be only one 'one'. Man is a separate being, but he is not an independent being. He exists only as he relates himself to the unique through his own consciousness of not being unique. Relation is the only admissible principle of duality. Thus the phrase 'house and garden' is dualistic; but the fundamental notion is 'house'. And the final notion is also 'house': garden stands between 'house' and 'house' as between source and head of identity. The modernistic hypothesis is monistic: man, feeling himself come directly against the 'one' by which he is a different 'one', makes experimental identifications of himself with it, in order to enjoy the dramatic sensation of personal uniqueness. And as the historical dualistic hypothesis 'man and God' was based on logic, the principle of experimental differentiation, so the modernistic monistic hypothesis is based on illogic, the wilful avoidance of differentiation: man makes himself brutally, satirically or sentimentally identical with the something else as he conquers the argumentative nervousness which produces 'God'.

You will be asking me: 'If to "see" God is merely the experience I describe, is there no "seeing" of the something else?' But in what sense do you use the word 'see' that you must put it between quotation marks? You are, that is, postulating a peculiar seeing – imaginative seeing. And so in my answer I must discuss the nature of sight. Man sees only what he understands. In imaginative seeing, understanding is optimistically made the equivalent of knowledge. Knowledge is complete awareness; understanding is local awareness. To 'see' the something else means to localize it in the human setting: to claim that the human setting is capable of containing it. But you would perhaps say that by 'seeing' you meant, merely, any experience in which man might feel the something else as a presence without there being any self-deception in his feeling; in using the word 'see' you are perhaps trying to state the possibility in its lowest terms. I will, therefore, substitute the word 'feel', since 'see' is an ambitious word. With 'feeling' there can be no mistake; we are dealing, admittedly, with strictly local, limited faculties.

I would then say that there are two kinds of feeling. The first is to feel in the sense of concentrating your emotions on something immediately available for understanding: you make your understanding of it out of the emotions you have about it. The second is to feel in the sense of being affected without trying to understand: something is felt, you do not know what, and it is more important to feel it than to try to understand it, since once you try to understand it you no longer feel it. The first kind of feeling applies to what is easily incorporated in your understanding; the second, to what resists incorporation – what is 'bigger' than yourself. With the first, your localness – your humanity – is the authority; with the second, authority is in that which is felt. There is, I say, subjective feeling and objective feeling. Everything which yields to the understanding is subjective feeling; what does not yield is objective feeling.

Emotional experience is composed of these two kinds of feeling; but the vanity of understanding suppresses the second kind. In saying 'I feel that,' man is declaring his intention to possess that which he feels. To say 'That is felt by me' precludes the possibility of possession. Having defined the two kinds of feeling, we can now distinguish between two parallel kinds of seeing: there is intelligent seeing and blind seeing. To try to see the something else intelligently is to humiliate the intelligence; for the something else cannot be 'understood'. But to see blindly involves no humiliation; the senses are merely reporting the existence of 'something else'.

Woman constitutes for man complete experience. In her the two kinds of feeling are provided for and they may operate without interference one by the other. She yields to subjective feeling, but in so doing defends against human understanding that aspect of her which is accessible only to objective feeling. But the more intelligent man becomes, the more repugnant does objective, non-intelligent feeling become: the more insistently does he interpret woman as an element of himself, entirely adaptable to his understanding. What he does not understand in her he dismisses as some vagueness in her structure; she is a being of his own kind, merely less firmly outlined. Even when he becomes modernistic and womanish – in his attempt to be everything – he perpetuates in this spiritual farce the historical impression of the nature of woman: he fancies that he is being woman as well as man in being less decided in form than himself.

Primitive man felt subjectively only in self-defence, he confined his understanding to a circumscribed number of things – to what was necessary for his physical sustenance. About everything else he felt only objectively. And he felt objectively, as well, about the things he understood, without relating the two sets of emotions. Thus he may seem to hold contradictory notions of the same thing: notions which seem contradictory to the civilized investigator because he tries to relate them. But one notion is the result of subjective feeling, the other of objective feeling; one is governed by convenience, the other represents what is impersonally felt. Particular burial-rites, for example, may seem to contradict the general notion of death; but to the primitive mind there is no contradiction. Similarly, woman (what the psychologist calls 'sex') was the greatest objective experience of primitive man. But he imposed on himself certain self-protective rules of behaviour toward her, a certain understanding of her. He was intensely preoccupied with her, but he allowed himself to understand only enough of her to protect himself from destruction in her. The phallic totem is not, as the psychological interpreter has it, a glorification of the male sexual apparatus; it is a sign of tremendous preoccupation with the female, more impersonal than personal.

The civilized mind is predominantly subjective. It is not merely self-protective; it is self-assertive. But man has cultivated subjective feeling at the expense of objective feeling; and no matter how 'much' he understands, he cannot change objective into subjective reality. He cannot 'be' what he is not, be more than he is. In the primitive mind, I have said, subjective and objective feeling went on unrelatedly at the same time. For objective feeling to exist in the civilized mind, it must succeed the subjective period, since it is the habit of the civilized mind to be wholly absorbed in the subjective: to have objective feeling it must *stop*. To 'see' the something else it must stop. But, instead of stopping, it goes on, from subjective period to subjective period; when it cannot go on, it repeats itself, rather than stop. My answer is, then, that if man will stop, since he has reached a stop, he will 'see'.

The subjective and the objective cannot exist relatedly in the same subjective period of the human mind: the objective cannot be incorporated in the subjective. But when the mind stops the objective succeeds; and only through the objective can the subjective be ordered and determined. In feeling objectively man is admitting the something else; and when the admission is made by him, in his highest degree of self-consciousness, at his limit of subjective power, he is saved from the suicidalism of mere consciousness, mere life as an end in itself. In stopping he is asking a question about himself instead of making affirmations; he is asking a question about his affirmations. Primitive man's personal existence was a dumb question. He required no answer because he made no challenging affirmations, only certain negative disciplinary affirmations about what he must not want, must not do. Civilized man's personal existence consists of challenging affirmations. And the civilized state of the mind is one of futile imaginariness unless it admits an end-of-consciousness: unless it anticipates a state in which the very affirmations of man's consciousness become a question seeking an answer.

Woman, I have said, constitutes for man complete experience. She is the material of both subjective and objective feeling; in her he may both understand and 'see'. But civilized man has used her only as an instrument of his subjectivity; as such she is what he 'loves', identifies with himself. The rest of the experience which she constitutes for him he evades sexually. In sex he makes his subjective experience of her the complete experience. In sex he dismisses the experience as complete in its subjective aspect: thus the euphemistic sexual conceit 'to know' a woman – that is, there is nothing more to know. With primitive man sex was not contempt of the experience woman constituted. He did not 'love' woman, understand her, identify her with himself. He was different from her; and by his difference he lived. But he feared to formulate his difference positively – make her the negative. In sexual relation with her he silenced the question – postponed the question – to which he feared to have an answer. But he did not use sex – the silence and idleness of sex – as a stimulant to subjective affirmations. In sex man neither understands nor 'sees'; sex is pure suspension of experience. And in sex primitive man was resting from his tremendous preoccupation with woman – his predominantly objective preoccupation; while in sex civilised man merely rests from his exclusively subjective preoccupation with her, which is fundamentally a preoccupation with himself. Woman constitutes for man complete experience; but sex is not 'experience'. Sex is suspension of experience. Primitive man, in suspending experience, suspended it in woman; civilized man suspends it in himself – the sexual act is the casting out of woman from his experience.

To return, then, to the problem of 'seeing' the something else: I have tried to show you that it involves a study of man's attitude to woman. There is no 'new' material of experience, no sudden strange apparition to be 'seen'; there is no 'more' material. There is available to man at every moment all the finally available material of experience. It is not a question of 'new' or 'more' material, but how he uses the material available to him, and whether he uses it all. You have asked me what must have seemed to you a fantastic question – about 'seeing' God. And I allowed it its full extent of fantasticness by changing it into a question about 'seeing' the something else. My answer to this question is that man can only 'see' the something else in 'seeing' woman. And whether it is less fantastic to envisage, in a sudden apparition, a completely unfamiliar material of human experience, than to envisage, in the accustomed apparition 'woman', all the humanly available material of experience, is a point that the spiritually perplexed commonly evade in lives divided between irregular mystical fantasy and conventional sexuality.

2

The Jews have always understood the dangers of spiritual ambition; it was as a magic charm against these dangers that they made God. Their God was *instead* of the something else, to stand between man and the something else, hiding it from the covetous spiritual appetite; which is why 'he' turned out so ill-tempered, overbearing, unlovable. They made the safest kind of God, which became Christianized into the most flattering kind of God. The Jews dealt practically, not idealistically, with the problem of reconciling the human will with the final, absolute law of things. The God that they made was – at least until post-Exilic times, when Christianization really began – strictly a God of immediate convenience. He taught them not spiritual strategy but spiritual propriety – to be morally irreproachable. He was not made out of spiritual opportunism, but out of the pressure of emergency; he was indeed the God of emergencies. The Jews made a figure of relative Immediate law, out of their sense of the absoluteness of final law. And they knew that they had done a terrible thing in making this God and that their God was a terrible God – a being of the occasion, a mere wisdom of the occasion. And he had, necessarily, certain devilish characteristics, because he was only a magical, pragmatic being, not finality itself.

To the pre-Exilic Jews God was the spirit of evil as well as the giver of practical advice. Only in post-Exilic times was a separate spirit of evil distinguished, as a result of Oriental influences – good and evil being distinct powers in Oriental religions. The story of the Garden of Eden reads like a post-Exilic interpolation – the serpent was a common figure of evil in Oriental myth.[2] The tree of the knowledge of good and evil could not have been an original Hebraic image. Truth to the Jews was an absolute – the Law; they indulged themselves in no romantic picturing of truth in conflict with falsehood. Only certain pragmatic uses might be made of the Law; it might be invoked with the object of determining right local behaviour. And so the God of the Jews was a god of periodical visitation. And the Jews used their power to invoke him sparingly, feeling that as he ceased to be a discontinuous emergency God he became devilish, their magic left their control.

The Christianized God was a continuous God – ideally present to all occasions. He administered not only the immediate solution but an ultimate universal happiness. The Oriental distinctions 'good' and 'evil' were sharpened. This was a God who must not only advise right courses of action: he must *make* right, turn wrong into right, 'save'. When man makes a god for himself, there is always something left over, something excluded, that the god does not contain: the something else, even, that it is the function of the God to remove. This cast-out element became, in the Christian religion, the Devil – the more dangerous ambitions of man. The Devil represented the immediate vanity and extravagance of spiritual ambitiousness as well as the intractable inhuman element of godhood that God Humane must hold off – the cause of the Devil, by its intractability. In the Trinity, the Holy Ghost is the Devil foreseen as ultimately good; Christ is the 'whole' man, human and supra-human – the triumphant product of the Christian God's technique of slow translation of all things into man. The Holy Ghost is millennium; Christ, eternity; God, patient futurism. A male patron of human ambition standing futuristically ahead of immediate life dims the irksome memory of the original spiritually restrictive female source of personal existence – the humiliating sense of having-been-child. Man calls his ancestors his 'fathers'; his male antecedents are inspirers to futurity, standing really before him rather than behind, 'getting' him more and more away from birth in mothers, whose identity presumably evaporates in parturition. The virgin-birth of Jesus represented complete disconnexion from irksome dependence on the female patron of origination.[3]

Jesus, in aiming at universal salvation, knew that he was making an experiment. As a Jew he felt the formidableness of the law which he was trying to soften in so final a sense. But he persuaded himself, in a manner suggesting Greek philosophical influence, that while an idea might as action be untenable, as thought it could have ideal probability. He translated the Hebrew God, the Critic of action, into a lenient God of thought, adding to the fixed Hebrew standard of immediate practicability philosophical connotations of futurity. And although Jesus's philosophy envisaged only an experimental manipulation of absolute law by the understanding, it was precisely on this ground that Hebrew orthodoxy opposed it: because it was an emotional philosophy and might lead to romanticism of action – as, indeed, it did. In all that affected immediate event the Jews conceived their God emotionally. But for the rest he was a severe intellectual symbol – within him lay abstraction, the unimaginable; only in the present was he a 'father'. And as an emergency improvisation he could become the Devil: he was the evil as well as the good angel of opportunity, since in daring to make him they had already broken strong primitive taboos against personal traffic with the unknown.

Bhudda, the Indian Christ, preached the gospel of decay and impermanence. Evil was matter; the good, the Positive, was the negation of evil, matter. In Hindu doctrine the good is merely the result of negation: it is made of matter, by spiritualization. To attain Nirvana is not to ascend to the good, but for the good to descend from abstraction into the evil: it is a state achieved *in* the flesh. Mahommedanism made a compromise between the Christian notion and the Indian notion; it tried to reconcile them both with the religion of Abraham and the law of Moses and to achieve world-conformity in God – becoming thereby the most fanatical as well as the most flexible of religions. It used the immediate-minded Hebrew code as a link between Christian experimentalism and Oriental inaction. In Mahommedan law the humanistic Hebrew reality is translated into a scientific reality – a primitive formula of factual realism to be constantly adapted to new sets of facts and successively reinterpreted by new prophets. Thus Mahommedanism satisfies Oriental belief in human impermanence and Christian belief in human progress and Hebrew belief in the reality of the moment. The Mahommedan God is a figure of varying, always newly definable law. Besides him there is the indefinable mother of the Book – the mysterious original of the law, construed as an implicit primitive being, not as an explicit finality; the Mahommedan mind construes only reasonable degrees of finality. Jesus proposed, as the Son of Man – as the ideal man in whom that which is lost is saved – to test philosophically the notion of active personal identity between the human and the other-than-human. 'If we are all good – that is, if we will to be one with God,' he reasoned, 'then we are as God himself; his personality and being is in us; he is the future, our father, we his ever-immediate expression.' But by 'God' Jesus meant something more than the opportunistic Hebrew God; he was not sure himself how much more he meant – he meant, in fact, as much as he might be allowed to mean. But two practical tests were necessary. First, he must have the complete support of the human will; second, he must have the consent of the god whom, in his philosophical vision, he allowed himself fondly to think of as the Greater Man, Man Potential. Jesus knew very well what he was attempting; he knew that success depended on his being able to make a strong emotional appeal to both 'sides': he foresaw the crucifixion and moved deliberately toward it. Catholicism interpreted his appeal as resulting in a qualified consent and concentrated shrewdly on stabilizing a tempered human will: God is the indulgent father of souls, or angelic nonentities, in whom he has trivial, even wrong, immediate being. Protestantism contested this interpretation on both counts. It was satisfied neither with the qualified divine consent nor with the self-deprecating human will it stipulated. In Protestantism human pride asserted a major will and a major fulfilment. Jesus, you see, had left the matter open; both the Catholic and the Protestant Church are equally Christian and equally provided for in Jesus's spiritual politics.

You will find in all this my answer to your sixth question – '*Does the Devil exist? Who is he? What is his relation to God? To Man?*'; and to your second question – '*Who and what is God (omnipotent, omniscient, infinite, indivisible, anthropomorphic, tribal)?*' And to your fifth question, although I have not spoken about 'daughters' – '*Has God sons (Buddha, Christ, etc.)? Daughters? What is their relation to God? Are they only a part of God, or is God only a part of them? (How does God show himself to Man?)*' About 'daughters': this question does not result from religious perplexity but from modern ideas of sexual equality – if men are entitled to be sons of God, then women are entitled to be daughters of God. The notion that a woman is as much of a human being as a man was a social levelling of those universal differences which were spiritually levelled in the notion of a humanized God.

Sexual equality was a practical result of the nineteenth century's passion for rationalistic simplification, the object of which was to determine what man was quantitatively and to dismiss all the remaining mystery as irrelevant to human thought. And if woman could be explained as a quantitative duplication of man, so much the less mystery. The nineteenth century was the last of the historical centuries; it extended into the twentieth century, as far as the Great War, which was the real end of history. The nineteenth century was the 'modern' century; the twentieth century is 'modernistic' – not a century at all but a suspended end-of-history. And the equality of woman with man is modern, not modernistic. Modernistic thought is a mystical romanticizing of modern thought, in which man is seen as the equal of woman, since she is the equal of man, and woman, nevertheless, as an abiding symbol of otherness. And if woman is mysteriously identifiable with the 'something else' as well as being, as it has been rationally established, the equal of man, then man may, through the intermediation of woman, identify himself with the something else; he is then himself, a known quantity, and also something 'mysterious' – ununderstandable. This mysticism was most naïvely propagandized by D.H. Lawrence, and most cynically by James Joyce.

And so as to 'daughters of God': they are a modern interpolation. Traditional religion did not commit itself about women; they were a cipher left undetermined. They were not acceptable representatives of the soul of man because woman was seen as a dangerous cipher, capable of anti-human determination. Rather, religion was useful to women as an instrument of self-negation. Women are not really comfortable in wearing human personality. They may feel all the human sympathies, be humanly knowing and efficient – but they do not feel comfortable. No matter how actively they assume traditional male roles, they are always something 'different': they are women. And, indeed, they only feel comfortable as something different. They were able to endure historical nullity as human forces because they were not human forces. The cloak of benevolent complaisance was a disguise under which they could always feel privately 'different', comfortable, fundamentally unreal in what they were 'doing' from the human point of view.

Women from the earliest of times have been used as conveniences of communication with unseen, inaccessible powers, but always in the sense that such exposing of self to dangerous mysteries, such destruction of the understanding as was required to become the slave of unseen powers, did not matter because the communicant was only a woman, in herself an

undetermined cipher – a nothing. Indeed, in a sense she was the slave both
of the unseen power and of man – as in early times the office of priestess
was often combined with the office of prostitute. The Sibyls had great
power and their communications were treated with great respect, but they
were not considered spiritual representatives of man. The Delphic
Pythonesses were not personalities; they practised divination of the will of
the god in a state of epileptic abandon, not of counter-will. A son of God
must have a 'will'; he must be aggressive on behalf of man. And what he
prophesies is something already plotted out, as Jesus's gospel derived
from Hebrew rabbinical tradition. Male prophets were concerned with
indicating new human potentialities. Female diviners merely 'knew'.
They went into anti-human trances, siding with man's gods against man
in their epileptic contortions and thus capturing weirdly the truths
secreted in the minds of the gods. Thus male prophets were necessary to
put the divinations of the Pythonesses into humane literary form.

The last part of your fifth question – '*How does God show himself to
man?*' – returns us to your question – '*What do men mean when they say
they "see" God?*' Let us examine in this connexion Moses's visual experience of God. God's first appearance to Moses (and here he is called not
the Lord himself but the angel of the Lord) was in a flame of fire out of the
midst of a bush. Such is the discretion of this passage that there are three
alternative figures suggested – the angel of the Lord, the Lord, and God.[4]
And first God appeared in fire, the devilish element. The reality of which
he was only a flashing improvisation tempted the mind to dangerous and
frightening spiritual adventures. Therefore the Jews were careful to
distinguish between fanciful and circumstantial sight; their business was
with a discreetly conceived emergency figure, not with a demonic halluci-
nation. And Moses hid his face, for he was afraid to look upon God – to
look long. Before God left Moses he told him where he should appear to
him again: 'When thou has brought forth the people out of Egypt ye shall
serve God upon this mountain.' Serve was here used to mean 'invoke'.
When Moses asked how he should explain God's command to the Jews
(when Moses asked himself how he should prove the invoked figure to be
true), God answered 'I am that I am.' This God was an empiric being,
available to the senses – not a subtle mind-maddening concept.

When Moses still pleaded the possible incredulity of the Jews, when he
wanted to see more, even against his better sense, at God's command he
cast down the rod in his hand; and it turned into a serpent. Moses's hand
became for a moment leprous; but, holding it against his bosom (the
bosom of his better sense, his heart as against his dangerous mind), his
hand became whole again. And this was the parable that he would use to
persuade the people to believe: to ask to know too much was unsafe. And
Moses used his parables to lead the Jews out of Egypt, the past, into the
present; whereas Jesus's parables were meant to lead people from the

present into the future. The land of Canaan was the promised, the reasonable present. Moses was equally the enemy of the future and of the past. But mosaic hard-headedness against futuristic fantasy gradually softened – already in David we find a pining for Christianity.

Moses knew that he must stage an impressive break with the past (the bondage of Egypt); and the Hebrew magicians made themselves as obnoxious to Pharaoh as they could. Pharaoh seems to have been patient enough, only wanting the Jews to keep to their work. And finally Pharaoh was so plagued that he let them go. The whole departure from Egypt depended on magic, on practical irrationality. And this is a curious capacity possessed by the Jews, the most rational of peoples: to know when to be irrational, when to lay an emotional check on the mind. In taking upon themselves a mission of historical self-consciousness they were attempting to deflate the future as well as the past: to formalize a world-magic of historical economy. Historical economy has been the persistent obsession of the Jews in history. But the people who were then Jews only in the tribal sense were reluctant to be Jews in Moses's sublimated sense, and he had to make great magic, and to close the Red Sea behind them, and to make the waters of Marah sweet, and to do a miracle of loaves (the manna-miracle), and to strike water out of a rock in Horeb. And the Jews have retained their power of realistic magic, of endowing the immediate with historical finality. They made a God in whom to concentrate the magic, by transforming their tribal pessimism into a fetish of practical optimism. And they became a holy people, by their very practicalness – spiritually intact in a disciplined, statically progressive immediacy of ambition.

When the Lord first came to Mount Sinai he only called, he was not 'seen'. And then he appeared in a thick cloud. But on the third day the voice of the trumpet was heard with accompanying thunder and lightning, and smoke was noticed on the mount – 'because the Lord descended upon it in fire'. It is possible that Moses now 'saw him' – though the people must not break through unto the Lord to gaze, and many of them perish. And then God spoke the laws, though the people heard only thunder and lightning and saw only darkness. And then God gave the judgements; for Jethro, the father-in-law of Moses, had advised him to stabilize the magic, to provide judges for 'every small matter'. Otherwise 'thou wilt surely wear away, both thou, and this people that is with thee'. Moses delivered the laws and the judgements to the people, and they accepted them. And then he wrote them down. And then he built an altar, and then he read what he had written; and again they accepted.

But still Moses was not sure whether he had sufficiently stabilized the magic. He went up again. And this time Moses, Aaron, Nadab and Abihu *and* seventy elders *all* 'saw' the God of Israel, as it were sapphire under his feet, as it were the body of heaven in his clearness – that is, the storm had passed and clear blue weather settled on the mountains. Moses had taken the seventy elders and two others besides Aaron into his confidence. But he must talk with God alone. He had told to the people, and read to them, the words of God; and twice they had accepted. Yet he was not satisfied; he must have them on tables of stone from the hand of God. So he went up to the magic mount again, taking Joshua with him as witness, though Joshua does not seem to have gone with him into the midst of the cloud. Here he received instructions for the making of the ark and the tabernacle and the altar, and for the ceremonies of worship, even to the composition of the anointing oil. For Moses knew that he could not hold the people by laws and judgements alone. He tried to surround this stark God of immediacy with an atmosphere of sensuous inertia. The God must foster, besides an immediatistic energy, a repose in immediacy – a charmed immunity from futuristic impulse. It was only after Moses had been instructed in these ritualistic details that God gave him the two tables of testimony.

But while Moses was studying this other magic the people grew impatient and incredulous and sought false gods again. And Moses threatened to leave them and find another people to be Jews. And he frightened them by breaking the stone tables. But he did not mean to leave them, only to weed out the uncertain: he provoked civil war among them and so reduced their number. Then the Lord appeared again, at the door of the tabernacle, in a cloudy pillar – though Moses spoke with him face to face. By now the people were tired and anxious to believe. And here we learn that, although Moses on this occasion spoke face to face with the Lord, he did not see his face: 'For there shall no man see me and live.' The people must have been asking, 'What is the face of this God like?' But the God would only show Moses his back parts: the front parts would reveal the intrinsic identity of the God, and Moses was careful not to know too much. Spiritual sanity and propriety forbade him to violate the incognito in which the absolute unnameable being appeared to him. 'God' was really the male-angel disguise of this being; Jacob, for example, wrestled with 'a man'. The ultimate figure was concealed in fire and cloud. To 'see' this would have been to transgress the limitations of time and intelligence. Such transgression was romantic futurity: stealing out of self, losing fear, and, inevitably, the security of location in the human.

3

George Bernard Shaw some time ago wrote a story in which an African girl goes in search of the Biblical God and finds that there is no fixed civilized notion of God. Irish iconoclasm of this sort must be understood as in itself defining a god which has no reality except as a point of intellectual leverage. To the Irish mind there is, in fact, no 'something else'. There is merely a human mind that divides wittily against itself, to provoke itself, expand itself. There is a human consciousness and a devil of provocation made out of the sense of inferiority which the consciousness feels. The sense of inferiority becomes the critic of the consciousness, identifying itself with a something else in which it does not believe and teasing the consciousness to expand. The English consciousness, whose object is to find true human adequacy, is the obvious target for Irish wit.

You ask: 'Does the Devil exist?' There exists devilishness. The Jews have a capacity for devilishness in so far as their reservations of confidence in both the human and the non-human may becalm them in an abstract neutrality between the two: devilishness is pure negativeness, sterile dividedness. The Irish have a more romantic, less metaphysical capacity for devilishness. There is a kind of Irish devil-type that identifies itself with 'the something else' in a mood of intellectual hostility to the inferior human consciousness, and of spiritual hostility to the coveted superior consciousness – which is non-human, presumably, only by the failure of human wit to be superior to itself.

Shaw is devilish in a merely journalistic way. He enjoys teasing humanity, but he is afraid to separate himself from it too strongly; in all dubious spiritual contingencies he hurries back to the despised human consciousness. James Joyce shows the human consciousness recklessly expanding, overflowing its limitations regardless of loss of sense. Anna Livia Plurabelle is the loose, expanded human consciousness become feminine; and not merely ununderstandable, but gigantically and power-fully senseless in the expansion. 'Anna was, Livia is, Plurabelle's to be.' And her spirit is 'eryan': 'Erin' is the punnish equivalent of 'Arya'.

What is Aryanism? In the *Rig Veda* words cognate with *arya* have a varying meaning of good and bad, with a central meaning of activity. Aryanism is the deliberate conjunction of opposites – the spirit of universal mixture. The last paragraph of Anna Livia Plurabelle is, in its reckless expansiveness, diabolically 'eryan':

Can't hear with the waters of. The chittering waters of. Flittering bats field mice bawk walk. Ho! Are you not gone ahome? What Tom Malone? Can't hear with bawk of bats, all the liffeying waters of. Ho, talk save us! My foos won't moos. I feel as old as yonder elm. A tale told of Shaun or Shem? All Livia's daughter-sons. Dark hawks hear us. Night! Night! My ho head halls. I fell as heavy as yonder stone. Tell me of John or Shaun? Who were Shem and Shaun the living sons or daughters of? Night now! Tell me, tell me, tell me, elm! Night night! Telmetale of stem or stone. Beside the rivering waters of, hitherandthithering waters of. Night!

And what is Anna Livia Plurabelle? 'Latin me that my trinity scholar,

out of eure sanscreed into oure eryan.' Nationalistic wisdom is challenged
to analyse the loose but single identity of the modernistic Aryan devil
whom Joyce characteristically makes a woman. In *Ulysses* Stephen
Dedalus represents the variety of contradictory impulses that hesitate to
unify themselves in the figure of Anna Livia Plurabelle. It is Bloom the
Jew who saves him from intellectual suicide in sex (from degenerate primitiveness) and gives him the courage of immediacy. A primary characteristic of Irish wit is that it does not mind being ridiculous; in *Ulysses* Joyce
was attacking the English fear of being ridiculous.

In the early Christian poetry of Ireland there is evident a conflict
between the devilish impulse to superiority and a fear of self-change in it.
The Christian symbol, vaguely associated with the Love symbol, was a
conventional means of quieting the fear and soon became absorbed in the
Love symbol. The Love symbol came to stand for identity with all that
was 'other', as well as for the confidence that human reality would not
suffer change in spiritualization. The dramatic equivalent to this concern
for personal immunity from the effects of spiritual traffic was sexual
chastity. The custom of sexless intimacy with holy women practised by
monks and priests survived in Irish Christianity long after it had been
suppressed elsewhere; it had been practised in the East by the early
Christians, but forbidden for some time even while it was being cultivated
in Ireland, where it lasted into the tenth century. And always in Irish
romance there is a characteristic abstraction of the concrete reality of
woman: she is merely the intellectually convenient figure. This is nicely
demonstrated in the early poem 'What Is Love?' from *The Wooing of
Etain*:

> A love much-enduring through a year is my love,
> It is grief close-hidden,
> It is stretching of strength beyond its bounds,
> It is the four quarters of the world;
> It is the highest height of heaven;
> It is breaking of the neck,
> It is a battle with a spectre,
> It is drowning with water,
> It is a race against heaven,
> It is champion-feats beneath the sea,
> It is wooing the echo;
>   So is my love, and my passion, and my devotion to her to
>   whom I gave them.

And Deirdre, who seems the most personal of Irish love-figures, is only
the unifying sign for the varied fields of conquest of the three champions
from the Red Branch.

Another early Irish poem, 'On the Flightiness of Thought', shows pride in the superior consciousness conflicting with fear:

> Shame to my thoughts, how they stray from me!
> I fear great danger from it on the day of eternal Doom.
> ....
> Though one should try to bind them or put shackles on their feet,
> They are neither constant nor mindful to take a spell of rest.
> ....
> O beloved truly chaste Christ to whom every eye is clear,
> May the grace of the seven-fold Spirit come to keep them, to
> check them.

In the 'Devil's Tribute to Moling', the Devil is the superior consciousness, Moling the fear. The Devil wants a blessing, but Moling says he has no right to one. Moling encourages him, advises him to *study*. 'Thine own study is not greater, and yet it helps me not,' the Devil answers. Then the Devil makes a hymn of praise to those who are holy, condemning himself. The Devil is rarely a serpent in Irish symbolism, but frequently a goat – as in this poem. St Patrick, in banishing serpents from Ireland, was asserting the human dignity of insubordinate intelligence; the serpent crawls on its belly, is driven to humiliating shifts of wit. St Patrick was, in fact, banishing nervousness and the sense of moral guilt. In the tenth-century *Saltair Na Rann* it is carefully explained that the Devil only took a place in the serpent's body for strategical purposes – to make a first unobserved approach to Eve. The most explicit modern instance of goatish diabolism in Irish literature is James Stephens' *The Goat Paths*.

4

Your third question – '*What is God's relation to Space? To Time?*' – brings up the scientific aspects of the general problem with which we have been dealing – the problem of human lesserness. Religious technique gets round the temporal aspects of human lesserness by futurizing time into eternity: the idea 'more time' seems to cancel the limitations of time. And as time is thus identified with a safeguarded extension of energy forward, space is identified with a safeguarded relaxation of energy backward, confirming the sense of accomplished temporal extension. Space in the religious sense signifies rest from activity without loss of the results of activity – spiritual triumph not merely as a high momentary felicity, but as a sustained possession of the whole range of spiritual extension from its lowest to its highest point. Space stands for Godhead – universality achieved by man; time, for the preservation of the human 'I' in this extension.

The scientific treatment of the problem of human lesserness is to reduce the human 'I' to a degree of extension that excludes all dubious 'other' degrees – degrees difficult to sustain. An enthusiastic reviewer of a book of sentimental philosophy recently wrote: 'This is an interesting attempt to explain man's place in the world of space eternity ... certainly the merging of life, time and space is fascinating.' The scientist does not view such an attempt as 'fascinating', nor is he concerned with the glamour of ideal results. His object is to determine the least duration man can be sure of, and not as the freakish, remarkable 'I', but as the least 'I', the common human factor. Instead of the large, generalized human type 'God', there is a particularized, immediately discoverable and enactable type that is not even called 'human' – because this involves a temptation to synthesis and God-making. 'Simply', the scientist tries to determine, 'what is the most common individual form?' And the answer is the atom, or whatever the atom can be made to split up into irreducibly. Then there is not 'I' manifold, but 'I' and 'I' and 'I' as an infinite repetition of the common type. And at the same time the problem of universality is solved; for the strict economy of energy by which existence is an infinite repetition of the most trivial degree of existence conceivable excludes the notion of extent of consciousness – in excluding the notion of sustenance of consciousness. The scientific individual computes its existence only against its own nothingness – not against an ideal duration and scope of existence.

The God-universe is an attempt to reconcile sentimentally the opposition between space and time; the scientific universe dispenses with these notions altogether. The reconciliation of space and time makes the third name 'God'; while the name 'space-time' merely states that space and time are contradictory notions and therefore self-cancelling. Science dislikes the burdens of compatibility. It makes distinctions with the object of proving the unreality of any principle of relation: it seeks an absolute of distinction, a quality that brings variant forms into mechanical inter association without organizing them into 'meanings'. The scientist says, 'Man is the absolute equivalent of himself. Man has no relation with anything but himself: he has relativity not relation.'

The scientific universe is, then, the repetition of a same circumstance, or differentiable, along a line that is not really a line but merely the number of repetitions. There is in this universe only behaviour and an infinite opportunity for behaviour. The individual is merely one of a succession of identical events all happening at once. There is variation in that there is a first number of the succession and, say, a thousandth; but it would be impossible to say which was the first and which the thousandth – one could start counting anywhere, and from one to a thousand would only mean that the counting had numbered a thousand identical events. Change (time) and position (space) are both cancelled as descriptive notions. The succession might be described in terms of change, or equally in terms of position; but the description would have to qualify itself by explaining that the change was not really change nor the position really position.

The scientific universe is composed of a succession of instantaneous events; and so long as there is at least one such event the succession is for itself infinite. The one event is the least imaginable motion between two points that it arbitrarily creates by being such motion, and so it is also an identical motion between any two such points; for as it is purely of motion it cannot stop – it is a succession. Nor is it exact to talk of the succession as a line that is not really a line. For it is not one such line, but an infinity of such lines on, top of, underneath, alongside of, before and behind one another – a surface without a content. The scientific universe has an extension that is neither spatial-composite nor temporal-continuous. It is identical in all its parts, and it is discontinuous. No single event depends on any other event, since the succession is really all one event in multiple repetition; and no particular event is the event, all the events occurring simultaneously and being mutually exclusive by the very fact that each one represents the other independently.

The scientific universe is the assurance that there is a next moment because there is this moment, and because the next moment has its start in this, is guaranteed in this, is really the same as this. And this free, perfect moment is not of space: it is only one moment, always the same next moment in the same position, though it has infinite occurrence. Variety of position means only numerical extent, as if to say: 'Let us reduce earth to the smallest conceivable space, so small that it cannot be called space. Then, though there are many of us, and only one spot, nevertheless we are all standing there; and it cannot even be called a spot, because, since all of us are standing on it, the notion of space is eliminated.' Nor is this free, perfect moment one of time: because, while there is a succession of moments, all the moments are equally this moment. They succeed each other in the sense that one is the logical predecessor of the other, but no new moment is entered into. It is already the new moment – already as new, as different, as 'next' as it can be in being the perpetuated same moment.

The scientific universe is a moving pause. It is a withdrawal from the problem of space and time, a self-isolation repeating the original derivation of life from a fundamental generality. It is particularity as its own generality; as if to say: 'I live because I have lived,' or, 'Having separated myself, I am separate.' Thus the scientific universe counts only the very first moment or fact of original life – the least living that can be called life; and it counts this not so much as the first moment but rather as the assured next moment after nothingness. If there is danger of man's being destroyed in his ambition to justify himself to a final value, then science offers a counter-security: to state himself only against his own nothingness, to be the smallest possible, safest self, rather than the largest possible, noblest self. And he who accepts the scientific universe can be at least sure that this moment in which there is neither space nor time is his own, for it is the moment of birth, of starting to live; the scientific universe is composed of startings which cannot be destroyed because they remain startings. Every old person who is depressed by being old cheers himself up by reminding himself that he was once young. And so the old historical universe cheers itself up by saying, 'I was once young, once I started: no one can take that away from me.' The scientific universe is man's cheering memory of his beginnings translated into a perdurable infant universe.[5]

And it is even the God that failed to equate the human with the non-human, even old-man God, who thus cleverly rejuvenates himself – even the spiritually rational soul of man (for man has many souls). And it takes all his cleverness – as it were all the cleverness of Einstein – to revive the infancy that he so carefully put behind him, to transform the immediacy of Moses into an immediacy which is merely the cancellation of the past that came after the first moment of life. Always the Jew, and always some-what in the sense of man caricaturing himself, gives man what he deserves. And when this seems to man to be the thing he wants, then the Jew becomes a hero. Old-man-God-Moses-Einstein by a clever magic gives man back his infancy. God is clever, but not dishonest, in the words of the Einsteinian epigram.

In the magic of Gertrude Stein it is not the first moment of life that is immortalized but the last: the last historical moment as a finality in which the human consciousness enjoys the absoluteness of its failures. As the Einsteinian gospel is the gospel of first childhood, so the Steinian gospel is the gospel of second childhood: the human consciousness is cheerful even in its oldness, its intellectual bankruptcy. The scientific universe of Einstein is a magic-making to give an illusion of perpetual immediacy in the first moment of human consciousness; the psychological universe of Gertrude Stein is a magic-making to give an illusion of perpetual imme-diacy in the last moment of human consciousness.

And every such offered universe is a strategical alternative to truth. And for every kind of human evasion of truth there is such an alternative offering. For man may choose any 'way' he likes. And in the gospel of Gertrude Stein there is no lie, nor in that of Einstein. It is possible to enjoy a momentary illusion of immortality in either of them. Each is a 'true' magic: it is possible to make such magics. Many millions of people are, in fact, being cheered up by these magics, though they may not realize it: they are being given both what they want and what they deserve. Various alternatives to truth are now being offered, but these two at least do not lie – that is, they do not really lie against truth. A person may tell a lie to himself in order to give himself a particular illusion, but to pretend to oneself is not really to lie; to lie is to attack truth with a pretence. A lie that has only the object of cheerfulness is not a lie. The lie, or universe, of Joyce, however, is indeed a lie. Its object is not cheerfulness, but insolence against truth; and it requires no magic to sustain it, only the dismal persistence of a single joke – the wilful mistake. It is a parasitic structure, availing itself of the psychological framework of Gertrude Stein's universe for support, and, for substance, of all the intellectual refuse which sober minds reject.

5

The word 'God' may have sympathetic phonetic connexion with the Sanskrit past participle *hūta*, from the root *hū* meaning the implored one, the invoked one – as if to say, 'O what? O who?' (which in themselves may have sympathetic phonetic connexion with *hūta, hú*). The categorical word in Sanskrit for 'the most important human idea' is *deva* – with which compare the Welsh *Duw* (God) but also the Welsh *diawl* (devil). Deva itself was undoubtedly dualistic, even as 'devil' can, as in devilish, have the sense of remarkable excellence. The English devil, the Anglo-Saxon *dēofol*, the German *Teufel*, the French *diable*, the Latin *diabolus*, the Greek *diabolos* – all contain echoes of *deva*; and so does 'divine', from the Latin *divus* or *deus* (God), or *divum* (heavens). The Hebrew *Jahveh* or *Yahweh* – 'the name which is not uttered' – suggests both *deva* and *Diovis pater* (Jupiter, Jove); the Hebrew reading of the tabooed word is *adonai* – perhaps chosen because of its phonetic nearness (*ădōnāi* is also used as a reading of 'Jesus' where it is regarded as a tabooed word). The phonetic approximation existing between all these words imitates the approximation in attitude toward a 'something else' existing between various frames of human consciousness – attitudes ranging from fear to praise but agreeing in a central attitude of perplexity.

The English 'God' comes from the Anglo-Saxon *god*, derived from a general Teutonic word (of obscure origin) with a definitely concrete emphasis, as to say 'the thing': there is an attitude of direct dealing with the something else. The phonetically associated word *gōd* meaning 'good' carries an emotional implication of godliness The sense of direct dealing with a mysterious force, making friends with it if possible, is demonstrated in the use of good as a propitiatory word – as to call fairies the good people, or to address someone with whom one is irritated as 'my good man'. 'God' is suggested in the name 'Goths' (Anglo-Saxon *Gota*) –which may have meant 'these strange, terrifying beings with whom we must deal.' If the Goths so described themselves, then their name may have been intended to strike active terror in the people whose lands they invaded. Many words phonetically sympathetic with the Anglo-Saxon *god* and *gōd* suggest a common perplexity of notion: as *gād* for goad (the apparently unrelated old Norse *gaddr* giving 'gad-fly'), and *gāt* for goat, the devilish animal, connecting with the Latin *haedus*, which is not unsympathetic with *hūta* – while the German *Geiss* for goat connects sympathetically with *Geist* for spirit (as indeed 'goat' with 'ghost'). While phonetic affiliations of this sort provide no logical clues to sense affiliations, they are symptomatic, nevertheless, of a basic emotional homogeneity in human thought.

When words for the 'other' notion tend toward abstraction, they lose the accent of perplexity. The notion is dogmatically characterized by the understanding, regardless of its resistance to rational characterization; in so far as the word fails rationally, it is merely a rhetorical idiom. Thus 'Fate', Necessity, Providence, Heaven, become idle invocations, as to say: 'There is no use in bothering about this notion. We will exercise our minds on more concrete perplexities.' (The Greeks had a separate altar at Athens on the Areopagos for the unthinkable aspects of divinity, as distinct from aspects in which it was more amenable to definition.) In poetical abstractions like 'Beauty' and 'Truth', the notion has been only sentimentally abstracted, but in the idealistic sense of being ultimately amenable to rational definition. And with all lofty or abstruse abstractions the word serves as a strategical limit to mental gymnastics: a boundary of the understanding with nothing on the other side which it recognizes as 'real', and therefore forming part of the understanding, an outermost part neatly encasing it in itself.

In Homer *theos* sometimes meant Destiny – an abstract, solemnly remote notion – but it could also mean Chance – a local personification of the incalculable course of everyday life; even as *theos* was applicable to familiar deifications as well as to the general principle of deity. Herodotus connected *theos* with the verb meaning 'put': therefore, the determining force. But Plato believed it likely that *theos* derived from the verb meaning 'run' – as the stars run: therefore the mysterious force. And it is possible that both these conceptions are contained in *theos*. It has even been suggested that the meaning 'heavens' in Plato's interpretation gave the Latin *dies*, for light, or day (as well as 'heavens'), and that Zeus derives from these associations rather than directly from *theos* as 'god' – another form of Jupiter is *Diespater*.[6]

The significance of all such phonetic affiliation is in the relation they suggest between notions which seem different because they are expressed in somewhat different combinations of sounds. The notions are all really the same notion: a central provocation to a variety of affiliated attitudes. These attitudes, when translated into mental behaviour, produce linguistic differentiations, all of which agree in their emotional ground. Thus *pan, pain, bread, Brot*, all represent variants of behaviour toward a notion which has a common identity in the emotions it arouses. Indeed, the very existence of different languages is due to differences of attitude toward the general notion of 'something else'; the multiplication of notions proceeds from the first distinction forced on man – the irritating quantitative distinction between himself and what is not himself.

And the final distinction must be an ordering, standardizing distinction – the first distinction as that which obtains ultimately and to which other distinctions must relate. But if man's first distinction is translated into the sentimental possibility of being different from himself, quantitatively greater, 'better', freer from his given limitations, then he is his own finality – a tragic or comic finality according to the duration he so conceives himself to enjoy; and the secondary distinctions of his consciousness degenerate into tragic or comic jargon. Thus contemporary humanistic finalities move either in the comic or the tragic direction. The comic and the tragic both express man's temptation to assert himself as finality either because, any other finality escaping him, he feels that he must round out the human drama with a mock-finality, or because he feels that if he does not assert himself as finality, another kind of finality will cut short his egotistic fancies – as the contemporary tragic mood is one of egotistic suicidalism.

L.R.

SUPPLEMENTARY ARGUMENT

T.M. – I agree that when man thinks about woman the result is either obscene or sentimental. But I do not admit that when man thinks about the 'something else' the result is either obscene or sentimental – though it may be terrifying. The realization is so terrifying, in fact, that it cannot be borne except in brief flashes; and so man invents taboos like 'God', or faith and religiousness, to keep him comfortable. I agree that woman is an indication of the existence of a 'something else' – perhaps even a proof of it – but I cannot agree that she 'is' the something else: she and man are too much alike, in too many finite ways. It seems to me that both man and woman are reduced by the something else to an unimportance which amounts to practical identity with each other.

L.R. – I do not mean that when man thinks about the something else the result is – presto – either obscene or sentimental. I mean that woman is something that man does not willingly think about; that when he does think about her the result is either obscene or sentimental; that when the result is obscene it is not essentially different from the status of irrelevance which the notion of a 'something else' has in his every-day consciousness – the disinclination to 'think about' results in both cases in a vindictive frivolity; that when the result, in thinking about woman, is sentimental rather than obscene, this is not essentially different from the reaction of guilt man has from his habitual summariness of temper toward the something else, however he construes it – in both cases he is trying to assuage a superstitious fear of retribution, to make things right with his conscience. This compulsion to make things right is the equivalent of your 'terrifying realization'; and this realization is not essentially different from man's unofficial reaction to woman – all men are fundamentally 'terrified' of women, though their terror is disguised in sexual bravado.

Man is terrified by the notion of a 'something else' as his judgement of his own meaning and value fails to seem true and final. He loathes the sensation of being 'watched', and yet he cannot help feeling that there is a watcher whose judgement of him is perhaps more valid than his own. He is aware of being watched by woman, but she is too exasperatingly near to be allowed to count as a figure of authority. He invents, therefore, the compromise figure 'God'. He can experiment with God, moving between surrender and resistance, without expressly committing himself – his behaviour in relation to God is all in the future. With woman he is at every point concretely and minutely committing himself; and so he is unwilling to attach any distinct, final significance to her as a presence – since unwilling to take final responsibility for his immediate behaviour. But if you agree that woman is 'an indication, perhaps even a proof' of the existence of a something else, then you are admitting that she is in some way the form in which the something else manifests itself.

If you agree that the something else must in some way manifest itself to man (that man is not an entirely free, lone being, a law unto himself), then you must also agree that manifestation must be relevant to the form of being at which it is directed; that the form in which the something else appears must be sufficiently opposite to maintain its otherness, and yet sufficiently intelligible to the human mind – sufficiently human-like – to make communication possible. Indeed man and woman are 'like' in many finite ways. You would not have the something else talk to man in *its* language: you would not suggest that man was capable of 'understanding' a language the terms of which were all of non-human meaning.

T.M. – I think of God (which includes death) as representing a notion so final that it makes all human values irrelevant. If it were possible to identify oneself with the something else, then it would be possible to consider the death-stopped notions of man as 'merely human' in comparison with the non-human; but how, being human, can anybody make such an identification and such a comparison? When you say that 'fate is the something else as indifferent to human values, a value to which to be indifferent, a value to ignore', I take it that you are referring to what man should do, not to what he does. Surely 'fate' is a value which man explores and placates, to which he is never indifferent and which he cannot afford to ignore – to which he is constantly making peace-offerings? A reflection of this attitude may be seen in such unconsciously philosophical remarks as: 'As soon as you get out of bed in the morning it's ten to one against you.'

L.R. – You say that you think of God as a notion so final that it makes all human values irrelevant. You are saying, really, that these values are something which man privately possesses without their coming, so to speak, under observation. God as including death is to you the fact of the isolation-in-self of human ways: of a final silence on the subject 'man'. My answer here is that God is to man, precisely, a convenience for the removal of human ways from observation. By a courtesy-argument the something else is supposed to be above petty interest in human affairs; death finally locks them away in human privacy. I say that the something else is not above such interest; that everything human undergoes judgement; that it is no more possible for man to dismiss his affairs as petty than it is for the something else to behave as a superior being above interest in them. The something else is interested in human affairs because they represent either an impossible apartness from the final generality or an explicit appeal to the something else to be included in the final generality – made somehow true.

About 'fate': it is odd that you should think that I am 'referring to what man should do, not to what he does'. In nothing that is written in EPILOGUE is there any insinuation of what man should do. There is a listing, from a final point of observation, of distinguishable varieties of human behaviour: what man actually does. We weigh the full implications of his behaviour, but without any purpose to suggest historical alternatives. What he does is already done. Your description of man's attitude to fate agrees perfectly with my definition: it is the something-else force felt as unprophesiably imminent; a force to be hoped against and magically avoided. Your 'exploration' and 'placation' reflect this exercise of human magic against the force; the existence of a large residue of unofficial daily life in which officialized spiritual confidence breaks down.

T.M. – I admit that man is capable of understanding only himself, and that he would do well to confine his efforts at understanding to himself; but in fact he does not. Granted that 'understanding' is made up of subjective feeling, I can't see what valid interpretation man can make of anything outside himself. I can see that if a person understood himself completely he *might* then be able to 'see' – have some right intuition about – the something else. Since I do not understand myself, the possibility of seeing in such a way remains hypothetical; and, being human, I look sceptically at any statement about other people seeing objectively. Do you mean that a man can not only understand himself but see the something else – by an act of will? Or by taking thought?

L.R. – Though man's mind is highly specialized toward the understanding, or containing of, himself, nevertheless he attempts to use this highly specialized apparatus on that which is not himself. We agree, then, that he cannot make a valid interpretation of anything outside himself; but in saying that we agree I must make you mean, by 'valid interpretation', a containing within his own organization of the something else. In attempting so to understand the something else he is not merely attempting the impossible but behaving with spiritual insolence. The alternatives to spiritual insolence are a pessimism like your own, grounded in modesty, or an unqualified curiosity toward truth, grounded in a more positive kind of modesty – the courage of humanly profitless wisdom. And whatever the choice, it is the result of an act of will. 'To take thought' is, indeed, to cultivate will. Whatever man is, he is by will. That you do not understand yourself is not an accident of your consciousness, but the kind of consciousness you have chosen.

T.M. – Is not man's instinctive disregard of woman rather an expression of his unwillingness to face facts which he feels are unbecomingly seamy? Principally, that he came into this world not trailing clouds of glory but a navel-string and an after-birth? rather this than direct disregard? It is his responsibility in the bloody business of birth that worries him, it seems to me, and tends to make him disregard the physical reality of woman and, at the same time, to exalt motherhood to a sentimental degree. Thus, when you say that 'the virgin birth of Jesus represented complete disconnexion from irksome dependence on the female patron of origination', I think you prove too much. It is the association of Joseph with Jesus that Christians mind, not the fact of Mary's being his mother.

L.R. – You agree, in fact, that man fundamentally dislikes his birth-dependence on woman, since the 'bloody business of birth' is not flattering to his vanity; it reveals him as an entailed being, entailed unpleasantly in woman. By sentimentalizing motherhood he makes this a purely fanciful entailment. The violence of birth reminds him that human life has the initial character of violence. The something else, in the form of woman, is irritatingly present to him; he is not a being unto himself. If he wants to be the being – the emphatic counter-being – 'man', he must state his desire against the reality from which he wishes continued separation: the very violence of his existence is a permitted violence. Sex is the first reckless statement of his desire, as a will to survive no matter how, or with what consequences. And he directs this statement at woman, who, in participating in the sexual act, temporarily silences the fact of a vigilant something else – her passiveness in sex is an uncritical allowance of the desire. And the uncritical answer to this simple desire is the simple consequence of continued momentary being, in circumstances which express the brutality of man's first blind insistence on himself.

I feel sure that you will be asking the question, 'Does not woman bear women as well as men?' To which I would answer: 'Woman bears women, yes – in response to the compulsion, as representative of the something else in the human scene, to be repeatedly present to it until it is made "right" – somehow consistent, true.' Woman as sexual instrument and child-bearer is the wrongest, the 'lowest' expression of her function as a right-making presence: she is letting the 'situation' develop freely, declare itself in all its quantitative explicitness. In his sexual relations with woman man is concerned only with personal existence, irrespective of the values that may govern it, regardless of its original wrongness (in the sense of violence). Then there comes to man, through a sense of the insufficiency of physical reality as a basis of existence, a self-protective desire to make things right. But he disregards woman as the presiding spirit of this right-making exactly because she is associated with the wrongness: he is more ambitious for himself, more 'idealistic', than the facts allow. And so woman lingers on in her sexual status, largely unused, while man invents for himself presiding spirits more flattering to his vanity; and things are not actually made right. And so most women are fundamentally unhappy because they do not immediately exercise their 'higher functions'. Yet women have an artful capacity for persuading themselves that they are happy, since their compulsion to make things right is also a knowledge that ultimately things must, somehow, be made right, and a sense of their power, however unused, to make them so.

Your suggestion that man's disgust with the 'bloody business' is due to his disgust with his own responsibility in it is the expression of a sort of civilized husband-guilt. The husband says: 'I have made myself a modest, quiet home from which I have excluded all those exhausting larger spiritual problems. My wife is a dear little woman, not the terrifying female figure of judgement that pursues the "great souls". I am all consideration for her, and she is pleased in me and grateful to me. She is the guardian of my peace of mind and also the gentle, contented mother of my children – thus giving me an assurance of modest continuity in other quiet, untragic homes like this.' Then comes the shock of the bloody business. 'What!' he exclaims, 'Is everything not all right, after all? Can my restrained, domesticated sexual relations with my wife be responsible for *this*? Is there no escape?'

As to Jesus and Mary and Joseph. Mary has little reality as the mother of Jesus – this relation is treated as fancifully as possible. The production of Jesus is exclusively the affair of his father, the Lord, and the Holy Ghost of experimentalism. He was given a natural birth only to ensure his acceptance as someone who had actually lived; not to put too great a burden on the faith of believers. If believers had been more advanced scientifically, he would have been presented as the result of a connexion between his father and a theological test-tube; that he lay in, and came out of, the womb of Mary is merely a manner of speaking. She does not really count as a mother: she was a Virgin. Jesus was got by a heavenly father – that is, by man futuristically in control of his salvation – on his rejected past: the Mary-gesture is the last goodbye to this past. Jesus himself had very little sense of the reality of Mary as his mother. On the cross he completely disowned her, throwing the more humanly entailed St John to her mother-feelings. Before that, you will remember, Jesus had already asked, 'Who is my mother?'

Among primitive peoples there is a strong feeling against associating the father with birth. Scientific field-workers assure us that the primitive mind does not associate birth with sexual intercourse: primitive peoples are supposedly incapable of this simple form of logic. But primitive peoples, who sustain themselves by just such simple logic as this, cannot really be so ignorant. Field-workers have here probably come up against a very strong taboo. The primitive instinct is against *mention* of physical fatherhood, although there is no taboo limiting discussion of the facts of sex. In the same way civilized children, even when fully informed of the nature of fatherhood, instinctively refuse to recognize it; although they like thinking that 'they came out of Mother' and advertizing their knowledge of sexual coupling. The civilized father fills much the same sort of equivocal rôle as the father does in many primitive societies, where the mother represents a static continuity of location and identity, the father a progressive continuity – something like historical time; when it is felt necessary, in such societies, to assert male connexion in order to confirm the child's identity as a socially active being, it is the mother's brother who is the male patron, not the father. A civilized child has a similar feeling of spatial certainty as centred in its mother; the father-sense comes late, just as the time-sense comes later than the location-sense.

T.M.–To the question *'Who and what is God (omnipotent? omniscient, infinite, indivisible, anthropomorphic, tribal)?'* you have given an implicit answer by showing how 'God' descended historically from the Jewish to the Protestant idea. You seem to say that God, being anthropomorphic, varies according to the racial attitude to the something else. 'The Mahommedan God is a figure of varying, always newly definable law. Besides him there is the indefinable mother of the Book – the mysterious original of the law.' This notion, which you give as the Mahommedan, seems to me to lead directly to the modern notion in which the 'figure of varying, always newly definable law' is represented by humanistic inter-pretations of Christ, Buddha, etc., and the indefinable figure by 'God'. The dialect in which this modern 'God' is being phrased is mathematical and physical rather than religious – a phrasing which amounts to a begging of the traditional questions. 'God' is being increasingly split into two parts: a Christly pseudo-human figure, more and more anthropomor-phic, and an unknown, undefined, shadowy omnipotence, further and further removed from human affairs. As the Christ-figure grows more tangible, 'God' grows less so; and the upshot, it seems to me, is that the modern religious-minded man 'takes God' on despair (rather than on faith) and tries to forget the notion, or soothe his irritation with its difficulty by making the Christ-figure more human, more familiar, more contemptibly 'one of ourselves'.

L.R. – I did, in fact, suppress a sentence about modern scientists being all good Mahommedans. But they do more than merely beg the traditional questions: they eliminate them. They have no interest in questions not immediately answerable, only in the immediate stabilization of life in an endless circuit – endless in that the movement is so economical as to be, in its self-protective negativeness, unstoppable. Scientific life consists of as little significant variation – as little aliveness to routine-disturbing questions of meaning and value – as can be consistent with being alive at all. This is why one frequently hears it prophesied that the last living beings will be insects; insects live on the scientific principle and have all the scientific qualities. Their immediacy has the value of eternity, by its economical concentration on the moment of life – on no more, no less. Thus the ant is 'wise and wonderful' – and Christ becomes more and more an ant-like ideal of virtuous efficiency.

It was recently proposed to ecclesiastical authorities in England that clergymen (Christ's vicars) should have instruction in the science of betrothal, marriage and parenthood, in order to be able to advise their parishioners in the more immediate as well as the more eternal aspects of life; and even Catholic priests now give eugenic advice. The modern clergyman, that is, must be psychologist and physician – the semi-modern clergyman-philosopher is not scientific enough. The splitting of 'God' into two parts is an accurate diagnosis: man is thus taking back all of himself that he has in the past experimentally combined with the notion of a something else, and treating the something else as a subject that does not enter into his field of interest, or universe, except as an ever-unimmediate metaphysical proposition. I am inclined to reject your word 'anthropomorphic' as too simple a characterization. 'God' is not merely deity in the form of man but the confused result of an attempt to combine the human with the non-human in a way favourable to the human. 'Anthropomorphic' is too 'bad', too scientific a word for a process not originally scientific – a process which did not mean to eliminate completely the notion of a something else, but rather to manipulate it. There is a reaction of despair in the discovery that the something else is not to be manipulated by the human will; but man does not long tolerate despair in himself. He tries to argue it away – though the more argument the cure involves, the less effective it is. Science is a laborious cure; but Einstein has greatly simplified its argument.

T.M. – You speak of Joyce's universe of irrelevancies. But the problem of a human being, as distinct from that of an artist, is that he is confronted with irrelevancy wherever he turns, and that the only clue at hand is himself – a part of the irrelevant picture. In other words: how can a man be the artist he must be without being the liar he cannot help becoming?

Thinking man cannot be indifferent (as science is) to the problem of finality; but how can he avoid suiting his frame of vision to his frame of mind?

L.R. – A human being is confronted with irrelevancy wherever he turns, you say. This irrelevancy is either his own, or it is the irrelevancy of other human beings. If he is articulately preoccupied with irrelevancy, then he is also preoccupied in a responsible way with relevancy – with the necessity of a making-right between man and something else which is not man. Words are the peculiar instruments of this making-right. Hence the aptness of the terms 'artist' and 'liar' in this context. For when a man who uses words is an 'artist', he is, cannot help being, a liar. An artist is, properly, one who does not worry about irrelevancy. He is so immediately conscious of irrelevancy and so ultimately unworried by it that, although his is the inarticulate language of irrelevancy (pictures, say), he is all the time asserting an ultimate law of relevancy. He is doing nothing to make things right, because he sees himself as the human, the weak one: he leaves it to someone else, something else, in the confidence that in the end all must be made right. The artist is, indeed, the true 'believer'. Joyce, in using words 'artistically', is making them articulate a consciousness of irrelevancy as truth – universalizing his sense of personal triviality. In asking how man can avoid 'suiting his frame of vision to his frame of mind', you are defending other human beings who are not so honest with themselves as you are – minds which prefer faking truth to seeking truth or admitting that they are not strong enough to assume this responsibility.

T.M. – The 'tight place' of being alive spells not only intellectual defeat to man (as stupider men than Socrates have admitted), but defeat all along the line, ending in death, his complete capitulation as a human being. Spiritual speculation, like all of man's activities, is an attempt on his part to translate his hopeless situation into less painful terms. Granted that this attempt is an admission of intellectual defeat, that it fools nobody but himself (and not even himself at bottom), what else is man to *do*.

L.R. – The 'tight place' spells defeat only when man tries to enlarge it into a luxurious spaciousness safe from criticism – from final evaluation. Science tries to save life from final evaluation by making the tight place as tight as possible; which is no less a fallacy than other shifts, since man cannot escape evaluation. By death man escapes the horror of succeeding eternally in all the insanities he attempts; only that which is consistent with truth (ordered totality) survives death. If he dispenses with death, man involves himself in endless, rather than merely mortal, insanities; he has hell. In hell man may do whatever he pleases without hope of ever being corrected. Primitive man feared death ; but the primitive fear of death is very different from the civilized fear. Primitive man made his life conform obediently to all the prohibitions implicit in his physical nature. He did not experiment intellectually, live 'doingly'; the fear of death was the fear of going beyond himself. Thus, primitive paradises were generally faithful reproductions of life, with the same kind of taboos and pleasures. – The primitive fear of death was really a fear of change, history, it meant an acceptance of the given limitations of life as the precious guarantee of life.

I must refer again to the psychologist-physician pretensions of the modern clergyman, to make a proper distinction between him and the primitive medicine-man. The modern clergyman is an arbitrator between religion and scientific principles which religion is not authoritative enough to put in their place as mere principles of animalistic well-being. Modern religion acquiesces in the primary stress that science lays on physical problems, if there is an exchange-courtesy paid to religion in the form of a vague acknowledgement that there well may be 'something else': science does not specifically deny this. And religion is even pleased that the acknowledgement is vague, that it is left free to work out the spiritual intricacies in its own way.

But the combination of practical and spiritual functions in the medicine-man was not strategical; he was really a psychologist and physician, and really a priest – not a subsidized thinker about hazy spiritual problems. The medicine-man made a working combination of the facts of life and the facts of death. Life emphasized possibilities: death, limitations. The medicine-man maintained an equilibrium between the possibilities and the limitations. The modern clergyman does not maintain an equilibrium, but rather a neutral space between the two sets of facts which prevents them from colliding. And he has the tacit permission of his congregation to experiment privately in softening the limitations that the second set of facts constitutes so long as his failures in no way affect the scientific security with which the modern world has been able to endow the first set of facts. The scientist, indeed, is the medicine-man with the priestly half entirely suppressed; while the modern clergyman is the specialized priest ingenuously and inefficiently assuming practical responsibilities after ages of disuse of the life-cultivating faculties, and by a sentimentalization of the priestly function that proportionately reduces his spiritual efficiency.

NIETZSCHE

Madeleine Vara

L.R. HAS WRITTEN THAT once the definition of the German spirit has
been made and the curiosities of German behaviour generally identified,
there is nothing left to record about the Germans, except instances of
Germanism to strengthen the identification. Nietzsche, as the 'particular
prophet' of the Germans, therefore supplies us with a complete psychological case. *Ecce Homo* is Nietzsche's critical summing-up of his significance as a spiritual force. Reading this book in conjunction with his *Poems*,
where he makes clearer confessions than elsewhere in his writings, one
finds an uncannily close correspondence between Nietzsche and man-
german as defined by L.R. It is so close, indeed, that if one did not stop to
make an aggregate consolidation in one's mind of the behaviour of all the
Germans with whom one has ever had intimate contact and so exemplify
L.R.'s definitions more generally, one would say at once that she had built
up her man-german from this single example. The homogeneity of the
Germans has been a matter of remark since the first histories of them were
written – as Tacitus writes, 'A race stamped with a distinct character: a
family likeness pervades the whole, though their numbers are so great.' It
is noteworthy that the four chief names for the race – *Deutsch, Allemand,
Teuton, German* – convey this sense of congenital relatedness. *Deutsch* and
Teuton are derived from the same word – meaning 'the people' in a corporate human sense. The Roman name for the race, as distinct from particular tribes, was *Germani*, which means 'the related ones'; it was a
mishearing of *Wehrmann* (warrior), but the Germans accepted it as appo-
site. *Allemands* or *Alemanni* is *alle menne* or 'all men' or 'the humans'.
Tacitus relates that their principal gods were Tuisto (the same as Teut)
and his son Mannus (Man), and that they sprang from the earth. That is,
from the beginning Germans made a generic identity between divinity
and humanity.

  Nietzsche was not only a German, he was increasingly conscious of what it was to be a German. *Ecce Homo*, his last book, is the most violent statement of Germanism on record; it was to him the most wonderful book, apart from *Zarathustra*, ever written. L.R. refers to the way Germans have of protecting themselves from a suicidal consciousness of their incoherence by telling themselves lies. Nietzsche piled lie on lie, but in the writing of *Ecce Homo* he must have understood himself, for the sequel was the madness that he had so long deferred: he allowed himself to disintegrate mentally and spent the rest of his life in an insane asylum. The Germans, as L.R. again points out, make a virtue of playing with danger. Similarly, Tacitus observed how anxious Germans were, even when sober, to submit themselves to risks: they would stake their lives and liberties on a dice-bout. And reading Nietzsche – a man who, by pursuing Germanism to a desperate extreme, broke down in insanity – is for Germans an excitingly dangerous thing. Did not Nietzsche himself give warning that he who breathes the rare air of his lofty mountain-heights must beware? 'The ice is near, the loneliness is terrible.' Such cold and loneliness are metaphorical of loss of the comfortable sense of family warmth. Nietzsche is tempting the Germans to the abnormal; and they enjoy the temptation.

Ecce Homo was written in a condition medically interpretable as *euphoria*, which means to feel the highest well-being and capacity just before a complete break-down. To begin with the physical background of this book is critically apt; Nietzsche himself was careful to explain his bodily condition by a running clinical commentary on the state of his health during the various periods of composition. The first chapter, 'Why I am so wise', is largely an assertion of his own physical soundness and of the identity of physical soundness with spiritual well-being.

My circulation is slow. No one has ever been able to detect fever in me. A doctor who treated me for some time as a nerve patient finally declared: 'No! there is nothing wrong with your nerves, it is simply I who am nervous.' It has been absolutely impossible to ascertain any local degeneration in me, nor any organic stomach trouble, however much I may have suffered from profound weakness of the gastric system as the result of general exhaustion. Even my eye trouble, which sometimes approached so parlously near to blindness, was only an effect and not a cause; for, whenever my general vital condition improved, my power of vision also increased.

He blames the original physical exhaustion on the German climate and German habits of over-eating, over-drinking, gathering round stuffy stoves, and on his own sedentary habits as a philological book-worm – from all of which he has long freed himself by escaping South. He makes no reference to his real ailment, a deep-seated venereal taint, though he must have been aware of it. 'I placed myself in my own hands, I restored myself to health … out of my will to Health and Life I made my philosophy.'

L.R. observes of the Germans: 'They nurse their shattered organisms with exalted invalid fantasies of hardiness.' *Ecce Homo* is one long diatribe against spiritual and physical uncleanness. 'I am gifted with a sense of cleanliness the keenness of which is phenomenal … I would die in unclean surroundings – I swim, bathe and splash about, as it were, incessantly in water, in any kind of perfectly transparent and shining element.' This bathing and swimming metaphor for spirituality is common to Nietzsche's writings; as all Germans give a spiritual significance to bathing and swimming. (Tacitus remarked on how much bathing the Germans did.) The Germans are also mountain-mad. By climbing they metaphorically express hatred of themselves for living in what Nietzsche (speaking in spiritual terms) calls the Flatland of Europe. Nietzsche's supreme praise for his *Zarathustra* is 'the loftiest book on earth, literally the book of mountain air'. Swimming and mountain-climbing take a high yearly death-toll of Germans: the number of bathers drowned in the Rhine, and of climbers killed in the Alps, is excessive. It is characteristic of the Germans, too, that once one of them gets drowned in a foreign river or killed on a foreign mountain his example is always followed by others: they do not intend to get killed, only to tempt a danger which the death of one of them has Germanized. Nietzsche knew the falsity of this climbing urge. He addressed the Germans in his *Dionysus-Dithyrambs:*

> Ye mount?
> Is it true that ye mount,
> Ye loftier men?
> Are ye not, pray,
> Like to a ball
> Sped to the heights
> By the lowest that's in you?
> Do ye not flee from yourselves, O ye climbers?

In the same poem he also writes:

> Only the poet who can lie
> Wilfully, skilfully
> Can tell the truth.

Nietzsche's clinical notes to the epitome of his books bear out L.R.'s observation: 'Physical pain is the strongest preoccupation of the German mind.' The wish to arouse universal pity for suffering bravely borne is a characteristic of Germans for which Nietzsche had nothing but scorn and of which he wrote at length; yet he could not avoid the national idiosyncrasy himself. The year, he said indeed, contained for him two hundred days of pure pain. Fear of physical indisposition makes the Germans of all people the most conscious of dietetic problems; and Nietzsche has not written twenty pages of this spiritual biography of himself as superman (the chapter heading is 'Why I am so clever'), before be feels himself obliged to note: 'In an enervating climate tea is not a good beverage with which to start the day: an hour before taking it an excellent thing is to drink a cup of thick cocoa, freed from oil.' In this strain he presses the double sense of the German word *Heiland*, which means both 'physician' and 'spiritual saviour'.

Nietzsche felt strongly in himself the German dietetic dilemma: the choice between the two extremes of 'bestial' meat-gorging and drink-guzzling and the 'nonsense' of vegetarianism, to which he lent himself for a time. The guzzling and sousing is the natural German habit – Tacitus commented on it – and Nietzsche rightly linked it up with German intellectual barbarity. Vegetarianism is the unnatural reaction, and Nietzsche rightly linked it up with the 'beautiful soul' movement which he equally hated. Yet on the one hand he boasts of his own youthful prowess as a student-drinker at Pforta University, and on the other hand praises his *Dawn of Day*, written shortly after his severance from German cookery and drinking, for

> ... that sweetness and spirituality which is almost inseparable from extreme poverty of blood and muscle.... The perfect lucidity and cheerfulness, the intellectual exuberance even, that this work reflects, coincides, in my case, not only with the most profound physiological weakness, but also with an excess of suffering. In the midst of the agony of a headache which lasted three days, accompanied by violent nausea, I was possessed of most singular dialectical clearness, and in absolutely cold blood I then thought out things, for which, in my more healthy moments, I am not enough of a climber, not sufficiently subtle, not sufficiently cold.

Nietzsche blamed vegetarianism, or malnutrition, for the spread of the enervating Buddhistic creed; and in modern Germany there has been a sympathetic affiliation between Tagore, Gandhi and Krishnamurti cults and the Rohkost creed. The 'beautiful soul' movement is apparently no modernism: the Germans have always been susceptible to Oriental religions. Tacitus was surprised by the presence of Isis rites in Germany – Isis, he said, was symbolized by a galley to denote that her worship was imported. He also remarked on the German desire to be thought well of by the outside world: 'They are peculiarly pleased with presents from neighbouring nations.'

The chief contradiction in Nietzsche lay in his alternate assertion and denial that he was a German. He loathed himself for being a German, and yet the immoderacy and self-contradictoriness of his loathing was characteristically German. He took refuge in the lie that he was really a Pole:

'My ancestors were Polish noblemen.' But his mother was pure German, and his father, a Lutheran pastor with connexions with a petty Court, had a pure German mother; the Polish strain was remote. He found comfort in the thought that when he travelled abroad he was never taken for a German, and usually for a Pole. Culturally he declared himself French. 'The Poles are the French among the Slavs.' 'I believe only in French culture and regard everything else in Europe which calls itself culture as a misunderstanding.' Referring to the *National Zeitung,* he says, 'a Prussian newspaper (this explanation is for the benefit of my foreign readers: for my own part, I beg to state, I only read *Le Journal des Débats*)'. Again, in one of his poems he describes himself as Genoese (by residence of a year or two), linking himself with Columbus. His Polish blood made it easy for him, he said, to be 'a good European'. Yet he was hungry and lonely for Germany and constantly slipped back in his writings into 'We Germans'. One of his poems, 'In Lonesomeness', is the most ingenuous admission of this hunger:

> The cawing crows
>   Townwards on whirring pinions roam;
> Soon come the snows –
>   Thrice happy now who hath a home!
>
> Fast-rooted there,
>   Thou gazest backwards – oh, how long!
> Thou fool, why dare
>   Ere winter come, this world of wrong?
>
> Now stand'st thou pale,
>   A frozen pilgrimage thy doom,
> Like smoke whose trail
>   Cold and still colder skies consume.

Nietzsche supplemented the poem with 'My Answer', as if the stanzas had been addressed not to himself by himself, but to himself by some critic in Germany:

> The man presumes –
>   Good Lord! – to think that I'd return
> To those warm rooms
>   Where snug the German ovens burn.
>
> My friend, you see
>   'Tis but thy folly drives me far, –
> Pity for *thee*
>   And all that German blockheads are!

In *Ecce Homo* he makes another accidental confession, at the end of a passage about his Polish blood and *'this* side of the Alps' and the German inability to understand music: 'I do not know how to think either of joy or of the South without a shudder of fear.' And in spite of his passionate invective against everything German he continued to award the highest praise to German individuals. By the time he came to write *Ecce Homo* he had dropped most of his previous admirations – Wagner, Schopenhauer, Goethe; but he could still applaud Heine, Händel, Bach, von Ranke, Ritchl, Schultz, explaining them as either of foreign extraction or as belonging to a race of strong Germans now vanished. He accounts for his former adoration of Wagner by saying that Wagner's music was 'the counter-poison to everything German': it was all wrong, a German drug, but if one lived in Germany, as he himself had done, one needed it to keep alive at all. 'If a man wishes to get rid of a feeling of insufferable oppression he takes to hashish.' Yet he had once prospectively linked himself with Wagner in posthumous fame. 'When, in the summer of 1876, I took leave of Wagner in my soul ... I took up arms, not without anger, *against myself* and on behalf of all that hurt me and fell hard on me.' One of his chief charges against Wagner's music is that it incites Germans not to marching or dancing, like strong old German music, but to a falsely spiritual *swimming*.

Nietzsche could not disguise the fact that German was the language in which he thought and felt and wrote. So he spoke of it as an obstacle the overcoming of which made his feats still more glorious. 'Before my time people did not know what could be done with the German language.' He boasted that he had even contrived to endow it with wit: the famous Monsieur Tame had spoken of his *finesses* and *audaces*. Yet 'in order to cross the threshold of this noble and subtle world one must certainly not be a German'. German dyspepsia 'utterly excludes all intercourse with my books'. He has been 'discovered in St Petersburg, Stockholm, Copenhagen, Paris, New York – everywhere but in Germany'. This curious appreciation of his work, in spite of the language bar, is due to the fact that 'my readers are all exceptionally intelligent men'. At this point Nietzsche cannot help making an appeal to Germany, as a poor misunderstood child cast off by his cruel parent. He writes winningly:

> Wherever I go, here in Turin, for instance, every face brightens and softens at the sight of me. A thing that has flattered me more than anything else hitherto, is the fact that old market-women cannot rest until they have picked out the sweetest of their grapes for me.

Nietzsche was a clever tactician and knew it:

> Deceit
> Is war's whole art.
> The foxskin

Is my secret shirt of mail.

This agrees with a statement in *Ecce Homo* about the natural depravity of 'us Thuringians', but is in flat contradiction with a neighbouring statement that he only fights honourable duels, with all fair and above-board.

His praise of everything French was well calculated. That a distinguished German classical scholar of good family and reputation had turned King's evidence against German culture was most welcome news to the French – still smarting from their defeat in the Franco-Prussian War. Nietzsche's master-stroke was the declaration that France had recovered her soul in this war. He even went so far in his flattery as to put Paris at the head of the places of 'pure dry air', followed by Athens, Provence, Florence and Jerusalem, where genius was climatically at home. French critics praised him extravagantly and the French Government eventually subsidized a translation of his collected works. Nietzsche knew that it was useless to flatter the English into accepting him as a superman; London is not among the capitals where he claimed to have been discovered. He seems to have decided that the best way of attracting the interest of Englishmen was to make disparaging remarks about their *niaiserie*, in the French style; he writes of them as 'mediocre', 'unsophisticated' and 'benighted'. He even uses the French sneer at the size of Englishwomen's feet; and defends French classical writers – Molière, Racine, Corneille – against the claims made for Shakespeare's wild genius. But he cannot avoid the jealous, complaining intonation which the Germans inevitably fall into when talking about England. 'England's small-mindedness' was the 'great danger now on earth': herself and her colonies were needed for the European mastery of the world, under the spiritual leadership of a self-confident Germany.

He knew that he would get fame in Germany by repercussion: that he would be honoured as a great misunderstood German who had been honoured by the outside world, and that his apparent anti-Germanism would be understood and forgiven. A further shrewd move was his flattery of the Jews. He called the German Jews the honourable exceptions in national Philistinism; rightly counting on them to make the home link. Much of the real impetus of the Nietzsche movement has come from Jews. The Editor of the standard English translation, Dr Oscar Levy, writes in his critical notes both as a militant Jew and a militant Nietzschean. He discounts the seriousness of the Nietzsche movement in France and expresses 'the firm conviction that if we could not obtain a hearing for Nietzsche in England, his wonderful and at the same time very practical thought must be lost for ever to the world – a world that would then quickly be darkened over again by the ever-threatening clouds of obscurantism and barbarism'. The Nietzschean cult in England has been confined to a very small group, mostly consisting of Scots; the one promi-

nent person to champion him has been Bernard Shaw. Because of Shaw he
has been accepted as a household reference, but at the price of being
treated as a Shavian paradox.

Nietzsche wrote violently against Hegel, only allowing him as a useful
counter-poison to German sentimentality. Tragic sentimentality is
another German characteristic. (The only other people in Europe to have
it mixed, in the same way, with blood-thirstiness and philosophy, are the
Scots.) He characterizes it:

> …Good-natured; incontinent in small pleasures; always ready for
> tears; wanting to be able to get rid of innate sobriety and strict atten-
> tion to duty and exercise; a smiling, indeed a laughing indulgence;
> confusing goodness and sympathy and welding them into one – this
> is the essential characteristic of German sentimentality; rejoicing at
> a noble magnanimous action; thoroughly self-satisfied.

This is the natural Germanism, the Germanism of the playwright
Kotzebue, he says, on which foreign elements are inappropriately
engrafted. Nietzsche's prose writings are the best possible evidence of this
contamination – for which he blames the Goethe cult. And in evidence of
uncontaminated German sentimentality there are his poems, even those
composed after his flight from Germany. For example, his two hymns to
Friendship; and his two poems on the subject of an Italian tombstone on
which was carved a relief of a girl stroking a lamb, with the inscription:
'*Pia, caritatevole, amorosissima.*' In the second of these poems occur the
following verses:

> To-day, to-day alone,
> My soul to tears is stirred,
> At thee, the pictured stone,
> At thee, the graven word.
>
> This picture (none need wis)
> I kissed the other day.
> When there's so much to kiss
> Why did I kiss the – clay?
>
> Who knows the reason why?
> 'A tombstone fool!' you laugh:
> I kissed – I'll not deny –
> E'en the long epitaph.

The anti-sentimental, blood-thirsty side of Nietzsche's Germanism is
manifest in his glorification of war and his description of himself in *Ecce
Homo* as 'the most terrible man who has ever existed', on whose appearance follow cataclysmic world-happenings. Looking about Germany for

companions in terribleness, he found them in Prussia, where there was an admixture of Slavonic blood.

> The Brandenburg nobility and the Prussian nobility in general (and the peasantry of certain North German districts) comprise the most manly natures in Europe. That the manliest shall rule, this is the only natural order of things. The future of German culture rests with the sons of Prussian officers. We require an inter-growth of the German and Slav races and we require too the cleverest financiers, the Jews, for us to become masters of the world.

Nietzsche is nowhere so inconsistent as in his alternate recommendations, as a non-German German, for the blending and for the non-blending of national races and cultures. 'Our present-day Europe, the scene of a senseless, precipitate attempt at a blending of races....' 'What I am concerned with – for I see it preparing itself slowly and hesitating – is the United Europe. It was the only real work, the only impulse in the souls, of all the broad-minded and deep-thinking men of this century. Only in their weaker moments did they fall back again into the national narrowness of the "Fatherlanders".' In preaching the necessity for a consolidated European culture he either assigns the leading part to Germany or excludes Germany altogether. 'Wherever Germany extends her sway she *ruins* culture.' Now he applauds Goethe for introducing foreign culture into Germany, now he deplores the result: 'German culture is a sort of cosmopolitan aggregate.'

Nietzsche, in his attitude to women, is divided between a desperate need for their society and a fanatic desire to stand alone. One of the strongest German traits is the recourse to women in time of anxiety. German women, as L.R. observes, are traditionally harassed by male self-preoccupation and exist only as vehicles of sympathy with male grievances against fate. Tacitus writes about the Germans' readiness to take the advice of their women – 'these, too, are the most revered witnesses of each man's conduct, and his most liberal applauders'; and about the tribal marriage-ritual – the husband presenting cattle and war-like gifts to the wife, the wife presenting the husband with arms, which he must not disgrace while married to her, and thus becoming the priestess of his honour. The wilful insensitivity of Germans toward their women in every-day life, mentioned by L.R., has in it an element of shame – shame of their dependence on women in moments of crisis. As in the time of Tacitus, Germans still have an uncomfortable feeling that 'something of sanctity and prescience resides in the female sex'.

Nietzsche advocated the total suppression of these feelings: Germans should learn to treat their women in the Oriental fashion, in the manner of strong men. Women's first and last function was child-bearing: in between, her function was to distract man and alleviate his troubles. In her distractive capacity Nietzsche insisted that she should take her cue from the man's desires, throwing prudishness to the winds: for 'love forgives all'. This is no easy task for her, he admits; man is so restless. She cannot keep his love unless she is essentially feminine, constantly whetting his sexual appetite by her fickleness. Such fickleness bars women from any part in public life or from any serious work. 'Women are so constituted that all truth disgusts them and that they try to be revenged on everyone who opens their eyes.' Yet 'the perfect woman is a higher type of humanity than the perfect man'. As for the divinatory and intuitive powers attributed to them, Nietzsche alternately pooh-poohed these powers and expressed the deep confidence in them that Tacitus mentions as a peculiar mark of Germanism. The most bitter of Nietzsche's many bitter charges against German women was that they were directly responsible for the barbarity of German culture; because they were such bad cooks, and because intellectual dyspepsia was identical with physical dyspepsia.

He gave them a complete exculpation, however, by saying that they really are not to be blamed; they are whatever man makes them. 'Man created woman – out of what? Out of a rib of his god, – of his ideal.' His own physical preference was for a majestic, contralto-voiced Germanic type – *petite* women were no women at all, he agreed with Aristotle. But this did not fit in with his intellectual demand for French daintiness and roguishness: he hated 'placid cows' as he hated the monogamic earnestness of the German marriage which had so impressed Tacitus. 'Bovine', 'cows', 'cattle', were his strongest words of anti-German abuse. He wanted to be a bird; he had a bird nature, he protested. And 'in order to become light and be as a bird, one must lose oneself – thus spake Zarathustra'. Nietzsche never succeeded in losing himself, only in contradicting himself; and the more self-contradictory he became, the more German – no soaring Napoleonic or Pindaric eagle, only a mad German ox entering into the spirit of the market-place by breaking loose from its herd and blundering into the booths.

POEMS AND POETS

Laura Riding

with questions and comments by Robert Graves

THE CRITICISM OF POEMS and poets may be called super-critical in that its material allows of more direct and complete judgement than material imbedded in the geological layers of history, on the excavation of which criticism must expend most of its energy. For in the criticism of poems and poets the material is already on the surface, and critical procedure is more obviously critical: it is in this sense that we can call it super-critical. Poets themselves do not merely lie on the surface like surviving monuments, as poems do; they walk about alive – living ghosts. And so in dealing with poets, rather than with poems, we are obliged to treat as it were *with* them, rather than *of* them. What is with poems an orderly distribution – as of intact relics which by their insistent survival deserve a fixed place in the landscape-present of finality – becomes, with poets, as it were, an emotional engagement of the self of poetry with its ghostly human selves; all the same ghost, really, in changing postures, while poems are the stable memorial individualities of this restless apparition.

CONVERSATION ON THE CRITICISM OF POEMS

Question – Will you first show how your definitions, which must necessarily be more final in the subject 'poetry' than in the more categorical, particular subjects, can be directly applied to the historical aspects of poem-writing and poet-being.

Answer – Definitions under the heading 'poetry' are indeed more explicitly poetic than the more conventionally critical definitions. What is the practical application of the explicitly poetic definitions to the routine-problems of the criticism of poems? Let us say that such definitions occur internally, within the first circle of poetic meaning, whereas the more categorically critical definitions occur in the outer historical circles. One way of answering your question is to say that with the criticism of poems the historical circles begin to disappear; that the method of applying definitions is here that of direct extension, or sympathetic elasticity, rather than of formal translation from the poetic into the critical.

[*R.G.* – What is the relation of this principle of extension to the minute analysis of Shakespeare's sonnet 129 we made in *A Survey of Modernist Poetry?*]

Answer – In that exercise in the *Survey* we were defending the integrity of texts against criticism which had only the object of softening their eccentricity as social documents. We did not offer this technique as a critical method; we meant to establish by verification of the text the reality which a poem may have apart from its social reality – a reality by which it is inviolable. We were defending the title of poems to attempt poetic reality in disregard of the anti-poetic pressure of social reality. And, as propagandists, we were defending only the title to attempt, not the results of attempt. We defended the textual integrity of a poem of Shakespeare's, as an instance of justifiable attempt – justifiable because the attempt is sustained throughout the poem. We were merely interested at the moment in keeping open the contemporary doors of attempt. The officious editing suffered by the particular poem of Shakespeare's examined provided a very full illustration of the social tyranny against which poetic writing must defend itself.

About the critical applicability of the poetic, the more final, definitions: the question is of their possible loss of meaning in the more remote uses of literary criticism – and so not merely a question of their practical usefulness but equally of the danger of their being corrupted and trivialized in such uses. Such a danger would exist where the interest in poems was mere scientific curiosity, to the prejudice of the poetically pertinent interest – the discovery and isolation of poetic content. Such a danger does, indeed, exist, if the critical removal from the poetic centre is based on a fear that too literal an acceptance of the central definitions might undermine patience with the historical texts. The only just basis for critical removal from the poetic centre is in the poetic inadequacies of texts which can be found only relatively good. But the critic of poems must *start* with a firm awareness of the absolutely good – of value. In the criticism of poems we might call this awareness, this sense of poetic definition, the first part; and the elasticizing of poetic definition toward the critical contingency, the second part. Hesitation between the two parts has characterized the behaviour of all the critics of the past. And they have dealt with their hesitation either by abrogating the first part, dissociating themselves arbitrarily from it in an Aristotelian mode of critical workmanship, or by softening the second part with experimental divination (the Platonic mode), blurring the critical function in philosophy.

The first part should be separated from the critical act not by any prejudice in favour of the second part, but merely by the recognized limitations of literary criticism. It is not that the critic must avoid the poetic sense in order to have the critical sense, but that he must deny himself use of the first sense except as a means of evaluating literary material, with the object of differentiating it accurately from absolute literature, or poetry. But he must first of all acquiesce absolutely in poetry – the poetic centre – in order to be able to conceive the secondary material relatively; he cannot make the acquiescence a sentimental corollary of literary criticism.

The real danger is the misuse of the terms of the first part: with the effect either of critical obscurity or of vulgarization of their poetic sense. But the danger will disappear in the restraint with which the critic applies these terms to the second part: if he applies them in such a way that the second part is not overburdened with the first nor the first corrupted with the second – if he limits himself to defining the impingement of one on the other. In this impingement a shadow-play of moral significances must be indicated, in which the poetic centre is the source of illumination for a view of poems as written with only a comparatively immediate sense of the poetic centre – as written in the unimmediate past. Criticism must show poems – texts – as removed from poetic reality – text – by their human immediacy.

Question – But to whom is the criticism of poems addressed? If it is addressed to the readers of poems, then there exist other problems besides the relation of the poem to value; there exists the problem of its historical reality, that is to say, its human reasonableness. And does this not imply considerations which, while of a critical order, must be stated in terms of historical value, rather than of poetic value?

Answer – The stipulated reader of the poem is really the critic who omits the perception of poetic value. The critic who insists on the reader is as it were hoarding the privilege of a kind of critical shop-talk with other critics which need not satisfy tests of poetic pertinence, but tests of human pertinence alone. But the human pertinence of a poem does not indicate value except as it shows the destruction of poetic pertinence in human pertinence.

In stipulating a reader-aspect you do, in fact, stipulate two kinds of interest in a poem: an interest in poems as historically intelligible, and as poetically intelligible. Certainly a view of poems as strictly relative to poetry rather than loosely identical with poetry presumes an idea of history distinct from an idea of value. But it does not presume a value of history. This is a value that critics invoke when there is no original acquiescence in the notion of poetry, and so no super-critical basis of criticism. Such critics value poems as they humanize the notion of poetry – for their humanity. The non-historical critic is concerned with the humanity of poems only as it spells a consciousness of not being identical with poetry even in the effort of identity.

We must avoid the danger of attaching critical authority to the opinions of critics merely because they seem to be governed by a scepticism toward the claims of poems to be poetry: their scepticism seems to correspond with our view of critical measure – the treatment of the *whole* content of any specific poem as critical content. But this view is very different from a humanistic concern in the poem as readable – from a merely literary concern. The criteria of readability that have composed the professional apparatus of critics in the past refer to the plausibility of poems as historical truth. The proper criteria of criticism are, indeed, secondary criteria – although its authority is founded in the primary criteria of truth. But these secondary criteria form no truth of their own independent of final truth; poems cannot be endowed, through the application of secondary criteria, with an independent historical truth. The secondary criteria of criticism are merely moral equivalents of the primary criteria of truth.

The critical aspect of value is to the poetic aspect of value as goodness is to truth. The critic must discover in poems, demonstrate by poems, goodness – values which are true for the exclusive human circumstances brought together in the poem. And the step between the true and the good, the transition from the poetic to the critical aspect of value, is not to be accomplished by a deliberate break with the poetic aspect. For then the critic must depend on historical criteria for the language of criticism, and the comparison he makes is not between the good and the true but between historical truth and poetic truth, so that he is talking in two languages, the second of which is in sentimental contrast with the first, rather than morally identical with it. Critical analysis which proceeds by the allegorical comparison of plausibility with truth results only in a contentment in plausibility as a practical substitute for truth; whereas critical analysis which proceeds by poetic, or intrinsic, comparison results in the dramatic effect of value. And it is the function of the critic of poems to dramatize the notion of poetry through the trivializing it undergoes in the human associations which condition poems. A poem must be shown to be as it were a comparison of the notion with itself at the disadvantage of human abbreviation: through the particularity of the poem, the generality – the size of the notion – is indicated. It is the poem itself which makes the step from the poetic to the critical aspect of value. It is the poem which derives the critic from the poetic centre. Poems themselves are the critical criteria, and their serviceability as criteria should be the test of their goodness: to what degree does the poem provide terms for a particularised statement of poetic value?

We must dispense with the idea of the reader in the historical sense. The direction of the reading, the dramatic address of the poem, must be toward poetry itself, not toward a human public with predispositions either for or against an absolute notion of poetry. Allowance for a human public with predispositions for an absolute notion of poetry results in critical extravagances; allowance for a human public with predispositions against an absolute notion of poetry results in concessions by the critic, on behalf of poetry, to human disbelief in poetry. In the first instance the critic would tend to make poetry comprise all the human notions of what is good, to define poetry itself as a morality, and in so doing sentimentalize – humanize – the notion. In the second instance the critic would tend to treat poetry as an abstraction; he would, indeed, by the exaggeratedly rationalistic character of his criticism, show poetic truth as acquiescing in its incommunicability in the merely human, conversational results of poems. The critic's work is properly one of intermediation between the poem and poetic truth. And in this intermediation he must show the address of the poem to be toward poetic truth as toward a public; the poem has no other public. Poetic truth is the only generality, the only judge of poetic effect, the only object of propitiation with which the poem can be legitimately concerned.

Question – How would you describe the relation between the writing of poems, in history, and their reality as non-historical acts – poetically rather than historically determined? The relation, in fact, between poetry as a historical conception and as an absolute conception?

Answer – 'Poetry' has been conceived as a human continuum made up of individual persuasions about finality; and thus, as a word, it has been used to describe the activity of poets rather than the inevitable point of rest at which the continuum will show itself to have been merely degrees of approach to absolute rest. I would correct the historical notion of poetry with a historical corollary: that finality, as the poetic subject, or cause, must be historically realized as the poetic object, or end. Poems anticipate (use as cause), in the form of human instances, the final event into which poetry accumulates through literary postponement. Poetry, the ideal end of the literary continuum, is an end; that is, it must happen otherwise than merely as poems, which are the temporal rendering of poetry. This explanation employs the idea of immediacy in a way that avoids possibilities of falsification: to describe *actual finality*. I.A. Richards's 'poetry as a means to value' asserts the historical benefits achieved by poems as the object of poems; he might better have said 'poetry as a means to a sense of value'.

Question – In this definition of poetic end which you make, what room is there for other ends or values? Does 'poetry', as the name of poetic end, exclude all the ends which have been historically identified with poetry: does it, in fact, exclude poems?

Answer – My definition does not exclude poems, but includes them by the subordination of their historically immediate, particular intention to what must be the general and final object of all poetic writing: an immediacy of reality, as superseding the more historically vivid but neverthe-less only approximate participation in reality which poems achieve. I reject, that is, only the glorification of intention – to the obscurity of the existence of the object which makes the intention possible.

Let us keep for the moment to the word 'end', associating 'value' with the *quality* of finality achievable by poems. In using poetry to describe 'end' oppositionally, I am ascribing vulgarity to individualized ends. I am distinguishing between end and free historical interpretations of end; the most deceptive of these being those which postulate 'pure' end – or poetic writing as an end in itself. My distinction is, also, an opposition of the notion of finality to the notion of futurity; Shelley is an example of a poet governed by futurity rather than finality. Abstract notions of poetry seem to endorse the notion of poetry as end; but the endorsement is deceptive. In the poems of Donne, for example, an abstract notion of poetry is subscribed to: cynically, as an ideal which sponsors the negation of human meanings. Poetic end has the force here of destructive finality. But where poetic end is a positive finality the human meanings of poems are critically redeemed in absolute poetic meaning. This explanation, besides clarifying poetry as end, should also supply a definition of literary criticism from the poetic viewpoint as against a definition of poetry from the literary view-point. For in asserting poetry as end we break down the categorical treat-ment of poetry and literary criticism – which makes 'poetry' only a verbal associate of criticism – and have *entity:* poetry as a standard of judgement governing the laws of poetic proportion.

Poetry as value is the demand for immediate response which poetry as end constitutes. Coleridge, for example, was tortured by his inability to meet this demand. He knew poetry but did not immediately feel it; his poems were desperate efforts to achieve a sense of poetic actuality by a deliberate emotionalization of his knowledge. Yeats seems absorbed in a similar sort of problem. But he does not, as Coleridge did, *know* poetry; poetry is with him a literary hypothesis, to be used as a background for emotional variety. The responsibility to demonstrate value which obsessed Coleridge so painfully (exactly because he was aware of his inability to do so), Yeats recognizes only as the professional responsibility to write poems which shall satisfy his own high standard of the complex sensibility becoming in a poet. I think it pertinent to name them together in this context because in both one is aware of an emphatic energy of poem-making – as distinguished from a serenely sustained consciousness of poetry; an energy which characterises the effort of value, whether the value-demand is authentically felt or not.

Question – Will you now redefine the notion of poetry and the notion of criticism you have been jointly developing here in a way to show how the notion of judgement is divided between them; and whether judgement is to be understood as a peculiar property of poetry, or of criticism. And will you clarify the difference between the relation of the critic, and that of the poet, to poetry?

Answer – Poetry is the only absolute to which comparative reference can be made; the only absolute which is not an abstraction. It is the basis of all comparison, the unique standard governing likeness. When a person says 'I like that,' he is using the notion of poetry as a sentimental model: the thing has likeness – it belongs somewhere within a range of interest centred in himself. The notion of poetry is the notion of an implicit identity of all distinctions in a final standard of relation. That which does not imply standard can have no reality as a distinction: it is freakish. Judgement is the force of interest with which the pole of identity is magnetized. By means of judgement, the different is endowed with coherence; judgement is at once the agent of unity and of diversity.

Criticism is not itself judgement, but the exercise of the principle of judgement implicit in the notion of poetry. Judgement does not consist of acts of dogma (taste), but of exemplifications of poetic liberality; the critic seeks to discover material which may be vested with truth according to its particular goodness – not merely to distinguish arbitrarily between the bad and the good. The critic is not interested in 'bad' poems. And with 'good' poems he is interested in more than in finding them good. He is interested in the verification of an order of poetic 'likeness'. Nor does he expect perfect poetic likeness, or identical truth, in the mere poem. He expects it only in what I have called 'text'; and text cannot be the work of a single humanly natured poet. The 'good' poem, in fact, is that in which there is, besides human likeness, an admixture of poetic likeness; as the 'bad' poem is that in which human likeness masquerades as poetic likeness.

The critic is preoccupied with the differences between poems and poetry. The poet attempts self-identification with poetry; the critic makes a comparison between the poem and poetry. The poet uses poetry, the language of identity, the critic uses prose, the language of differentiation. Yet the critic has a stronger practical identity with poetry than the poet has – though a less intense one in a personal sense: the critic starts from the poetic centre, moving away from it toward levels of incomplete identity, while the poet starts in the human scene and moves ambitiously toward poetry as toward an ideal self. Judgement is the clarification of the ambiguities with which poetic ambition is loaded; criticism is the prophetic assertion of the inevitableness of judgement. The critic prophesies judgement; the poet – with his poem – challenges judgement. Thus the critic furthers the action of judgement, while the poet lingers in the poem, obsessed with the consequences of judgement: the critic, so to speak, purifies the judgement-situation of the private morbidities of the poet.

Question – The critic has indeed an advantage over the poet in that he steps into the situation after it has been created – by the existence of poets and poems; his interest is pure, that is, free from personal concern. But is not this purity conditioned by the fact that he expresses himself in prose, and so diffusely; while the poet, however personally coloured his consciousness, must subject himself to the discipline of poetic expression – which means a concentratedness, an imposed unity of thought? So that, in this sense of language, the poet is being more severe with himself than the critic can ever be with him?

Answer – First, to repeat: it is the function of the critic to be liberal, not severe. The severity of a poet with himself is, moreover, a pressure upon himself to be superior to himself, while the critic must be content with the imperfections he finds, accepting their inevitability as the poet cannot. Prose is adapted to the acceptance of imperfections in a way in which poetic expression is not. Nor is prose necessarily diffuse expression; it should not be this in its use by a critic. Prose is the language of difference, as poetic expression is the language of unity. And prose is only diffuse when it sentimentally imitates the poetic obscuring rather than illuminating difference. Criticism must operate through prose since it is the measurement of compatible difference, a measurement of particular poems as combinations of variant material with the objective of perfect unity ideally undertaken by all poems. It is by this passive fidelity to the given material – which is the fidelity of prose – that criticism has active fidelity to the given end of poetry: by which its definitions have elastic range, are poetic definitions in being critically sensitive. Thus we can say that a central poetic statement becomes critical by the application of its quality of absoluteness as a quality of range.

Question – Is there any way in which the casual opinions that a poem provokes belong to the poem? I mean, apart from the larger nature of criticism as the reconciliation of difference with unity, what pertinence can casual opinions about poems have? What, if any, minor critical usefulness for their poems? Granting that they are 'just' opinions?

Answer – By 'just' opinion you mean, presumably, a kind of historical reaction determined by the poem itself – not by the historical prejudices of the critic; a reaction to the content of human experience in the poem. Such a reaction can be critically useful as a measure of the poem's responsibleness – its historical conscience. Because a poem is only a poem (not poetry) it must be disciplined with the human concerns from which the poet is to some degree freeing himself in it: he cannot make himself absolutely free. Opinions of poems, therefore, are useful in testing the human sanity of the poet – since opinions cannot exist of activities which dispense irresponsibly with human concerns. This is as if to say that the experience of Jesus, viewed as a poem, is unreal in its non-human aspect because, in proceeding from human to non-human concerns, he dispensed with human concerns, falsely suppressing them in his act of self-liberation: thus removing the possibility of opinions about his experience and giving it a false absoluteness. And the result has been, because of this absence of responsibleness, the uncritical reaction which is called belief. So my answer would be that opinions, as distinct from the orderly findings of criticism, may strengthen the historical authenticity of a poem.

Question – What is the significance of the preoccupation of the Elizabethan poets with criticism: that so many of them were themselves critics? Of the Elizabethan tradition of 'apologies'?

Answer – Elizabethan poets frequently were critics as well as poets, just as their poems were both personal and impersonal: they were, in the good sense of the word, critical poems – poems and their criticism together. The Elizabethan apology was not an apology for poetry but for poems; virtue was claimed for them, but no boast of mysterious absoluteness made. The apology was, in fact, to poetry, not to the human public. Romantic apology, in reviving the Elizabethan habit of apology, addressed the human public, and in this sense: 'See, this is not a frightening, indigestible notion of poetry that we present to you, but magnificent, inspiring human resistance to the notion.' Spenser, indeed, anticipated this note: he was properly an early nineteenth-century figure, rather than an Elizabethan, as Keats appreciated. Keats identified himself with Spenser critically, but this identification left his poetic problem unsolved. He resisted the notion of poetry 'magnificently', but remained still petulant and dissatisfied. He was torn between his desire to make a fine human show, and an involuntary reaction of surrender to the notion; surrenders in which he expectantly disposed himself, so to speak, toward spiritual rape by a vigorous poetic personhead imagined as in pursuit of conquests. Shelley tried to solve this problem of the two spectators (the human audience and poetry itself) by a sentimental compromise: a notion of poetry in which judgement was evaded by a philosophical equating of the human with the poetic.

[R.G. – What you say about Keats and Shelley provides a very useful clue to the peculiar resemblances and oppositions between them; I should like, when you have finished this conversation, to present a study of them according to these characterizations of yours. And I should also like to make a similar study of Coleridge and Wordsworth. What clue, within the kind of meanings you have been setting out here, would you suggest for them?]

Answer – For Coleridge and Wordsworth one should, I think, first of all consult the word 'pleasure'. In the poems of Keats and Shelley one is primarily conscious of what they are 'doing'; in the poems of Coleridge and Wordsworth, of what they are feeling, or trying to feel. The pleasure element in any poem is the pursuit of an experience which is against human reason and yet does not permanently affect or discredit human experience and identity: to enjoy an identity-sense different from the human and yet not to lose human identity – rather to decorate and confirm it. The essence of this pleasure is in the *unreality* of the enjoyed poetic identity as compared with the homely, secure reality of the human. Thus Wordsworth insisted on the preservation of human reality in poetic experience; while Coleridge was morbidly fascinated by poetic 'unreality' as it continually and challengingly broke into human reality, with the effect not of pleasure but of pain – pleasurable pain. Coleridge was not humanly brusque and self-protective, as Wordsworth was; nor yet poetically active enough to affirm poetic reality against human reality. He chose the way of paradox, opposing one reality to the other without having the courage to decide between them or the faith in himself to attempt a practical resolution of the paradox. He rested at pleasure, thus identifying himself with the comfortable majority of poets to whom poetic experience is, merely, the exciting human accident; with the difference that he knew that this meant poetic suicide.

L.R.

[Some of the problems dealt with in this study were originally suggested by Mr J. Bronowski in a private correspondence.]

COLERIDGE AND WORDSWORTH

Robert Graves

COLERIDGE, AS L.R. HAS INDICATED, accepted, although against his instinct, the conventional distinction between poetic reality and human reality. But while 'Life went a-maying with Nature, Hope and Poesy', he had believed in the possibility of an accord between the two. While still at the University he had decided not to pursue metaphysical speculation, but to seek a life of practical virtue and labour in ideal surroundings and in the company of chosen friends. He was always looking for friends. The closest friends he made were also poets, but not poets in his sense. They were stupid but ambitious men, clever enough to recognize that he had the very qualities which they needed to improve their own work: they could borrow from him. Southey was the first. Coleridge drew him into a scheme for forming a pantisocratic community with ten other gentlemen and twelve ladies in the backwoods of America. Coleridge wrote at the time:

> ... O'er the ocean swell
> Sublime of Hope, I seek the cottag'd dell
> Where virtue calm with careless step may stray,
> And dancing to the moonlight roundelay,
> The wizard Passions weave a holy spell.

But Southey abandoned this colonizing scheme as impracticable, and Coleridge never recovered from the set-back. It returned pantisocracy to the barren region of speculation from which he had tried to escape: moonlight and the wizard passions, failing to reconcile themselves with virtue calm and the cottag'd dell, became disconnected poetic unreality again.

He next won the friendship of Wordsworth. Wordsworth had himself recently made a failure, but a more complete one than Coleridge's. He had known an overwhelming sense of guilt from his desertion, at his uncle's orders, of Annette Vallon and her unborn child, despite his pledges of perpetual love. He had also deserted the Girondin cause to which he had pledged his revolutionary sword. These experiences had been Wordsworth's plunge into poetic unreality, and he set himself to destroy all incriminating evidence of them. The story appeared, as a tale told him in France, in 'Vaudracour and Julia'. Though giving an account of the closeness of the tie binding the two lovers and the spiritual collapse of Vaudracour after he had been separated from Julia by filial obedience to family orders, he so distorts the actual happenings as to acquit Vaudracour of all infamy and assist the drawing of the moral of human reality: the love was too idealistic, and should have remained unconsummated. In one other early poem, 'Nutting', this sense of guilt also appears, though the culprit is only a ragged boy and the wrong only done to a virgin nut-tree 'tall and erect with milk-white clusters hung' – whimsical guilt.

In the third book of the *Excursion* there is a confession of guilt by 'The Solitary'; yet his account of his blameless wedded life and subsequent poetical activities does him only credit. So with Wordsworth himself: a sense of guilt prevailed over all his elaborate self-excusing. 'The Solitary' is unbalanced by his wife's death: despair drives him to revolutionary politics and to Rousseau-istic experiment. Both activities proving fallacious remedies, he retires to the country-side to commune with Nature. He tells his visitors:

> Stripped as I am of all the golden fruit
> Of self-esteem: and by the cutting blasts
> Of self-reproach familiarly assailed:
> Yet would I not be of such wintry bareness
> But that some leaf of your regard should hang
> Upon my naked branches: – lively thoughts
> Give birth, full often, to unguarded words:
> I grieve that in your presence, from my tongue
> Too much of frailty hath already dropped

Coleridge had not been base. He had not wilfully retreated; he had merely not been able to find strength to cling to the 'unreal'. Strength came to mean human companionship and assistance. Wordsworth assumed a righteousness proportionate to his sense of guilt; and Coleridge, only aware of guilt in himself, did not realize, when he wrote to Southey that Wordsworth was the greatest man he had met, what his righteousness hid. The failure of the revolutionary principle in France to achieve ideal results seemed an *ex post facto* justification of Wordsworth's desertion of the cause, and of his own abandonment of the American plan. Between them the two poets made this amendment to Godwin's ethical idealism, to which they had both been committed (the words are Coleridge's):

Those feelings and that grand ideal of Freedom ... do not belong to
men, as a society, nor can possibly be either gratified or realized
under any form of human government: but belong to the individual
man, so far as he is pure and inflamed with the love and adoration of
God in Nature.

So, instead of practising pantisocracy on an ideal shore, he decided to
content himself with Wordsworth's scheme of deducing morality from
Nature, as observed in the English countryside, and using this morality to
soothe spiritual dissatisfaction. But Wordsworthian Nature did not satisfy
Coleridge; poetic unreality still beckoned. Yet by himself he could do
nothing, he needed Wordsworth's help. So he persuaded Wordsworth to
collaborate in *Lyrical Ballads*, which was to consist of poems of two sorts
– those dealing with natural, and those dealing with supernatural, incidents. He made this concession to Wordsworth: that the supernatural
incidents were to be put under the discipline of the natural emotions that
they would excite. Coleridge's 'Ancient Mariner' has the wedding-guest
as the human standard – for whose benefit the mariner, a sinner redeemed
from torment by the love he has suddenly felt for some beautiful water-
snakes, attempts to confute poetic unreality with moral counsels. But the
poetic unreality of his story has infinitely the greater stress.

   Among Coleridge's other contributions to *Lyrical Ballads* was 'The
Foster-Mother's Tale'. Here he tells of a youth who became very learned
and 'ere his twentieth year' had 'had unlawful thoughts of many things'.
He was put into a dungeon for heresy (dreaming there of green savannahs), but escaped to America; where he sailed alone in a boat up a great
moonlit river, to live, a naked man, with the wild Indians: and was never
seen again. In spite of the formal censure of the youth's behaviour, this
constitutes a strong statement of poetic unreality. Wordsworth countered
it, in the second edition of *Lyrical Ballads*, in which it was reprinted, with
a strong restatement of human reality – the poem 'Ruth'. 'Ruth' is a tale
about a romantic young man, who, having lived in mistaken idealism
among the American Indians, sang of *real* green savannahs to an English
maiden. He begged her to go back with him as his help-meet. But he had
learned the vices of the Indians, who were far from noble savages, and so
came to betray her. His ship sailed without her. She went mad. Then,
recovering somewhat, she lived an innocent life as a rustic tramp, playing
on a pipe made of a hemlock and communing with Nature; and
Wordsworth promised her a Christian burial when she came to die.
Coleridge had also written the first part of *Christabel* in the same year: it
was a still stronger statement of poetic unreality – the 'frightful' beauty of
the woman Geraldine, the witch who infected with her wickedness the
modest dutiful Christabel of his pretended preference. Not being able,
without violence, to subject the poem to the human discipline which he

had contrived to introduce into the 'Ancient Mariner', he did not offer it
for inclusion in *Lyrical Ballads.*

'Lewti', though at first included, was cancelled at the last moment:
poetic unreality was idealized in it as a beautiful Circassian for whom a
lover vainly sighed. For 'Lewti', 'The Nightingale' was substituted. In it
Coleridge made his most formal disavowal of the witch, whom the
nightingale's song had evoked in her aspect of Melancholy, saying that
Melancholy was an idle illusion – for 'as thou my friend and thou, my
sister' (William and Dorothy Wordsworth) have learned, the nightingale
(poetry) was really a merry bird. To hold the other view would, he said, be
to profane Nature's sweet voices, always full of love and joyance. But the
poem itself, after the first three lines, which show the witch's influence, is
a proof of the destruction of his poetic energy by such disavowals. The
commonest symbol in Coleridge's poems of the haunting presence of the
witch is the moon. It occurs at the emotional peak of 'The Ancient
Mariner', *Christabel*, 'The Foster-Mother's Tale', and 'Lewti'. It is the
main theme of 'Dejection' (written four years after these poems), where,
again addressing Wordsworth, he again tries to overbear melancholy with
joy; but the moon has taken the shape of an Indian canoe and the Virtuous
Lady Joy is routed. He records in this poem that he has been unable, in
spite of Wordsworth's inspiration, not to think of what he needs must feel.

The only poem in which he dared to find the moon good was 'Frost at
Midnight'. But he wrote it not for himself but for his newly-born child,
for whom he invoked the spiritual independence that for him seemed
unattainable. In this poem he forgot all his Wordsworthianism; as he did
in 'The Three Graves', written at the time that *Lyrical Ballads* was being
prepared (but not included there). In 'The Three Graves' Coleridge
savagely identified the sun, Wordsworth's god of joy and duty, with the
mad vulgar mother who curses her two sensitive daughters and her son-
in-law to perpetual unhappiness in spite of every virtuous endeavour on
their part. In 'Kubla Khan' he made his most complete recantation of
human reality, indulging in a luxurious wantonness that came near to
devilishness. 'Kubla Khan' was written in the *Lyrical Ballads* period, but
held back for a number of years, with the other unsuitable poems, until
after his breach with Wordsworth: and then only published at the request
of Byron, whom Wordsworth had taught Coleridge to regard as a representative, with Shelley, of the Satanic school of poetry. Even then he
excused its composition as due to opium, following the distress of mind
produced by the calumny and ingratitude of men who had been fostered
in the bosom of his confidence (Wordsworth not yet among them).

When friends failed him Coleridge was always lost. As early as 1797, in
his poem 'To the Rev. George Coleridge', published as the dedication of
his *Poems*, he tells how much he has already suffered from disillusions and
betrayals in his friendships:

... through life
Chasing chance-started friendships. A brief while
Some have preserv'd me from life's pelting ills;
But, like a tree with leaves of feeble stem,
If the clouds lasted, and a sudden breeze
Ruffled the boughs, they on my head at once
Dropped the collected shower; and some most false,
False and fair-foliaged as the Manchineel,
Have tempted me to slumber in their shade
E'en 'mid the storm; then breathing subtlest damps
Mix'd their own venom with the rain from Heaven,
That I woke poisoned.

He then eulogizes the dedicatee as his earliest friend, whom he has loved as a brother and revered as a son. But in one copy of this book Coleridge wrote above the dedication: 'N.B. If this volume should ever be delivered according to its direction, *i.e.* to Posterity, let it be known that the Reverend George Coleridge was displeased and thought his character endangered by the Dedication. – S. T. Coleridge.'

Shortly after writing 'Kubla Khan' he went with the Wordsworths to Germany. Parting from them there he took up metaphysics again, though he admitted its devilishness.[7] On his return to England he showed a sudden surprising energy, writing vigorously on politics for the daily press. He renewed his friendship with Southey; and it was at this time that Southey gave him the first three stanzas and two further stanzas of 'The Devil's Thoughts'. Allowed this licence by a friend whom by the standard of his own human deficiencies he could regard as a model human being, Coleridge let himself go as a devil, putting the responsibility of his elaborations of the theme on the blameless origin of the nucleus. This poem, and the later 'Two Round Spaces on the Tombstone', and 'The Rash Conjurer', have all a vigour which directly belies his pious affectations of childish innocence in 'Something Childish but Very Natural', 'My Baptismal Birthday', 'A Child's Evening Prayer', 'Answer to a Child's Question' – with which they are contemporaneous. The child poems were written in momentary reaction against metaphysics and in sycophantic imitation of Wordsworth's childishness – which was proper to Wordsworth's narrow-minded obedience to authority. In any case, his vigorous mood did not last long. He lost his concentrating force and wrote less and less. He even had to depend on Southey for the support of his family – Southey who had abandoned his idealistic principles and become an industrious hack-writer, and was about to accept a pension from the Government for political services; and who had, moreover, an unfavourable opinion of Coleridge's work and habits. Coleridge and Southey were married to sisters; it was Southey who had forced Coleridge into marriage – with a woman who proved to be chiefly interested, as Southey was, in worldly success.

Coleridge's inevitable break with Wordsworth was long delayed. At first there had been a fair exchange. In return for Wordsworth's friendship and moral stimulation, Coleridge had given him not merely a scholarly background to work against, but constant critical help in the use of language. (At the time of the breach Coleridge complained: 'I have loved with enthusiastic self-oblivion those who have been well pleased that I should, year after year, flow with a hundred nameless rills into their main stream.') But Wordsworth had now little more use for Coleridge than had Southey, who had practically given up poetry for the journalistic successes of prose. The Napoleonic wars had made a patriot of Wordsworth: he portrayed an ideal England where duty and liberty met, a symbol of an urbanely poetical human reality. Coleridge had followed, but timidly. Patriotism and nature-worship in Wordsworth turned to preaching; and preaching ended in ecclesiasticism. He had some time before, for final self-justification, paid a brief visit to Annette in France, in company with his sister Dorothy, explained himself, and then returned to marry a Lake Country neighbour who made him a devoted wife.

In the self-complacent *Prelude*, addressed to Coleridge, and written at a time when Coleridge had fallen far behind him in popular success, the affection and gratitude expressed are little more than what he might have granted a wise old family servant, now in decay, but who would be interested in the record of his young master's successful march to eminence. Only at the end does he give him credit for being a poet too, playfully recalling to him the time when, before turning their minds to more serious tasks, they had 'wantoned together in wild Poesy' – Coleridge's 'Ancient Mariner' and *Christabel* being linked with 'The Idiot Boy' and 'The Thorn' – and encouraging him to use the few remaining years of his life in raising a monument of glory to himself. He, Wordsworth, has shown the way and the two together will instruct posterity: 'Prophets of Nature, we to them shall speak / A lasting inspiration.' Coleridge, aware that since those wanton days he had written practically nothing, and aware of Wordsworth's huge output, replied with 'To William Wordsworth', in the decayed family-servant style, humbly grateful for mention in a work which seemed a classic as soon as written. He said that on first hearing it read he had burst into tears, thinking how he had wasted his own life; but that the tribute had given him some hope again and he now apologized for scattering poison-flowers of self-depreciation among the triumphal wreaths which were Wordsworth's due. There is a reference to Wordsworth's revolutionary visit to France, encouraging the legend that Wordsworth, glorious in his performances there, had only left because the revolutionary cause seemed hopeless, and was '... Thenceforth calm and sure / From the dread watch-tower of man's absolute self.'[8]

A few years after the reading of *The Prelude* came the breach, subsequently repaired for good manners' sake, but in reality a final breach. Coleridge had lost confidence in Wordsworth and in himself; Wordsworth only in Coleridge. Coleridge continued to lament his own idleness; particularly he wished that he could have finished *Christabel*. But the second part, completed on his return from Germany, had turned out tedious and discouraged a third part. 'Work without Hope draws nectar in a sieve, / And Hope without an object cannot live.' He was a 'Delinquent Traveller' and, no longer fit for 'America' (for true poetic experience, he meant), thought himself fit only to be enrolled among the criminal 'founders of Australian races'. But in 'The Delinquent Travellers' (one of his best poems) he claimed for his unregenerate aberrancy, or delinquency, a higher poetic merit than for Wordsworth's reformed social delinquency. And he reasserted, however cynically, what he had expressed many years before in 'Frost at Midnight' – a confidence in himself as the destined father of poets, successful where he failed:

> – The Rogues! I see it in their faces!
> Receive me, Lads. I'll go with you,
> Hunt the black swan and kangaroo,
> And that New Holland we'll presume
> Old England with some elbow-room.
> Across the mountains we will roam
> And each man make himself a home:
> Or, if old habits ne'er forsaking,
> Like clock-work of the Devil's making,
> Ourselves inveterate rogues should be,
> We'll have a virtuous progeny;
> And on the dunghill of our vices
> Raise human pine-apples and spices.

He still clung by habit to the idea of friendship and virtue.

> Old Friends burn dim, like lamps in noisome air.
> Love them for what they are: nor love them less
> Because to thee they are not what they were.

But he knew that he was for his fellows only a devil now – a cast-off, boring devil. In a piece called *Luther – de daemonibus* he wrote:

> 'The angel's like a flea,
> The devil is a bore – '
> 'No matter for that,' quoth S.T.C.
> 'I love him the better therefore.'
> *   *   *   *   *   *   *

As for the progeny of the first travellers to Australia: they have indeed turned out so virtuous that a few years ago the City Council of one of the Western Capitals burnt all its early archives. 'Human pine-apples and spices' could not be bettered as a characterisation of the modern Australian. Coleridge's son Hartley did become a poet, but he repeated his father's failures. Coleridge's sons of the spirit were the pre-Raphaelites, headed by Dante Gabriel Rossetti. Of these only William Morris had the healthy energy for carrying the group's idealistic principles into orderly practice. But his Coleridge-like poetic beginnings – 'The Defence of Guinevere' – were soon lost in his growing success as an importer of practical beauty into Victorian everyday life – his printing, furniture, fabrics, etc. He continued to write, but what was not prose social propaganda was interior-decorator verse, applauded by the same 'liberal' public that had applauded the hard-working Southey.

KEATS AND SHELLEY

Robert Graves

KEATS'S CHIEF INTEREST was the relations of the poet with poetry, but his poetic imagery was predominantly sexual. Poetry for him was not a philosophical theory, as it was with Shelley, but a moment of physical delirium. The figure that L.R. has used in characterizing Keats ('He expectantly disposed himself, so to speak, toward spiritual rape by a vigorous poetic personhead imagined as in pursuit of conquests') is one that occurs constantly in his poems. The first occasion is in 'Sleep and Poetry':

> O Poesy! for thee I grasp my pen
> That am not yet a glorious denizen
> Of thy wide heaven; yet, to my ardent prayer,
> Yield from thy sanctuary some clean air,
> Smooth'd for intoxication by the breath
> Of flowery bays, that I may die a death
> Of luxury, and my young spirit follow
> The morning sunbeams to the great Apollo
> Like a fresh sacrifice; or, if I can bear
> The o'erwhelming sweets, 'twill bring to me the fair
> Visions of all places ...

Keats's contemporaries found in this sort of writing a quality that they interpreted as moral perversity. The slamming reviews which depressed him so much, because postponing the moment of poetic ecstasy which he identified with the moment of poetic fame, resulted rather from this particular impression of perversity than from general obtuseness to his craftsmanship, or from prejudice against him as Leigh Hunt's protégé. Perversity, to the English mind, means any confusion of the usual functions and prerogatives of the two sexes, and Keats never seemed to be playing a *manly* role in his poems. Although he was male-minded enough in ordinary sexual business, as his letters to Fanny Brawne, and his song 'Give me women, wine and snuff', show, the critics were right: he did mix the sexes in his poems. But this was not a sign of sexual perversity. It derived from Keats's personalization of the notion of poetry as an active female figure, and from his disavowal of the traditional rape which the poet, as male, made of Poetry – poems, in that imagery, being the poet's children begotten of the Muse. He rejected traditional poetic psychology because the ecstasies it provided were banal and repetitional: not because he *knew* the nature of poetic experience, but because he had a vulgar greed of it and felt, rightly, that it could not occur within the known, exhausted poetic conventions. So he reversed the traditional position, making Poetry, as a dominant female, pursue the youthful, womanish poet with masculine lustfulness.

Endymion was the stock classical figure of human youth and beauty lying asleep, secretly beloved by the watching divinity – the Moon. Keats, who had said that if poetry did not come to a poet as naturally as leaves to a tree it had better not come at all, used Endymion as the figure of a poet who, by putting himself into a recipient attitude, won gratis 'the overwhelming sweets' for which his soul longed Keats used to court poetical inspiration by dressing up in traditional poetic robes and laurel crown. Endymion first learns the technique of attracting goddesses by a study of Adonis in his bower; a heavenly guide conveys Endymion there and, as if to give him a foretaste of amorous delights, cossets him with sweets (always associated in Keats's poems with poetic seduction) – wine alive with sparkles, juicy pears, cream sweeter than nurse Amalthea skimmed for the boy Jupiter, and a bunch of blooming plums, ready to melt within an infant's gums. From Adonis's bower it was no long journey, by eagle-ride part of the way (to point the connexion with the seduced Ganymede), to a mossy bed where Endymion could fling himself on his back and presently clasp a naked waist above him. It was Dian, and he whispered to her:

> O known Unknown! From whom my being sips
> Such darling essence, wherefore may I not
> Be ever in these arms?

The reviewers called *Endymion* 'indecent'. They wrote as classicists, and they were right in calling the poem indecent from a classical point of view: Diana should never have been equated in her sexual technique with Venus.

Hyperion started in a more 'manly' fashion. Hyperion was the Sun-Titan, an inexperienced youth, not yet converted into Apollo, the god of Poetry; the poem gives an account of this metamorphosis. Keats is said to have interrupted the writing of this poem because of the bad reception of *Endymion*. But *Endymion* was disliked because it did not show him a good man; whether Keats was judged a good poet or not depended on his showing himself first of all a normal male being. Critics did not analyse the nature of his abnormality, but merely saw him as conceited in some way that was not regular. In a letter to his publishers, the more conventionally conceited, over-manly Byron wrote, for God's sake to send him no more Keats: accompanied by abuse so indecent that it has been deleted by editors. The principal epithet that stands is 'mannikin'.

Keats was aware that *Hyperion* was more spiritually ambitious than *Endymion* and may have argued that it would be still less favourably received, for in *Hyperion* he was poetically identifying himself with the god of Poetry. (The reaction of shame is recorded in his poem of apology to Delphic Apollo for having put on his laurel-garland.) But Keats did not understand that it was the mawkish quality of his ambition that critics disliked rather than the fact of his ambition. Hyperion is, in the end, not much more of a man than Endymion. He does not become the god of Poetry except by quasi-sexual relations with a female principle of reality described as Mnemosyne or Memory. She is an awful goddess, a supreme shape, and comes on him while he is half-asleep. He gazes into her eyes and:

> Soon wild commotions shook him, and made flush
> All the immortal fairness of his limbs,
> Into a hue more roseate than sweet pain
> Gives to a ravished nymph when her warm tears
> Gush luscious with no sob ...
> ... So young Apollo anguished.
> His very hair, his golden tresses famed
> Kept undulation round his eager neck.
> During the pain Mnemosyne upheld
> Her arms as one who prophesied – At length
> Apollo shrieked – and lo he was the God.

Keats toned down this passage when he eventually published it, leaving out the ravished nymph, and making the climax less final: 'Apollo shrieked – and lo from all his limbs / Celestial ... ' At 'Celestial' the printed version broke off politically, as if he had cast his pen down in despair on reading the notices in the *Quarterly* and *Blackwood's*. In 'Sleep and Poetry' Keats had already begun this technique of sexual counter-changing; the confusion is shown most clearly in the short-circuit made between the female spirit of Poetry, the slumbering Endymion, and Apollo the mighty:

> A drainless shower
> Of light is poesy; 'tis the supreme of power;
> 'Tis might half-slumbering on its own right arm.

The very archings of her eye-lids charm
A thousand willing agents to obey.

Keats's second volume, *Lamia, Isabella, The Eve of St Agnes and Other Poems*, was given more favourable notices because Keats had disguised the indecency by taking the sexual figure one stage further. The conventional imagery had been of man the poet raping woman, the Muse; Keats's perverse improvement on this had been woman a mannish Muse, raping the womanish poet. He now showed a definitely female figure inviting rape by a definitely male figure; but he told the story from the female point of view. By doing this he avoided the charge of perversity: he showed himself yielding to female temptation as an apparently normal sexual adventurer, though to change his Muse into a conventionally feminine Muse he had to lay on her all his own sexual coyness. In 'The Eve of St Agnes' Madeline lies asleep but amorously expectant, while Porphyro heaps up the extravagant jellies and candied fruits and syrops and spiced cakes in gold and silver vessels. Then she listens to his serenade of 'La Belle Dame Sans Merci' (by which the identification between Madeline and Poetry is clearly made) and finally allows him to throb like a star among her dreams. The sweetmeats in these rape-scenes stand for the 'beauties' of poetry on which Keats laid more stress than on poetry itself. The 'beauties' were 'verisimilitudes', or the ore with which every rift should be loaded: the poetic object was an illusion of glory, made out of the material at hand, in which the Muse was expected to indulge the poet. 'The Eve of St Mark' (not included in this volume) was written in the same vein. Bertha sat alone in her room in the Minster Square at Canterbury. Everyone was at Church, and the streets were deserted. The stage was set for the lover to come along with his sweetmeats and musical instrument; to which blandishments Bertha could not but yield. She only kept her virginity by Keats's failure to finish the poem.

Isabella and *Lamia* are both poems of poetic disappointment and self-pity. Isabella is the spirit of poetry luxuriously grieving for the poet who has been murdered by the 'ledger-men' – i.e., the materialists, the rationalists, the critics. They even rob her of the sweet-basil that grows from his dead head. Lamia, who to classical legend was a frightful demon-succubus, Keats made into 'poor Lamia', the spirit of poetry whom old Apollonius, the philosopher, stares at, sees as a snake and banishes from sight.

Philosophy will clip an Angel's wings,
Conquer all mysteries by rule and line.
Empty the haunted air, and gnomed mine –
Unweave a rainbow, as it erewhile made
The tender-person'd Lamia melt into a shade.

Lamia is as if the morbid, freakish figure of poetry infuriated by neglect – by the want of such sexual flattery as Keats imagined fitting tribute from the poet.

Keats wrote in a letter to Woodhouse that a poet was functionally irresponsible and had no identity, only yearning and fondness – allowing himself to be pressed upon and annihilated by stronger identities with whom he came into contact.[9] In a letter to his brothers he glorified Shakespeare, in the same strain, as possessing the supreme poetic quality – '*Negative Capability,* that is, when a man is capable of being in uncertainties, mysteries, doubts, without any irritable reaching after fact and reason.'[10] Keats felt himself torn between two demands (what L.R. calls the two 'spectators'): the demand of the critics and the sweeping demand of poetry itself. Between these two demands he equivocated with that fluttering complaisance which he calls 'Negative Capability'.

Shelley championed Keats as a victim of critical cruelty, seeing him as performing something like his own philosophical arbitration between 'the human audience and poetry itself'. Shelley displeased contemporary critics for reasons opposite to those for which Keats was damned. It was not his professed atheism and Jacobinism that outraged popular feeling, so much as his spiritual hermaphroditism. L.R. has explained how he tried to reconcile the opposite sympathies to which the poet is exposed: by a sentimental compromise in a notion of poetry in which judgement was evaded by a philosophical equating of the human with the poetic. Shelley, indeed, at one time debated whether he should become a professional philosopher or a professional poet; and, though he chose the latter career, he tried to combine the philosopher and the poet in a Satanic character of superior physical and mental powers. In his *Defence of Poetry* he puts Bacon among the great poets and Shakespeare, Milton and Dante among the philosophers of the very loftiest power. Queen Mab is his first Queen of Poetry: and she does not have love-relations either with Oberon or with some mortal youth. She merely imbues the soul of a girl called Ianthe (Harriet Shelley) with a righteous, philosophical view of human affairs; the verses are annotated with astronomical data, recommendations for a vegetarian diet, and thoughts on the nature of time. Queen Mab appears later as The Witch of Atlas, an energetic spirit who flies about with a winged monster of her own creation, called Hermaphrodite. Hermaphrodite is the poet-compromiser:

> A sexless thing it was, and in its growth
>   It seemed to have developed no defect
> Of either sex, yet all the grace of both, –
>   In gentleness and strength its limbs were decked;
> The bosom swelled lightly with its full youth,
>   The countenance was such as might select

Some artist that his skill should never die,
Imaging forth such perfect purity.

Near the end of the poem Shelley gently rebukes Keats for conceiving the
poetic personhead as sexed as, therefore, a being unpropitious for the
harmonious levelling which should be the poet's object:

'Tis said in after times her spirit free
  Knew what love was, and felt itself alone –
But holy Dian could not chaster be
  Before she stooped to kiss Endymion,
Than now this lady – like a sexless bee
  Tasting all blossoms, and confined to none,
Among those mortal forms, the wizard-maiden
Passed with an eye serene and heart unladen.

But the Witch is only a fanciful presentation of the Spirit of Poetry. The
poem ends:

These were the pranks she played among the cities
  Of mortal men, and what she did to Sprites
And Gods, entangling them in her sweet ditties
  To do her will, and show their subtle sleights,
I will declare another time; for it is
  A tale more fit for the weird winter nights
Than for these garish summer days, when we
Scarcely believe much more than we can see.

First must come the serious business of smoothing out antagonisms of a
more immediate sort. Mary Shelley criticised the poem as having no
human interest; and he replied with some joking verses, acknowledging
the ineffectiveness of his vision:

How, my dear Mary, – are you critic-bitten
  (For vipers kill, though dead) by some review,
That you condemn these verses I have written
  Because they tell no story, false or true?
What, though no mice are caught by a young kitten,
  May it not leap and play as grown cats do,
Till its claws come? Prithee, for this one time,
Content thee with a visionary rhyme.

But he never managed to synthesize into a single figure the poet, and the
philosopher, and the Promethean man of action on whose strategy the
miracle of salvation seemed to depend.[11]

R.G.

A NOTE ON THE PASTORAL

Robert Graves

THEOCRITUS WAS A PROFESSIONAL poet, attached for a time to the court of Ptolemy Philadelphus at Alexandria, and later to that of Hiero, tyrant of Syracuse. His more formal poems were panegyrics and hymns; the Eclogues were merely 'occasional verse', half-humorous accounts of the shepherds and goat-herds he met when on holiday in the Sicilian countryside. He selected on the whole the more sentimental passages in their lives for poeticization, but invented no Arcadian Golden Age for them. The Arcadian Golden-Age pastoral was a development by his Greek imitators. If the effect of the eclogues is cheerful, it is because the climate of Sicily and its political security at this time gave the shepherds an easy enough life – they had plenty of time for piping, unhappy love-affairs and their traditional contests of verse-improvization. Theocritus lets them talk broad Doric and use coarse expressions. They know nothing of philosophy. No worship of nature as such is ascribed to them, though they have superstitions about the Nymphs and Pan. Their life is not ideal-ized as superior to the town; and indeed, by contrast with the people of Syracuse, they appear foolish clowns. In the Twentieth Idyll, Eunica, a city girl of Syracuse, when made love to by one of the most eligible of neat-herds, spits thrice in her own bosom (as if to avert the ill omen that meeting a lunatic brings), and tells him that constant pipe-playing has roughened and deformed his lips and that he stinks of goat. The famous First Idyll, which contains Thyrsis's elegy for the dead shepherd Daphnis, is in no less realistic a vein than the Fifteenth Idyll, which describes the comic adventures of two Syracusan country-women on a visit to the Adonis festival at Alexandria.

Virgil's Eclogues were a formalizing of the more narrowly bucolic Idylls of Theocritus. He used the bucolic situation as a convenient rostrum for moral philosophy; and though he kept a careful eye on the correctness of his shepherds' costumes and professional habits, he gave them smooth lips and let them smell of civet rather than of goat. Moreover, when they mourn for Daphnis in the Sicilian style, they do not mean Daphnis but Julius Caesar. And in the last Eclogue, Virgil's patron, Gallus, is wafted to Arcadia, where he sits in pastoral fancy-dress, mourning for Lycoris – in real life an actress in low comedy who has left him to go off with a soldier. The country deities gather pityingly about Callus, and in this context the 'Where were ye, Nymphs?' is borrowed from Theocritus: 'Quae nemora aut qui vos saltus habuere, puellae / Naïades?'

The Virgilian pseudo-shepherd was imported into English poetry by a scholastical Scottish monk, Alexander Barclay. The manner of early English poems had been bare and direct; they were written in the shadow of a world of brutal fact – a cold, foggy world with only an occasional May Day or Christmas-tide interlude to relieve it. Their notion of poetry was a notion of physical defeat. In popular and provincial poems this tradition survived late. The Church, in consolation of this gloomy view, tried to make the holy world of Scripture, and especially the Gospels, the supreme poetic reality. The popular poetic response was to bring Biblical characters into the immediate English countryside. Thus the English shepherd was an important figure in early popular ballad and carol because of his connexion with the Nativity; but remained an English country oaf, smelling of his flocks and smeared with tar:

> The shepard upon a hill he satt;
> He had on him his tabard and his hat,
> His tarbox, his pipe, and his flagat;
> His name was called Joly Joly Wat,
> For he was a gud herdes boy.
>   Ut hoy!
>   For in his pipe he made so much joy.
>
> The shepard upon a hill was laid;
> His dog to his girdell was taid;
> He had not slept but a litill braid,
> But '*Gloria in excelsis*' was to him said.
>   Ut hoy!
>   For in his pipe he made so much joy.
> . . . . . .
> 'Now must I go there Crist was born;
> Farewell! I cum again to morn.
> Dog, kepe well my shepe fro the corn,
> And warn well "Warrocke" when I blow my horn!'
>   Ut hoy!
>   For in his pipe he made so much joy.

'Jesu, I offer to thee here my pipe,
My skirt, my tar-box, and my scripe;
Home to my felowes now will I skipe,
And also look unto my shepe.'
            Ut hoy!
    For in his pipe he made so much joy.

'Now farewell, mine owne herdes man Wat!'
'Yea, for God, lady, even so I hat;
Lull well Jesu in thy lape,
And farewell, Joseph, with thy round cape!'
            Ut hoy!
    For in his pipe he made so much joy.

The use of allegory in sermons and devotional books had only a super-
ficial influence on popular poems. *Piers Ploughman,* for example, is cast in
allegorical form, but the characters are ordinary English countrymen and
their problems are ones of immediate social behaviour. The mediaeval
popular poet tended to record only his own direct experiences. The court-
poet, however, leaned toward allegory; but he converted it to more and
more unecclesiastical ends. He borrowed from contemporary continental
practice a new poetical world called 'The Kingdom of Love', which was
geographically localized on a legendary Mount Cithaeron to which access
could only be had in dreams. It was ruled by Love, a capricious, all-
powerful Deity, whose severity to the lover could be somewhat mitigated
by the intercession of his mother Venus (a parody of the Catholic ritual in
which Mary intercedes between Christ and the sinner), and was haunted
by powers such as Envy, Despair and Poverty (borrowed from ecclesiastical allegory), whose business it was to make the lot of lovers more difficult. The month in this kingdom was always May and the Kingdom
consisted of a Royal Palace (some rooms of which were devoted to famous
poets and orators) surrounded with interminable pleasure-grounds where
the love-making knights and ladies wandered. Yet this poetical world still
kept a certain correspondence with the actual world. The scene was not
impossibly fanciful, but merely a prolongation of summer well-being
enjoyed in the gardens of royal palaces. The flowers in the parterres were
the familiar rose, lily and pink, the rich clothes were the court-wear of
state occasions and fine weather. Court-poems were a sort of sweet
conserve of brief summer joys for use with the salt-meat staple of the bad
months. After a time poets tired of the sameness of their adventures in this
Kingdom of Love, and especially of the morality figures that occurred in
them, and so tried to find a more poetically, not merely climatically,
appealing Mount Cithaeron. They found it in the pastoral imported by
Barclay, which had no relevance at all for their world of experience –
Corydon, Phyllis, the Nymphs, Apollo, banks of asphodel, the parsley-

crown, the vineyard, and the lizard on the rock, being entirely un-English.

Barclay's treatment of the pastoral was moralistic. He borrowed not from Theocritus, but from Virgil through the fifteenth-century Baptista Mantuanus, who had adapted the Virgilian eclogue to the satire of court and city life. In his Fourth Eclogue Barclay attacks his contemporary, Skelton, as a 'rascolde poet' who had an immoral muse and who pandered to the taste of princes by celebrating viciousness. This is probably a reference to Skelton's *Tunnyng of Elynour Rummynge*, written in recollection of his sallies into low life, in company with Henry VIII, from the ideal pleasure grounds of the royal palace of Nonsuch near Leatherhead. Skelton was almost the last classically educated English poet who could forget his Classics when looking at the countryside and not see Margery Milke-Ducke as Phyllis and Jolly Jacke as Corydon, or find 'behind every bush a thrumming Apollo' (John Clare's criticism of Keats). Shakespeare was not classically educated, but picked up his classics as he went along; his treatment of country-people changes considerably as he proceeds. In his early *Love's Labour's Lost* he caricatures the euphuists, showing in Costard's letter, read by the King, what the literal result would be if a *real* countryman tried to be a pastoral swain. Here also occur his Winter and Spring songs, which are critical demonstrations of *real* pastoral lyric: with Dick the Shepherd blowing his nail and Marion's nose all red and raw. Later, however, in *As You Like It*, the aesthetic pastoralists are favourably contrasted with the true countryman: the Clown is gross and stupid, not even idiot-wise like the fools in the tragedies, and only serves as a butt for Touchstone's euphuistical ruffling. In *The Winter's Tale*, one of his last plays, Shakespeare has all but capitulated to pastoral fashion. The shepherd, as Perdita's foster-father, is promoted to blank verse – hitherto all Shakespeare's countrymen have had to use country prose full of broad *a*'s and *zed*s. Even a country-dance of Satyrs is introduced. There is still a clown, but he is merely the low comedian. Finally, the island in *The Tempest* is a pasteboard Arcadia: no clowns and, instead of shepherds, classical gods and goddesses who descend by stage-machinery.

The Elizabethan university-wits rejected Barclay's Mantuanian pastoral in favour of that of the Neapolitan Sannazaro: as better suited to their sophisticated literary purposes. (Barclay and Googe were from their point of view stuffy, old-fashioned writers spoiling good material.) They used the Arcadian scene as the ideal seat of literary leisure:

> Then amongst flow'rs and springs,
> Making delightful sport
> Sat lovers without conflict, without flame;
> And nymphs and shepherds sings
> Mixing in wanton sort
> Whisp'rings with songs, then kisses with the same

Which from affection came.
The naked virgin then
Her roses fresh reveals,
Which now her veil conceals.
The tender apples in her bosom seen;
And oft in rivers clear,
The lovers with their loves consorting were.

But they linked the pastoral with another contemporary fashion – Euphuism – and made it ancillary to prose oratory. For Greene, Peele, Lodge (from whom the scenario of *As You Like It* was borrowed) and the rest, the shepherds were scholars proficient in the various schemes and tropes of rhetoric learned from Sherry, Priscian, Donet, Alexander, Mosellanus and Sysenbrotus; which they applied, however, not to philosophy or theology or legality, but to the logic of love (thus giving Mount Cithaeron a Renaissance education.) In Greene's *Menaphon,* a representative example of this technique, academic niceness in prose writing is the important consideration:

Well, abroad they went, *Menaphon* with his sheephooke fringed with quell, to signifie he was chiefe of the swaynes, *Lamedon* and *Samela* after: plodding thus ouer the greene fields, at last they came to the mountains where *Menaphons* flockes grazed, and there he discoursed unto *Samela* thus; I tell thee faire Nymph, these Plaines that thou seest stretching Southward, are pastures belonging to *Menaphon:* there growes the cintfoyle, and the hyacinth, the cowsloppe, the primrose, and the violet, which my flockes shall spare for flowers to make thee garlands, the milke of my ewes shall be meate for thy pretie wanton, the wool of the fat weathers that seemes as fine as the fleece that *Iason* fet from *Colchos,* shall serue to make *Samela* webbes withall!; the mountaine tops shall be thy mornings walke, and the shadie valleies thy evenings arbour: as much as *Menaphon* owes shall be at *Samelas* command, if she like to liue with *Menaphon.* This was spoken with such deepe effects, that *Samela* could scarce keepe her from smiling, yet she covered her conceipt with a sorrowful countenance, which *Menaphon* espying, to make her merrie, and rather for his own advantage, seeing *Lamedon* was a sleepe, tooke her by the hand and sate downe, and pulling foorth his pipe, began after some melodic to carroll out this roundelay.

Poetic writing had merely to be witty and 'sugared'. Thus the first verse of Menaphon's roundelay:

When tender ewes brought home with euening Sunne
Wend to their foldes,

And to their holdes
The shepheards trudge when light of day is done.
Upon a tree
The Eagle *Ioues* faire bird did pearch,
There resteth hee.
A little flie his harbour then did search,
And did presume (though others laught thereat)
To pearch where as the princelie Eagle sat.

Sidney belonged to this school, but he was more classically inclined than the others: he inserted in his *Arcadia* three or four gentlemanly imitations of Theocritus.

In the *Shepheards Callender* Spenser tried to escape from this rhetorical paralysis and to make the pastoral a more serious – or at least superficially a more serious – poetic mode. Improving on Sidney's classicism, he engrafted the classical pastoral, in all its impure variety, on to native English rusticism, thus supplying a looser and yet more immediate pastoral technique. His Colin Clout, borrowed from Skelton, and his Piers, borrowed from Langland, graze their flocks in fields where Kentish and Arcadian trees and flowers and deities are all mixed up together. Spenser here gave authority to his composite, year-long poetical world by locating it in an idealistic folk-loreish atmosphere – substantiating this atmosphere with quaint dialect words and obsolete forms borrowed from 'Old Tityrus' (Chaucer); it was essentially the same world, enlarged to more than Mandevillean range, over which the Faerie Queene ruled. Sidney, as a traditionalist, criticized Spenser in his *Apologie for Poetry*:

> The Sheapheards Kalender hath much Poetrie in his Eglogues, indeede worthy the reading, if I be not deceived. That same framing of his stile to an old rustick language I dare not alowe, sith neyther *Theocritus* in Greek, *Virgill* in Latin, nor *Sanazar* in Italian did affect it.

But Spenser, by the plotting of this self-sufficient lunatic world, won the name of 'the Poets' Poet', and Sidney is chiefly remembered as the dead shepherd of a classically incorrect pastoral of Spenser's.[12]

R.G.

From *Epilogue Volume II*

HOMILETIC STUDIES

Laura Riding

All rules are not calculated for the meridian of every state. If all bodies had the same Constitution; or all Constitutions the same Alteration; and all Alterations the same Times, the emperick were the best physitian. If all States had the same Tempers and Distempers, and both the same Conservatives, and the same Cures, Examples were the best directions, and Rules digested from those Examples, were even almost infallible. The subject of Policy is Civill Government; the subject of that Government is Men; the variableness of those Men disabsolutes all Rules, and limits all Examples. Expect not therefore, in these, or any of the like nature, such impregnable generals, that no exceptions can shake. The very discipline of the Church establisht, and confirm'd by the infallible choice, is not tyed to all times, or to all places. What we here present you with, as they are not rocks to build perpetuity upon, so they are not rocks to split beleefe upon it: it is lesse danger to rely upon them, than to neglect them.

– Francis Quarles, Enchiridion.

THE DISCUSSION OF PERSONAL QUALITIES has gradually, from being an informal and familiar colloquy, become an external science, with sober frankness replaced by diagnostic shamelessness: it has become 'psychology'. Psychology has disintegrated the natural person, disentangled the constitutional strands, and attempted to recompose them again not into constitutions, but into patterns of behaviour. In the old homily tradition which preceded psychology, the determination of qualities, the resolution of character, was a process dependent on personal choice. This is why the appeal for certain qualities and against others was moral, not scientific. The natural person was an inviolable unit: all modification or strengthening must take place from within, be an act of character. In psychology the person is emptied of his personal content, which is cast upon the public laboratory table and, after a thorough elimination of all private contexts, reassembled into a mechanism of prearranged responses. The incalculable, autonomous element has disappeared – that element to which homily once addressed itself and which is character.

Psychology dispenses entirely with the notion of character. It is such a notion that we shall attempt, by these and further studies in this narrow genre, to reinstate – narrow, because in it we are necessarily restricted to the definition of purely private truths. Such truths will not serve in the definition of larger, public truths; it should not, indeed, be necessary to define them, since they represent what one should be able to take for granted with maturity. And the traditional homiletic writer recognized this, by his manner of elderly sententiousness: he protected himself from the accusation of presumptuous interference by assuming that his audience was below the age or experience-level of maturity. But we cannot now easily take for granted a given character-product in people; we cannot pretend to assume, with every person of reasonable age, a minimum private coherence. Psychology has thrown away the person, our guarantee that what is being done and said is peculiarly, personally, of now, and plunged event and truth back into its primitive state of chaotic detail. We think well, and the happenings and intellectual realities of our time have an educated accent. But they scarcely seem to have anything to do with us, because we are scarcely *we*.

Our persons have grown ghostly under the influence of psychological analysis, which composes a common, public person out the old privately vested qualities. It is for this reason that our happenings and intellectual realities – our public world of event and truth – collapse into chaotic detail: we invalidate the person, by which alone they can be morally sustained. We do, and say, and then disappear personally, so that what we do, and say, can have no internal application. Event and truth must be public realities; but they cannot be this unless apprehended by a personally identifiable population, each of us grounded in private integrity of consciousness.

It is not only that we are cowards in deserting personally the public realities which exist for us and by us, but that we cannot run away, indeed, if we would. That is, persons enough must abide by them as well to articulate them as to sustain their literal application. Let us here say this much for psychology: that it purifies the essential population of superfluous, fictitious persons – of the crowd. But there must remain, then, the 'persons enough'. And these have a responsibility, toward *their* world, of self-possession – which is to say, of character.

L.R.

STEALING

Robert Graves

THERE ARE MANY FORMS of theft: some tolerable and even admirable, some reprehensible, some quite intolerable. And there are many debatable cases. The ethical question has been confused by the simplified definition that the Law has been forced to make of theft: the abstraction from others of such property as has market value. The penalty imposed varies, roughly, according to the market value of the property stolen. In the old days in England the theft of goods of the value of five shillings or over automatically carried the death sentence with it. (Merciful juries used therefore sometimes to find that a stolen guinea was worth only four shillings and eleven pence.) The Law has been softened, but market value is still the ruling consideration. There are others: whether it is a first offence, whether the thief is a minor, whether the theft was accompanied by violence. But certain fundamental considerations play little part: the degree of mental annoyance caused to the victim, and the whole question of title, which the very fact that thieves exist proves to be ambiguously formulated. The thief who snatches a woman's handbag from a shop-counter – purse, keys, glasses, private letters, shopping-list and all – is likely to cause far more acute mental annoyance than a thief who abstracts some valuable work of art from a public museum. Yet the difference in gaol-sentence if both are caught is between weeks and years. And in one case the thief is violently and personally challenging the woman's confidence in the fact of possession; in the other he is merely playing a game of chance over something that seems attached to nobody in particular.

Mental annoyance is difficult to assess, and so is the 'sentimental' value of objects stolen. The Law cannot take into account the plea that a gold-headed cane, of which an exact reproduction could be made at a cost of five pounds, was worth a hundred times that amount to its owner because it belonged to his father. As for the stealing of intangible things which are not translatable into market value, the Law generally confesses that it is equipped to deal only with economic values, not at all with emotional ones. A wife or husband may be awarded monetary compensation for stolen affections; but this does not really represent an evaluation of love; rather, of the incidental economic loss which loss of love has entailed.

There are three main kinds of thief: the thief who prides himself on confounding property distinctions, who steals for the sensation of freedom and power it gives him; the thief who has shame in his thieving, who steals something that he feels he has no right to; and the thief who neither knows nor admits that he is one, stealing from mere vagueness of property-sense. Dillinger and Bonny Parker, the American public enemies, took pride in their thieving. They robbed from the rich and did not adopt the Robin Hood practice of giving the spoils to the poor; the act of daring being sufficient end and justification. This kind of major stealing, in which the thief conscientiously accepts outlawry, and often becomes a hero of ballad literature, should be distinguished from stealing by swindle, which is mere effrontery within the social constitution. Such minor thieves make no positive attacks on property, but merely avail themselves of weaknesses in the laws or the protection of property. If these laws were fool-proof they would presumably be honest men: their daring is in the comic, not the heroic vein. Horatio Bottomley was of this swindler class and, among his intimates, it is said, jocularly proud of it. ('Suckers have to learn their lesson!') An office-boy once came up before him, charged with stealing a one-and-sixpenny postal order from an entry to a John Bull competition. Bottomley said indulgently, 'Well, I suppose he has to begin somewhere.'

The second kind of thief is represented by the well-dressed shop-lifter who figures regularly in the news and usually faints for shame when charged – the impulse-thief who cannot account for the act even to herself, except as a temporary loss of her sense of the social realities. A private luxury-drama got the better of her for the moment; but in her normal mind she respects the property limitations against which she has unwittingly rebelled.

The thief who neither knows nor admits that he is a thief seldom comes into court. And this is the most dangerous sort. The things he steals are, precisely, those whose market value is not economically assessable. He is the thief of one's privacy, patience, time, energies, and of one's very identity. How are such thefts licenced? The theft of one's privacy is licenced by the general axiom that man is a gregarious creature and enjoys, or should enjoy, casual visits from his neighbour whenever he is not ill, engaged in intimate love-making or working concentratedly at his trade or profession. He is held to represent a certain amount of social pleasantness which it is his duty to share with his fellow-creatures – who call on him in a vague sense of self-insufficiency which they credit him with feeling too: like themselves, he must need 'company'. They are only fulfilling recognized conventions of social interchange: they are not really interested in his personal problems, nor would they own to any burden of serious responsibility towards him. To this neighbour-theory is added the theory that any aberration from the normal that anyone makes is 'news' and public property (social pleasantness heightened to social excitement); the person who first gets hold of the news is not only no thief but entitled to a reward from the news-hungry public. And nine out of every ten people seem ready to share themselves with the public to the most generous extent – the hatchet-slayer calls in the newsmen and asks anxiously, 'This is front-page stuff, isn't it?'

The theory of the gregariousness of man is held most strongly in the country, where everyone who refuses to go further than 'good-morning' and 'good-evening' with his neighbours is considered a mystery and a social danger; and invasions of his privacy will take place in a hostile and surreptitious way. Once a new-comer opens his door to the first caller (the local parson), his time and energies are at the mercy of all neighbours of the same social class, who feel entitled to a share in his humanity. And even in city neighbourhoods, where one is not expected to know the occupants of the flat above, or the flat below or opposite, there is always the State – intruding, on one bureaucratic pretext or another, with inspections, demands, subpœnas and forms to be filled in. The State's theft of time and energy are excused on the plea that everyone is a member of the State, possessing through it a claim on all its other members; national community, the basis of the assumption of social community. If a private citizen regards himself as the victim of thievish officialdom, the remedy is held to lie in his own hands as a voter. And besides all this, there are the thefts made in the name of Business, Politics, Charity – invasions of privacy, draining of energy, wasting of time, legitimized by an intensification of the neighbour-theory. That this organized theft continues shows that the people who consider themselves private property are numerically unimportant.

The question of what one can rightly call one's inalienable own, safe from encroachment, becomes extremely confused in the case of private amenities. There is a general democratic view that each of us is entitled to an average reasonable amount of personal control of his immediate surroundings. The too 'particular' people are regarded as freaks and trouble-makers. Between one person and another there is assumed to exist a no-man's-land of property over which no one has any special control. If, for example, we do not like the architectural renovations which are being made in a favourite old street of ours, our objections must be raised on the grounds of impersonal architectural taste: they represent our opinion, to which we are entitled, but no right to be consulted in the matter. That it is a favourite old street 'of ours' is only a manner of speaking. The architectural effect is a general property only remotely subject to our personal control through municipal authority; the detailed reactions of citizens can play no part in this authority. Presumably, however, such reactions have a certain validity within our immediate field of residence. What, actually, of our purely local amenities can we call our own?

Few amenities are protected by Law. One can perhaps bring a successful action, on financial grounds, against a glue-factory that is built next door to a tea-garden, or against a kennels built next door to a hospital for neurasthenic patients; and there are such things, in Law, as 'ancient lights'. But there is no remedy against the spoiling of the view of a private house by the building of a gas-works or a modern-Gothic castle. There is no way of preventing a neighbour from erecting some structure in his garden which commands a view of one's own and so destroys its privacy, unless his actions when posted there are of a noisy or menacing kind. It is possible, again, to bring an action against a neighbour for stealing flowers from one's garden, but not against a neighbour who steals the affections of one's cat by giving it richer food than it gets at home. It is possible to bring an action against members of the fashion-trade who take surreptitious notes of the new models at a private pre-view; but nobody can claim justice against a neighbour who plagiarizes one's individual way of dressing and thus steals from one the special sense of looking fastidiously like oneself. It is possible for an author to take action against a publisher for a plain infringement of copyright, but nobody can take action against a person who tells one's story or joke as his own, and thus steals from one the peculiar flavour of wit which is part of one's social identity. It is possible for an inventor to take action against a manufacturing company for a plain infringement of patent, but nobody can take action against a person who copies the interior decoration of one's house and thus steals its dignity of being peculiarly one's own.

In everything which concerns private taste we are, in fact, entirely at the mercy of public depredation. If we enjoy a particular view, we are powerless to prevent its being spoilt, exactly because our liking rests on taste, not on strictly material considerations of comfort. If we fancy a particular combination of colours and express this in the decoration-scheme of our sitting-room, we are powerless to prevent a plagiaristic attack on this amenity that we have made for ourselves, because it is only a matter of taste the sensibilities associated with taste not being seriously recognized in the public-property register. We are not really in personal possession of a view on which we have endowed great care of eye and which has played a significant part in our local orientation; or of a care-fully devised sitting-room colour-scheme. We are only in possession of a taste for a view of a certain kind or of a taste for a certain colour-scheme; and taste is so 'subtle' a possession that it can have no official sacredness.

The two proverbial charters licencing plagiarism are *de minimis non curat lex* – meaning that people must not make a fuss about trifles, it being sufficient satisfaction to know that the police protect one's house from burglary; and the proverb 'imitation is the sincerest form of flattery' – implying that the real object of a sensitive personalization of one's existence is to call attention to oneself, or to influence dominatingly the ways of others, not the moral object of being oneself as responsibly and honestly as one can. If imitation were said to be the sincerest form of respect, that might be refuted in intelligent argument. But the sneer in 'flattering' imposes shamed silence; perhaps one has, after all, been aggressively self-demonstrating. The remedy is to seek forms of self-expression which shall seem more naturally, less theatrically, individual.

It is commonly supposed that a crowd cannot be reduced to a single integer by a process of division. It can. The integer of the crowd is the thief. Crowds gather outside a church where there is a wedding, or outside a hospital when an ambulance drives up, with thievish anxiety to steal some of the private feelings of the principals. For the crowd exists by virtue of the theory that everyone has a share in certain common possessions. And these common possessions are so vague in substance that the collective sense of ownership is not satisfied by them; so that the crowd swoops down on the private experience or entity and claims it thievishly for its own. 'News' is one manifestation of this methodical thieving; fashion another. Fashion is the pseudo-honourable convention by which something private is publicized. And the original inventor? But the fashions that the crowd adopts are seldom original inventions, nearly always vulgarizations of such inventions by some super-thief. The super-thief has an eye for what is 'different' and knows how to convert the different to the stylish, or the topical, without going through any the processes by which the different was arrived at. He would not reproduce the original even if he could; is only interested in reproducing its 'atmosphere'. These super-thiefs are the greater public characters, from dictators downwards, and need the three qualities that the Elizabethan pick-pocket had to possess – an eagle's eye, a lion's heart, a lady's hand.

The matter is complicated by the question 'Isn't everyone a thief?' For there is, if not a precise, immediate, collective property, at least a common stock or 'cultural inheritance' on which even the most inventive person must draw. The inventor of the phosphorus-match, for example, merely combined two previous discoveries – the tinder-box and the ignitability of phosphorus by friction. A person with a personal way of dressing does not make the stuffs of her dress herself or design the buttons, or the jewels, or the gloves. The most original poet starts with given language and certain inherited metrical conventions. That there is nothing new under the sun is a sweeping consolation to the uninventive and would, if true, be a justification for theft. But it is not true. There exists, certainly, a common historical background. But what we, in the present, individually do or are constitutes specific additions and manipulations of our background. The crowd has a collective claim on the past, but not on the present. A living person is something that cannot be collectivized except through what he specifically offers to common stock: which is not himself, but only a statement about himself in relation to the world he lives in. Such a statement may help others to understand their own meaning; but one's way of being is as uniquely private as one's hand-writing, features or gait. It is true that there are hundreds of thousands of people whose subservience to a conventional pattern has made them approximate to one another very closely. But there are inevitable differences in people, and in so far as these are not altogether suppressed they are, however slight, their authentic title to existence. In some small respect, at least, everyone is an original, and no thief, though on crowd occasions this originality tends to disappear, because of the thievish collective atmosphere.

What stealing is legitimate? The taking of property that never had or has temporarily lost an individual owner – the raw material of living – is not stealing. Buttons and trimmings, for example, are exposed for public sale in a great variety of colours, materials and shapes. A person carefully chooses a certain set of buttons and a certain trimming to suit a certain dress, the raw materials of which were also carefully chosen from a shop counter. No stealing there. Stealing occurs only when someone deliberately appropriates the effect of someone else's carefully assembled dress, disregarding its special personal association. Accidental thefts occur by coincidence and similarity of circumstance and temperament; more often by a lazy indecisiveness of mind in which memory-impressions of things seen or heard exert a strong hypnotic power.

Nature provides convenient symbols of the legitimate thief and of the illegitimate thief; the illegitimate thief is the cuckoo, which saves itself the trouble of nest-building and the care of its young, the legitimate is the hermit-crab which uses discarded sea-shells to cover its unprotected softer parts. And then there is the jackdaw, the doubtful case. The jackdaw steals in a haphazard and altogether irresponsible way, cheerfully decorating its nest with whatever bright object it can get off with. It may be a bit of broken glass or one of a pair of diamond earrings that someone has left lying near an open window. The cuckoo must have a vivid consciousness that what it is doing is stealing, but the jackdaw is merely carried away by vanity; it would be difficult to lay an accusation against it of conscious intent to steal. In literary stealing the tendency is to view the thief as a jackdaw, with indulgence: literature being presumed to be a necessarily jackdawish profession.

Stealing brings its own punishment. Nobody with sensibility enough to realize his offence as theft is permanently easy in the ownership of what is not really his own, though the outlaw may try to be romantic about it –

> Furto cuncta magis bella;
> Furto dulcior puella,
> Furto omnia decora,
> Furto poma dulciora.

On the other hand, does anything that is an integral part of a person's life get stolen? If a literary style or a way of dressing can be so exactly reproduced that there is nothing to choose between copy and original, must we not conclude that the original was not so original, after all – only a pattern of common-places? Objects of sentimental value are tokens of either clear or uncertain memories. If of clear memories, then the object is a superfluity; if uncertain memories, then still less integral a possession.

Love is the greatest single force that makes people thieves. Love, in its popular sense, I mean – the desire to take complete possession of the loved one. Such love leads many an otherwise honest man to imitate the ways of the loved one so closely that he hopes to appear a second self to her: her favourite flowers, tunes, poems, colours and localities will be his favourites, and his objects in life merely male parodies of her female ones. This may be called the swindling technique of love and is to be distinguished from the robbery with violence glorified in the melodramatic novel: which in actual life is resorted to rarely enough. If the swindler is not repulsed and succeeds in winning a woman's affections by these means, there is likely to have been swindling on both sides: such a love-match might be described as the association of two thieves, each happy in the possession of the other's purse. Jealousy in love is rage that something remains to the loved one that has evaded theft; for example, former friendships or occupations or even affection for a favourite cat or dog. All successfully married couples tend to have a common gait, a common smile and a common hand-writing. As individuals they have almost ceased to exist; what they have stolen from each other and held in common pool has turned into a synthetic mediocrity, lacking in all personal freshness of accent.

In painting and literature thefts are sometimes due to possessive love; if not sexual love, at least to disciple-love. The victim of the theft is likely to feel embarrassed and annoyed, as a woman feels when a covetous stranger makes formal proposals to her. But as social custom exacts that a woman shall simulate compassion in a case like this, rather than express her boredom or anger, so with disciple-love which takes the form of close imitation of style or matter. The 'master' seldom says, as he should: 'Run away, thief, and manage with what you have!' This is usually because he himself began as a thief, and therefore looks upon such stealing wistfully, as a wholesome characteristic of youth. Nor is disciple-love the only cause for plagiarism. It is often prompted by an envious desire in the thief for the reputation enjoyed by the person plagiarized, a naïve reckoning that if he can outdo the master in his own field, he will then be the famous one. Sometimes, also, by light-hearted experimentation: 'What does it feel like to write or paint like So-and-so, and then like So-and-so?' A sort of fancy-dress gaiety.

On naturally honest persons, or on thieves converted to honesty by dissatisfaction with their spoils, the prevalence of stealing all about them forces a conscientiousness that may become almost morbid. The fact that a friend has a green tea-set is argument against buying a green tea-set oneself, even of a different green and a different design, and even if green is the colour that the tea-table happens to need. Or, the discovery that two words in a line of a poem that he has just written are matched by the same two words occurring in a line of a poem by someone else will sometimes make a poet alter his line, even if the sense and contexts of the two lines are completely different, and even if those two words are the most natural ones to use. The Chinese have a proverb commending such scrupulousness in avoiding even the appearance of theft: 'When passing through a neighbour's orangery, do not pause to lace your hat; when passing through his melon-patch, do not stoop to lace your shoe.'

R.G.

IN DEFENCE OF ANGER

Laura Riding

ANGER IS A MUCH ABUSED emotion – in the two senses of 'abused': people make ill use of anger, and in Christian morality it is classified with the disreputable emotions. Jewish morality allowed it always in God, and in human beings when the provocation was an offence to piety; it allowed anger in God, and in the righteous. Christ was behaving Jewishly when he grew angry in the synagogue with the Pharisees because they objected to his healing the man with the withered hand on a sabbath day. This was the early Christ; the late, the Christian Christ would have waited for the man to come to him and healed him quietly and modestly, not provoking controversy.

Anger according to Christian definition is an immodest display of righteousness. It is, certainly, a strong criticism, as wrongful, of something someone else has said or done or failed to do or say. In Christian morality categorically adverse criticism is avoided. A wrongful deed is made a ticket of entrance to a future of better deeds: everyone must have his chance – and more chance and more chance. For anger, forgiveness must be substituted, because (the Christian assumption is) one would oneself prefer forgiveness to anger, since critical denunciation is so discouraging. Thus, the Christian distinction between right and wrong is weakened by the tenderness with which wrong is treated with the result that Christian reproof, resting largely on suave, unangry insinuations, is, in its indirectness, more unpalatable and more offensive to the dignity of the criticized person than direct anger would be. Christian notions of right are themselves suave insinuations of what is right, rather than direct assertions.

Anger is a precious emotion. It is perhaps the only critical emotion. By anger I do not mean the fury of hate. I mean that spontaneous rejection of something which is an act of solemn, not vindictive, dissociation from it. Anger does not include hate or deeds of vengeance. It is, strictly, an instinctive withdrawal from an association, dictated by an absolute disagreement with some element in it: critical accuracy forces one to break the association, painfully – anger includes pain, but not hate. Anger is mental pain physically articulated.

Anger does not last, as pain does not last (at least, mental pain). Anger is precious because it is an immediate, undeniable clue to what our minds (so much more cautious in rejection and resistance than our bodies) will not tolerate. It is precious because it is momentary: it is a momentary act of dissociation which makes a basic review of an association possible – compels a basic review. Anger has, properly, a constructive sequel of clarification. It represents surprise at the appearance of some unsuspected element in an association, an element which was not consciously acquiesced in. The whole association is momentarily at stake because, to the angry person, it is less valuable than the principle on which he consents to it. The kind of association in which anger occurs may vary: it may be a close personal relationship, or an association through assumed membership in the same social or professional body, or one based on an axiomatic assumption of membership in humanity, or on a courteous assumption of membership in a liberally inclusive order of intelligence and decency. But anger can only occur where some association exists, whether implied or specific. Its occurrence precipitates a re-evaluation of the association; it is precious because it makes the association severely immediate, bringing it out of the kindly past or the lazy future and setting it on the work-table of the present.

To foreswear anger, and with it, necessarily, the right of protest, is to sacrifice one's critical sensibilities to an ideal of genial vagueness with other people – in which there can be no real pleasure, only a feeling of temporary security from irritation. For it is impossible to people who possess critical sensibilities to remain long insensible to something in which offence inheres; and no association can be free of the possibility of offence. Associations are living, variable experiences. The capacity for anger is proof of one's own aliveness in them and responsiveness to their variations. One can only be beyond anger when an association has been closed, or has never really existed. To refuse to be angry with someone about something which does in principle arouse anger means that one disacknowledges relation with the person, from disrespect. To forswear anger is to forswear respect, to abandon all expectation of critically satisfactory association with people. Unangry disrespect may be the correct attitude to some people; but a wholesale renunciation of anger implies a disrespect to one's own power to evoke association of a critically satisfactory kind.

With some anger, dissociation is its effect as well as its action; there is no return to a reassembled association. If anger concludes an association, then the association has been a mistake, having existed only to demonstrate its impossibility. And the anger felt is hypothetical and private – what one would have felt if the association had been real. True anger is an incident of communication. It occurs publicly, retaining the presence of the person concerned within reach of reassociation. Nor is anger easily aroused in circumstances where its expression must be private, where there is no habit of intercourse in which it can figure as a mutual interlude. One is, for example, only hypothetically angry with those who commit offences against others, if one has no personal contact with the offending and offended persons. One judges, but one does not feel. The judgement is consciously applied to the situation from without, as to history; it is not unexpectedly and immediately provoked in one. We may dramatize the situation for ourselves in a hypothetical and private anger, but our public expression will be a historical statement; so-and-so has committed this or that offence against so-and-so. We cannot declare, in anger: 'What you do is wrong!' The gesture of anger must look toward a possible next step of repair. Anger which occurs in utter private instantly recalls itself, for it cannot exist without a belief in its constructive effectualness.

For this reason it is very difficult to feel angry with injustice proceeding from some political source, from some person of official authority with whom one has no personal relation. Anger in such a case would be ineffectual; one could only feel it privately, fancifully, soothing oneself with a picture of what one would feel like if the situation were personal and one's feeling of anger, therefore, a power in it. What one would feel in a case of official injustice, would be something closer to war than to anger: a sense of outraged privacy, not of outraged affinity. But one would probably not feel an emotion of war, either. War, like anger, must believe in its effectualness in order to exist. The emotion of war must look toward a possible next step of destruction of the interfering force. One would, probably, feel impersonally calm, as many people on trial in a court of law manage to feel impersonally calm, in the persuasion that they are facing injustice rather than justice: they feel that what is going on does not really concern them, and, having no physical power against the interference, flatter themselves into a mood of irony which names the interference a contemptible irrelevance.

Moralistic counsels against rebelliousness and anger are essentially recommendations of the ironic mood: to regard provocations as trivialities and be superior to them. But to the person who has been subjected to violent interference the attitude of superiority means death, for his desire is to be left alone in living privacy; the only decent recommendation would be to urge him to have the courage to be unhappy. And to the person whose anger has been tempted the attitude of superiority also means death, for his desire is to communicate with people in living associ-

ations worthy of intellectual respect. It is extraordinary how much suicide
has been recommended to us in graceful moralistic guise. Let us, by all
means, kill ourselves if we grow tired of ourselves; but not because others
have grown tired of us – certainly not if it is our anger that wearies them.
Our anger is a measure of our hardiness, and their capacity to endure it a
measure of theirs. When people nervously shrink from it in others, it is
perhaps a sign that they are tired of themselves. The discussion of anger
may, in fact, properly include the recommendation of suicide – but not to
the angry.

Anger combines judgement and emotion in a single impulse. It is
significant that in a code of moral decorum where allowances are made for
impulses of nearly every variety of unreasonableness, the one impulse
which is inspired by judgement should be disallowed. Even hate is held
excusable, and purchases a morbid sympathy – because it is incoherent,
unreasonable and exaggerated, and therefore, like madness or illness,
something that one can ignore or be concerned with at convenience or
caprice. Anger cannot be ignored; it challenges the whole surrounding
situation and demands an intelligent positive attention. It is logical and
precise, being moved by the genius of exactitude, not of fanaticism. And it
is extremely coherent – anger which is incoherent is not true anger, but a
mixture of several emotions. To show anger about something, therefore,
arouses immediate hostility. One is seen to be exercising judgement at
close personal range; and Christian decorum, which pervades the modern
world, frowns upon all judgement but a perpetually futurized Last
Judgement.

One may, the rule goes, give free rein to one's delight with something
but not to the presumed opposite of delight, anger. But, in truth, this
permissible delight – our common formalities of approval, whether of
books or pictures or deeds or food – is no opposite of anger. Examine it in
its most strenuous expression – in, say, any ordinary literary paper. What
are its conclusions? That something has been well done, or that something
shows great talent, or that something is intellectually or emotionally
exciting: but never that the something approved of must be closely,
precisely, responsibly and permanently included in our conscious order of
things. The customary delight of approval assumes no sustained
conscious order, no existing critical government in which everything and
all are intimately concerned. On the contrary: we are assumed to be joined
in a tentative, accidental and comfortably distant way that imposes on us
only occasional mild attention to others and the activities of others. We
are, conventionally, freed from any obligation of approval so strong as to
constitute a strong link, or any obligation of disapproval so strong as to
constitute a strong act of severance. There is no provision either for anger
or literal approval in our so-called critical formalities – which are only
gestures of figurative appreciation. Our conventional delight represents

no exercise of judgement; it is no critical finding-right, as anger is a critical finding-wrong. It is a finding, rather, that something annuls the critical sensibilities and diverts the mind from the responsibility of judgement. It is a finding-comfortable, and its opposite is indifference, not anger: the ignoring of that which it is not comfortable to contemplate. Anything that challenges the critical sensibilities to pledge themselves either to intimate acceptance or rejection falls, by our habitual standards of criticism, outside the bounds of normal seriousness. It is found erratic from a critical point of view because tiresome from a social point of view; social impatience is, paradoxically, the material out of which critical patience is formed.

The common remark of the person whose critical criterion is social comfort, to the person who places anger before social comfort, is: 'Why mind what other people do or say? Why not be indifferent to provocation, above it?' The key-word in this spurious appeal to one's dignity is 'mind'. Can one genuinely not mind – force one's mind to ignore – something which has for one the quality of a personal offence, acquiescence in which would be equivalent to acquiescence in a lie about oneself, or about one's values? One can only ignore the provocation if one does not take oneself or one's values seriously. The common-sense appeal to one's dignity is a spurious appeal because it appeals to a spurious dignity. One's dignity, it implies, is safer if one does not take oneself seriously, because in doing so one risks looking the fool. But true dignity can survive such risks. True anger does not, in fact, run a person into such risks, since it occurs on a level governed by critical, not conventional, values, where the effect of foolishness is not included in the range of descriptive terms. Foolishness can be an effect only on a level governed by conventional values – inelastic formulæ of social toleration. On this level it is possible to describe as a fool someone who appeals for social toleration of something not authorized in its narrowly genial catalogue of indulgences – something which is either too earnest an affirmation or too earnest a refutation. But on the critical level on which anger has effect there can be no appeal for toleration of earnestness. Earnestness is a required condition both for those who act and those who witness on this level. The descriptive terms for the effect of anger here – and it is here alone that it can have a describable effect – can refer only to the degree of agreement or disagreement it evokes. One can say that one disagrees entirely with a person in his anger, but one cannot call him foolish. For in giving attention to anger one is concerned, like the angry person himself, with the values at issue and not at all with the laws of dramatic (by which I here mean social) appropriateness. It would be more logical to advise the person whose criticism is made up of these laws to ignore anger, since it takes him to a level where he can only stumble in critical blindness, than to advise the critically sensitive person to ignore provocations to anger.

With anger dignity shifts from the social to the critical level: it is vested in the values at issue. The social dignity one has in one's relations with people is real only if it corresponds with an internal character of earnestness; only if it is the incidental manifestation of that major dignity by which we have the courage to form, on our own responsibility, definite critical decisions, and have definite critical reactions. Dignity is a matter of self-confidence – the trust we are able to place in our reactions and decisions. To make dignity the ground for avoiding occasions in which our reactions and decisions must assume explicitness is to make it, by turns, the comedian's arrogance or the comedian's humility. Social, or dramatic, dignity, should be a token that in a given crucial occasion we can be relied on to behave coherently, to form decisions about goodness or rightness and have reactions about badness or wrongness. We all live together, surely, make a world together, surely, in fundamental earnestness, not in comedy? Is the air of dignity with which we act socially a comic invention, or the result of our being, each of us, ready to face responsibly the difficult occasions when they arise? I think it is the latter, but that we are so anxious to save our energy for the difficult occasions that we treat every occasion at first, cautiously, as an easy one, and thus affect a laziness which, because it becomes a general habit, is a dangerous temptation to general inertia.

Life consists essentially of the difficult occasions. The easy occasions which compose the inessential routine of life are a temporal padding; whatever dignity surrounds them is an aura deriving from the dignity inherent in the difficult occasions. By difficult occasions I mean those in which we rely on judgement rather than on social habit, those in which we must behave originally and which are the integers of our consciousness, as the easy occasions are mere fractions. Social habit emphasizes and extracts the minor aspects of a situation; its rule is the evasion of idle emotional and intellectual stress, with the ideal object of saving emotional and intellectual energy for the destined difficult occasions. The facility of social technique is likely to deceive us: we are inclined to use our expertness in it for the entire evasion of the difficult occasions. But it is for these occasions that we live, and social habit has, properly, the object of protecting them from vulgarization in accidental reactions and decisions, not of forestalling them utterly.

Judgement on its positive side is the act of finding something good in particular according to values based on a principle which is one's knowledge of what is true in general. We develop such a principle, such knowledge, by faithful attention to and respect for our consciousness, which represents our given obligation and right of comprehensive familiarity with the world we live in. We develop the critical values implicit in the principle by faithful attention to and respect for the difficult occasions of life: they supply us with instances of comprehensive force, whose particularity we can generalize, from our knowledge of what is true in general, as good, or bad. And if one finds something good, one can also find it right, and if bad, also wrong – in so far as it concerns oneself. But a thing must be found good, or bad, before it can be found right, or wrong. We must approve or disapprove of it critically before we can approve or disapprove of it personally; otherwise personal approval or disapproval is a caprice which may well involve us in indefensible positions – positions in which we are at the mercy of others, since our own caprice invites theirs. The name of this good-and-right-finding which is a combination of critical and personal approval is satisfaction. We are on safe ground in expressing satisfaction because those who may be moved to dispute it must, if they wish to make their disagreement articulate, participate in the difficult – that is to say, comprehensive – occasion of judgement to the same degree as ourselves. An intimacy of concern must be established; there is no possibility of attack from without. It is only mysterious opposition, motivated by a concern unknown to us, which is dangerous. Our own clarity of mind (and true satisfaction can exist only in clarity of mind) exacts a relevant clarity from those who would disagree with us.

I have thus described the nature of satisfaction and its invulnerability from idle attack because anger is of the same order as satisfaction ; and one of the strongest grounds against anger is the danger of personalistic attack it exposes us to, in being a personalistic manifestation. Emotion is personalistic; emotion invites emotion; the emotions of others, when in conflict with our own, can be dangerous to us. But anger is an emotion only in the sense that it is a critical statement produced by emotional means. Anger is the name of that act of judgement which is a finding-bad-and-wrong. It is personal only as satisfaction is personal – by a personal intensification of an original critical concern. And it is an emotion, rather than an act of thought, only because judgement does not work characteristically by negation: this is why anger is momentary and has as an immediate sequence, a re-evaluation of the spoiled situation in positive terms. Anger, like satisfaction, occurs on safe critical ground. It occurs in clarity, and the response of disagreement must have an intimacy of concern with its object of the same clear degree as anger if it is to have effect as a response. Anger cannot fear the mysterious, privately generated response because it is itself produced in the open air of judgement.

One takes precautions, needs them, only if one is oneself doing something dangerous, arbitrarily emotional. Someone, in response to our anger, inflicts a personal wound on us, it can have no importance or reality in the context of our anger. It can have only the importance and reality of an accident. To warn people against anger as something dangerous can have no more specific meaning for anger than the sentimental generalization that everything is subject to accident can have for any coherent process. An accident is an event irrelevant to the particular process we are engaged in. The only way to avert accidents is to improve the coherence of our processes – cancel irrelevancy with relevancy. We do not sacrifice any of our essential processes because we agree in the general proposition that everything is subject to accident. Anger is an essential process. It has the essentiality of judgement, and of any organized articulation of sensibilities. Those who warn us against the dangerousness of anger would do better to advise us to perfect its organization: if they are really interested in our safety. But they are probably less alarmed for the private safety of anyone than for the disturbance, by anger, of the fixed social course of events, which provides for only a limited quantity of experience. Anger does, indeed, create experience, though it does not create accident. And perhaps these warnings are useful, after all, to those who have such fear of experience that any excess of it beyond the effortlessly endured social quantity is equivalent to accident: descriptions of the dangers of anger may make them shy of anger and the angry, though the original intention has undoubtedly been to frighten anger and the angry out of society.

But has anyone the right (it may be asked) to assert on his own authority that this is good and right and that bad and wrong? We live: and with a high degree of deliberateness. We cannot but, in honour, make this deliberateness a responsible one. In living as we do by the method of consciousness, we are assuming, each, tremendous authority. We endow ourselves, each, with a royalty of life; and at our stage of consciousness we cannot without indecency shirk the royal gestures of satisfaction and anger. It would be well enough to issue counsels against anger if a large part of our population stood, by self-definition, in the relation of mental slaves to ourselves. But then we should also have to issue counsels against the exercise of judgement. And I am sure that none of us would make personal dignity, or responsibility, so scarce an attribute. None of us would call the world so poor and uncertain a place. Do we not all feel a respectful interest in one another – respectful, that is, unless specific ground is given for disrespect? If not, why is it that so much of our activity – activity of all kinds – takes serious cognizance of the reactions and decisions of others?

We are all, really, respectfully interested in one another. Other people represent to us potential events of importance – something more than sources of accident; they inspire in us expectations of satisfaction. We prescribe the nature of satisfaction as our judgement develops, but not the number of people with whom we can enjoy common satisfaction: this is ever the benignantly uncomputed number. When we are angry, which is to feel cheated of a particular satisfaction promised to our judgement by a particular situation, we are opposing to the immediate chagrin an insistence on the general possibility of satisfaction – or our emotion would be despair rather than anger. Anger is concrete hope in the midst of disappointment; without anger we should be overwhelmed by our disappointments instead of stimulated by them into assertions of the general possibility of satisfaction.

But people with a capacity for anger are undoubtedly a problem to people who do not like to be exposed to observation and judgement and yet wish to circulate freely in the world. It is significant that counsels on the theme of anger are not addressed, generally, to people who do not like their behaviour to be taken into account, but to people of critically developed sensibilities: these are asked to isolate their sensibilities, not the others their behaviour. Anger, as I have said, is a precious emotion, and should be an object of great tenderness. Aristotle somewhat felt its value, but he saw it more as a part of the healthy emotional material which should be the endowment of the average person than as an important critical faculty. 'He therefore who feels anger on proper occasions, with proper objects, and besides in a proper manner, at proper times, and for a proper length of time, is an object of praise.' But what of the improper occasions, of anger with improper persons? Where is to be found the counsel which urges the improper objects – namely, people of careless behaviour – to isolate themselves or their lapses from the attention of the critically sensitive.

Anger is a precious emotion, but it is also a generous one, as judgement is a generous faculty. The person who possesses the faculty of judgement possesses it exactly because his field of potential satisfaction is extensive and not niggardly: the extent necessitates judgement as a large place necessitates government, and a very small place does not. The field of anger is as extensive as the field of potential satisfaction; it is, indeed, the same field. To restrict the action of anger is to condition judgement with a miserliness of energy toward the dissatisfying; and judgement needs no such protection – anger (and those who possess the faculty of anger) needs no such protection.

They keep telling us not to waste anger. ('Be not mortally angry with any for a venial fault. – He will make a strange combustion in the state of his soul, who, at the landing of every cock-boat, sets the beacons on fire.' – Thomas Fuller.) They might as well tell us to be careful how much we think, lest we use up our minds. No one who feels anger is angry that he has been made angry: true anger does no one any more harm than satisfaction does. No one feels anger unless the provocation is interesting, as no one experiences satisfaction with what is not interesting – not pertinent to one's conscious experience. The provocation to anger is interesting because it raises the question of satisfaction in an urgent and immediate form. There can be no danger, ever, of wasting anger, for it is not the spending of a waning physical store but the exercise of a progressively heightened mental sensibility. Every incident of anger improves, rather than impairs, its functional excellence.

They keep urging us not to excite ourselves on dull subjects. But they mean, by this, only to divert our attention from the careless or inadequate or inappropriate: they know very well that dull subjects do not excite us. The person who supplies the provocation may be in the main a dull person, but the subject of anger cannot be dull – if it were, we should feel not anger, but boredom. In so far as a person raises a subject of anger he is not a dull person. Why do they not leave us to our anger? We do not complain. And what cause have they to complain, when the result of anger is as clear a definition of what we hold good and bad, right and wrong, as if we had experienced satisfaction, and not anger?

I myself am always grateful to the anger-provoking situation, for the clarity it produces – whether it is my anger or someone else's. My only complaint, in relation to anger, would be that there is not enough of it. It is a remarkably infrequent occurrence, considering the frequency of exhortations against anger. I love seeing a person in anger as I love hearing a person think: we do not often so honour one another. And so do we all, really, love to witness one another directly. But we conceal our curiosity in the social fiction that we are only casually interested in one another; we advertize the fiction that we may conceal our curiosity behind it and protect it from rebuff. This is one of the reasons why plays and cinema dramas excite us: we can look directly at the characters, and in the theatre-dark let our curiosity loose without social embarrassment. And no dramatic representation can have such reality for us (given adequate verisimilitude) as a display of anger or a character shown in the act of thinking aloud. For these are more intimate, more integral self-manifestations than either distress or pleasure, hate or love, or any other pair of living occasions.

I have written in this strain on anger as one familiar with anger in herself. I do not get angry often, but sometimes; because, of the difficult occasions which compose my experience, there are many more which satisfy than which do not. This is somewhat to my credit, for the care I bestow on the difficult occasions, but in great part to the credit of those who share in them with me and with whom I reap the common fruit of satisfaction. And I am so grateful for my good luck that I am prepared to take some bad luck along with it; I am prepared to reap, sometimes, the lonely and not unhealthily bitter fruit of anger. It is good, sometimes, to feel as lonely, and vigorous in loneliness, as anger makes one feel. Anger is, I think, the only condition of loneliness which does no damage to one's inward vigour – on the contrary, it purifies and rehabilitates it. The anger, even, of another person toward us somewhat fans our own vigour: we too are made lonely by it, since it momentarily severs association, and thrown [*sic*. throws us?] upon our separate resources. I would rather have another person angry with me than coldly antagonistic; anger declares the bond which it breaks, while cold antagonism refers to no bond, being only the assertion of a fundamental incongruity of persons. My only reaction to cold antagonism is one of self-blame, that I have ignored the fundamental incongruity and so made its assertion necessary: as one blames oneself for having sown seeds of expectation in any ground that proves itself barren.

But I write in defence not in praise of anger; I do not wish to seem an epicure of anger. It is a pity to have cause to feel angry, but better to feel angry than affect indifference about something that one is expected to accept and cannot, in conscience, accept. Nor can anger easily degenerate into a habit of intolerance. Anger is a loyal defence of one's convictions against a breach of loyalty by someone who might have been reasonably expected to share in them with one. It is not an arbitrary demand of loyalty. There must always be, with anger, an unexpected defection, by someone else, from a standard it was natural to regard as mutual. No one grows angry over a difference of opinion arising from idiosyncratic personal difference, though he may grow intolerant and petulant. What produces anger is a sense of betrayal and of being asked to co-operate in a betrayal of some established generality of conviction.

To be habitually petulant about something is to own to private arbitrariness of conviction and to demand, tyrannically, indulgence or submission – the petulant person does not care which. Anger is self-protective rather than tyrannical. It expresses shock and a resolution not to let the defection of another person from a common ground of conviction influence oneself toward defection. It preserves the critical basis of association from sentimentalism. If a person is constantly returned to solitary guardianship of his convictions, he cannot become petulantly aggressive about them unless he changes them from convictions, which are values sensitive to universal impressions, to opinions, which are private dogmas closed to universal impressions. For anger, and one's convictions, to undergo such a drastic degeneration, one must have gradually grown so uncommunicative in one's convictions that idiosyncrasy and petulance are their only public characteristics. If this has happened, that is, the fault is with intellectual arrogance and personal vanity, not with loyalty to conviction and its emotional concomitant, anger. I am here concerned with anger, not with petulance, the emotional by-product of idiosyncrasy – or with any other counterfeit anger.

I do not think it is difficult to distinguish between petulance and anger. The confusion, if it occurs, must derive from a disrespect to anger which has affected the integrity of our vocabulary. If someone glorifies petulance into anger, he is ridiculous; and our respect for anger should prevent us from associating it with the ridiculous. True anger is never ridiculous. We cannot say of a person that he has let himself get too angry: there are no degrees in anger, as there are no degrees in judgement. One is either exercising the faculty of judgement or of anger, or one is not. Anger is noble and whole-hearted, as judgement is noble and whole-minded. We should greet its appearance in ourselves as a sign that thought has made its way into our very bones. Indeed, I should be inclined to make the bones, rather than the heart, the seat of anger. Is this not what we have meant, and laboured, to be: all-of-a-piece beings? That which distresses the mind should make the very bones – our mutest parts – protest? Since what rejoices the mind gives the bones peace, this is surely not too much co-operation to expect from them.

Francis Quarles, from whose *Enchiridion* the head-piece to these homiletic studies is taken, says of anger: 'Naturall anger glances in the breasts of wise men, but rests in the bosome of fooles: in them, it is infir-mity; in these, a sinne : there is a naturall anger; and there is a spirituall anger; the common object of that, is the person; of this, his vice.' But there are not two angers. For that anger which is an infirmity and not a power to detect the wrong quickly, with the feelings, is no anger at all; it is a hasty, disorderly emotion of any kind except anger. What Quarles here says of natural anger applies to lust, cruelty, enthusiasm, pity or any other accidental emotion. But anger is never accidental; it is quick, but not hasty. It can occur only where there is an order in the feelings inspired by an order in the mind. Our feelings supply our minds with information about what is, and out of this information our minds make a knowledge of what should be. Our minds then educate our feelings, giving them the only kind of knowledge which is emotionally intelligible: a knowledge of what should not be. It is by this knowledge that anger acts.

Minds move in a leisurely way: to know what is true and be sensible of the good, the right, requires leisure and patience. Therefore, minds are not expertly equipped for the detection of the bad, the wrong. A principle of truth has a constant and complete occupation of the mind and leaves no room for a principle of falsity – which cannot exist, except by emotional invention, and then only for the immediate emergency. A knowledge of what should not be can have no constant existence: truth can make no other provision for falsity than the denial of it when it appears, by the detection of its badness and wrongness. The bad, the wrong, must be detected with speed and impatience, since to ignore them is to tolerate them and condition the true with the false. For this kind of detection we must rely on our feelings, on the spontaneous evocation of a principle of falsity in imitation of a principle of truth – on the faculty of anger.

The mind is continuous; the good, the right, details of the true, are continuous subjects. The feelings are discontinuous; the bad, the wrong, details of the false, are discontinuous subjects; a principle of falsity must be discontinuous. Nothing can really shock the mind; it moves with an almost complacent rhythm between contemplation of what is and realiza-tion of what should be. And yet, because life is not a closed situation, because between these two poles of event (what is and what should be) there are occurrences to which neither our sense of facts nor our appre-hension of ultimates can allow reality – things which are mere impossibilities: because of the necessary experimentalism of life, we must remain susceptible to incongruous experience and be able to dispose of it in some way consistent with our mental rhythm of reality. We must be able to belittle (with our humour) or see as otherwise than it seems (with our love) or utterly deny (with our anger) that which falls upon our minds with destructive strangeness, and against which we have no other defences than our feelings. Anger deals with that which is most incorrigibly strange; it is our most critical weapon of defence against the impossible.

I see no reason for calling anger a 'spiritual' weapon. By 'spiritual' we generally mean, and in the passage quoted Quarles means, a weapon wielded only abstractly. True, anger delivers no blows. (Vengeance is not the result of anger, rather of humiliated pride – the angry person is offended in his judgement, not in his personal vanity.) Its method is not one of attack, only of self-severance from the provocation. Yet anger is a concrete and natural gesture; it is no mere speculation, but something we do. In anger we assume a posture which has the critical effect of 'No!' One cannot rest at 'No!' 'No!' has only a momentary reality – the next moment it vanishes in the positive rhythm of the mind. But in vanishing it makes the reality of the provocation vanish along with it; and while it lasts, moreover, it is as absolute as thought in its power to legislate for the person who feels it. Anger is, in fact, a terrible faculty – thanks be to the good sense of our bodies for it. But may we not be caused to have overmuch of it. For the body has a natural wildness, even in its good sense: no doubt we shall be saddened when we remember, later, the cruel parts that we had, of living necessity, to play.

L.R.

THE EXERCISE OF ENGLISH

Laura Riding and Robert Graves

1

PEOPLE PERCEIVE: THEY ARE AWARE of differences between this and that, between themselves and other people. The different realities of perception are at first understood only in terms of their difference one from the other: the perceptive faculties are merely acted upon, merely see. What is the whole? To the person who merely sees, the whole is the unknown. The person who merely sees because he shrinks from the responsibility of making a personal definition of the whole is the artist; the whole is the mystery he is afraid to profane by interpretation.

To combine the realities of perception into an understanding, or personal whole, is to make language. Uncombined, the whole is 'reality', the unknown. Language describes reality in terms of human capacity for knowing it. The different realities of perception exemplify human incapacity to know wholly. Language organizes perception into human equivalents to reality, into notions of reality. In language the human and the real make a compromise. In language and in language alone are all the problems solved.

There are many different speeches, but there is only one language; and this is English. Speech is spoken, language is written. The exercise of English is the writing of English. The exercise of speech is the use of words for other purposes than those of language; while the purposes of writing are identical with those of language. And so the words of a speech differ from the words of a language. And speeches differ among themselves; they differ according to their purposes. Different speeches are of peoples with different purposes. Nor is it exact to say that language has, like speech, purposes. Language has an end. The difference between a purpose and an end is as the difference between life and death. Life is a purpose. Death is an end. Speech is the use of words for a purpose, for all the purposes into which it is possible to vary the conglomerate purpose *life*. Language is the use of words for the one purpose that can outlast all purposes: the reconciliation of purposes. This is not a purpose, but an inevitability. Consciousness moves beyond the living satisfactions. There is no satisfaction beyond these, only reconciliation. Consciousness automatically chooses death because it is more finally satisfying than life. Death is an end; language consciously pursues this end, as speech wilfully pursues the various purposes which make up life.

Speech subordinates truth to the purpose; and it passes with the fulfilling of the purpose. Language remains; when there is nothing but language left, language is truth. Speech has grammar, a convenience of sequence for words used in capricious living senses; language has relation – an internal grammar in which the living senses are reconciled. English has relation, not grammar. English has in it all the speeches; its purity is a consciousness of the impurities of the speeches. In English the living mind sacrifices purpose to end: the end of surviving life, or mere perception. To survive perception is to have coexistence with reality in a knowledge, or whole, that can be encompassed by the human mind: reality rewards the whole-seeking human mind by taking on finiteness.

The non-human part of language is the word; the human part is words. Language is the understanding of the word with words; speech is the understanding of words with words – the human part of language understanding itself, agreeing with itself. The agreement of the human with itself is logic, and the system of logic is grammar, or the exclusion of discord. The agreement of the human with the real and of the real with the human is truth, and the system of truth is relation, or the inclusion and ordering of discord. Truth is expressed reality – language. I do not say, sentimentally, 'The English language is truth.' The English language is the history of truth: it is the historical antecedent of truth. Immediate truth is poetry. But before words can become poetry they must become language; and it is in English that this transformation occurs.

Spoken English is the experimental mixing of the speeches, the education of words in the uses to which language may *not* be put. For this reason English as a speech is the most conversational and idiomatic of speeches; as a speech, that is, English is an understanding of the nature of speeches. English is a language, and therefore also a complete indication of all that is not language – as anything that is good is also a definition of what is bad. English is a language and therefore also a standard of language.

2

The communication between the human and the real takes place in language. In expressing itself the real is not using a speech of man; it is using man's understanding of it as the form of its address to man. In language the human mind seeks ideas of reality, with only one reservation – the survival of the 'I' in the idea; this is, in fact, implied in the term 'idea'. Reality proportions itself to the human understanding by means of ideas: an idea is the result of an adjustment between two different elements. English is the language of ideas. Ideas are definitions of reality in terms of the human understanding: reality as the human mind is capable of integrated perception of reality. Language is reality in human degree.

English is the language of ideas. An idea is a name: the unification of a conglomerate impression. 'I call this conglomeration X,' says the perceiving agent, 'because when I perceive it I feel X; I give it the name of my reactions to it. I try to identify myself with it, and the name is really both of us: the name includes me. If I can make no identification whatever, then I give it no name; it is unknown to me.' Language is a catalogue of the identifications which the human mind is able to make between itself and reality. It cannot make complete identification, because it is only a derivative aspect of reality integrating itself sympathetically (not identically) with it; the identifications are sympathetic identifications; language is not a word but words. *The* word is the name of reality. The human mind cannot conceive reality absolutely. It can only conceive it sympathetically, in words, in particular effects – in names.

In a speech the 'I' of a word is the individual 'I' of a special humanity standing in a special reality of its own. It is the 'I' of one humanity as against the 'I' of another, not the representative human 'I'. English is the language of names, of unifications; speeches achieve only perceptive syntheses. An English word possesses the character of the experience as well as that of the experiencing 'I'; it is a concept. The word of a speech possesses the character only of the people of the speech: it is itself an 'I'. In English the human 'I' is merely the pronoun of inquiry. The combination of the pronoun with the fitting answer makes the name, or noun.

English is the language of nouns. It is an analysis of reality from the human point of view, without being a humanization of reality. It is a practical expression of reality, not a theoretically perfect expression. English is reality imperfectly expressed – an incomplete questioning of reality answered as fully as the questioning allows. The sense in English of an impossible perfect expression that can only be proportionately achieved is the Greek gift. The sense of limitations is the Latin gift – a flat ruling-out of the impossible; Latin is the rhetorical discipline of English. French is ironic conceit in English – the use of words of merely interrogative force as words of declarative force: the strategy of eloquence is the French gift. French makes extravagant identities between the human and the real which carry with them their own negation: 'We are extravagant; but we are only speaking metaphorically. Our purpose is a theatrical sensation.'

English is literal, it is a language. Truth in French is merely a refinement of the concrete. Truth in English is a proportion between the concrete inquiring apparatus and abstract (not wholly conceivable) reality. French is metaphorical. English is plain. French is adjectival; English is of nouns. English words that are not nouns are conjunctives serving nouns.

German is a speech of verbs. German tries to lift up the concrete apparatus *in toto* to the abstract level, as French tries to bring down the abstract to the concrete level. French gives an effect of inappropriate lightness; German gives an effect of inappropriate earnestness. But there is in the presumptuous French adjective a saving sophistication: it knows that it can only pretend. The German verb is not aware of its presumptuousness. It represents a stupid will to reach the abstract level, to achieve the impossible. And because the will is stupid, it seems honest. Thus the French have a reputation for being false, though they are only theatrical: while the Germans have a reputation for honesty, though they are only stupid – and far less innocent than the French. The German will is to impose the human on the real, to conquer the real, be the real. German speech is pseudo-impressive; French speech is ironically eloquent.

English is not a speech; it is a language. Language stands between concrete, external human consciousness and internal, unexpressed – and therefore 'abstract' – reality. The German places its 'I' arbitrarily in the abstract. The French leaves its 'I' in the concrete, making only metaphorical identifications with the abstract. The English 'I' moves out of the concrete to a level intermediate between the concrete and the abstract: the level of the humanly possible. We might similarly discuss other speeches in relation to the English language, but French and German serve best as direct bases for comparison, being both speeches that seem, beyond other speeches, *personal,* and therefore endowed with the qualities (such as responsibility and coherence) which we look for in a language.

3

Nouns are the vocabularistic basis of the English language. A foreigner wishing to learn English might well learn all the nouns first: this would distinguish for him the English habit better than general exercises in translation. A Frenchman wishing to communicate the notion *C'est la vie!* who knew only that *vie* in English was 'life', would be obliged to concentrate in the utterance of the single word 'life' the meaning which in the French is only theatrically insinuated. If he were told that the translation of *C'est la vie!* was 'Such is life', he would be side-tracked by the adjectival appeal of 'such'; and the emphasis would fall on 'such'. In the English phrase no variation of emphasis is possible. 'Such' prepares gently for the strong idea 'life'; 'is' provides for the slow, not too emphatic utterance of 'life'. In English the phrase is an act of realization, even in a flippant context; in French it is a flippant gesture, even in a serious context.

'The book of life': here are two nouns which together constitute a third noun – a third naming. Accuracy of implication is safeguarded by the literal sense in which the word 'book' is used; 'life' as a word carrying in it the danger of facile abstraction is disciplined by the opposition of the more concrete 'book'. 'The book of life' is not an enlargement of the idea 'life', but a concentration. A book has pages, chapters, a beginning, an end, natural and unnatural turns: it is, like life, a protracted entity. 'The book of life' presents the idea 'life' as life is actually a book. The characteristics which 'life' has in common with 'book' are not goodness or badness, interestingness or dullness, only such characteristics as are intrinsically book-like – such as cohesiveness in spite of variety of contents. It is not the irony but the truth of the comparison that produces the phrase. 'Book' and 'life' are combined into a new precision of reality; the 'I' is stood anew in the entire phrase.

Le livre de la vie: it is not possible in French to say this purely. *Le livre – la vie*: they do not co-operate. One feels for an adjective: '*le livre confus de la vie*'. Not 'book' and 'life' as a new degree of understanding of both 'book' and 'life', but merely life in the sense of *a* confused book. 'Book' and 'life', indeed, fall away; we are left with an adjectival sensation – confusion. 'Book' is here, that is, hopelessly concrete, 'life' hopelessly abstract. In French there is an adjectival barrier between nouns, and it is the so-called 'abstract' nouns which suffer from the isolation: the face of the barrier is turned toward the concrete noun. The natural French noun is the concrete noun; in English the concrete and the abstract are equally natural.

Or, *La vie, c'est comme un livre*: life is like *a* book. A book, a concrete object that one employs for one's convenience at any hour of the day, is being compared to life, an abstraction. Life, with other abstractions of its kind, is something outside the daily experience of speech. It is introduced only as a luxury emphasising the sufficiency of the concrete – this is the purpose of the introduction. *La vie, c'est comme un livre:* the mind glows beneficently at the concrete goodness of *livre*. We have here a contrast, not a combination. Combination is poetic, contrast is witty. The poetic in French becomes the witty. Well, life is like a book. And how do you make that out? *Because* it is either dull or interesting. There is no third naming in which the other two are absorbed. 'Book' stands off sharply from 'life'; 'life' creeps ingratiatingly over the adjectival barrier, leaving its abstract self behind, and becomes an exceptionally dull or exceptionally interesting book. But would not one say 'Life is like a book' in English? One would not. In English one does not put all one's eggs into one basket: because there are a great many eggs, and a great many baskets to put them into.

Das Buch des Lebens: *Das Buch* is an abstraction, *Das Leben* is an abstraction. And both are also concretions: the thing 'book' as well as the idea 'book', the action 'to live' as well as the idea 'life' – a book as well as the book, living as well as life. The German noun is a verbal reach between the lowest and highest point of conceptual power. The uttered word 'book' represents *only* the 'I' straining to connect impossibly the book of perception and the abstract book, to make a complete identification between the human 'I' lifted out of the book of perception, struggling in verbal suspension between this and the abstract book, and the 'I' of the abstraction – the 'I' of reality. The German 'I' tries to be the perfect 'I' implicit in the abstraction: it tries to be reality itself. The English 'I' never attempts to be more than the humanly personal 'I'.

Das Buch des Lebens: the very thought of it tires. *Leben* demands an unimaginable stretch between the concrete level and the abstract level. The English word stops where the imagination fails, the German word recognizes no limit of imagination: the imagination must follow the effort. *Das Buch des Lebens*: *Leben* excites in *Buch* a passion of verbal duality. We have not only two words *Leben* but two words *Buch*. The four words suggest some fifth word carrying on the dramatic action of the four: 'What does *Das Buch des Lebens* do?' *Das Buch des Lebens* perhaps weighs down on the mind like … We come to a sixth degree of self-tantalization. The book of life weighs down on the mind like a whole heavenly *library*. And then there is the key to the library – in the Berlin Museum perhaps. And then there is the deciphering of infinite hieroglyphs of meaning which shall be found there; which should not be impossible, only all very hard work.

In English 'the book of life' would be the culmination of a process, not the beginning of a process. All antagonism to the abstraction is worked out before the denominating phrase is uttered. And it is not so much antagonism to difficult reality, as a testing of human powers; antagonism is worked out in the understanding of these powers as limitations. In English no word must be loftier or more debased than any other. English words are all in the same degree: the human degree of the real. Language is conditioned by human integrity; the human mind places itself in reality only as it is possible to do so sanely, without contortion, without witty pretence or the vehemence of disappointment.

There is then in English a central standard of naming, a studied measure of possibility between the concrete and the abstract. Words that satisfy this standard are the true words, the primary poetic words. Words that do not satisfy it have validity as critical words. The human 'I' in every word is, indeed, a critical consciousness, and as such it has a critical identity with reality itself. Reality and the human mind agree in the object truth: truth is the standard. In every English word it is the same 'I' conscious of standard. The 'I' in the concrete word that fails to achieve name-value keeps the word out of the primary poetic vocabulary: makes it adjectival. The 'I' in the abstract word that resists personalization similarly keeps it out of the primary poetic vocabulary: makes it as a verb.

Any word in English must be a 'good' word: it must indicate, if not directly exemplify, standard. It is a name; or, if it has not the careful confidence of a name (*i.e.*, is not a true noun), it is a mobile instrument in the confirmation of words of stronger name-value than itself, or an instrument in the subordination of words of no stronger or even less strong name-value than itself. English is thus a language with a central faith or nucleus of established names accompanied by a flexible critical apparatus: the critical apparatus is used by the names to form themselves into a truth-structure which the human 'I' in the names may sustain coherently, personally. The critical words represent both the reticence of reality toward the human and the honest incapacity of the human toward reality; as the names represent their mutual sympathy. And thus language becomes a habit of integration, of reconciliation, and finally of poetry.

4

The following passage from an essay by the late Lord Birkenhead illustrates the action of critical words in English; not only in self-subordination, but in restraint of the nouns they serve. The effect is that wilful prosiness and indirectness called 'characteristically English' which the English are apt to produce when they use language against its poetic possibilities, from a nervous embarrassment with the intensities lurking in words.

No inconsiderable portion of my reading leisure has been spent in the company of swashbucklers and pirates, and I have succumbed deliberately and often to the imposture of the detective tale…

I will attempt no prediction now. Yet it seems to me not unlikely that our descendants will declare for pleasure rather than for pain in the realm of fiction, and that those books possess the secret of survival which are clear and kindling, and tell a story plainly and without undue circumlocution. My advice to youth has always been to set out adventurously and my advice to novelists is the same. I have risked some censure elsewhere for reminding adventurous youth of the opportunities which await it. I was blamed, as candid commentators often are, for telling the truth. I do not take naturally to perverted meekness or loose-thinking or the shirking of facts, and I resent the exalting of arm-chair theorists into arbiters of conduct in times of crisis. I cannot accept the hypothesis that success awaits the pusillanimous, or that nations which bottle up their ambitions will grow to greatness.

Before I was of age I had read all Scott's novels more than once.
I had galloped as often with the Three Musketeers from Boulogne,
and dived with the Count of Monte Cristo from the Chateau d'If
into the midnight sea; and I cannot but believe, in reference to my
own career, that no inconsiderable portion of any success which I
may have achieved derives from the impulse of these magicians and
the example and emulation of their heroes.

We are first presented with three names – each of a critical rather than poetic
character, each structurally involved in the machinery of low emphasis:

No inconsiderable portion of my reading leisure
The company of swashbucklers and pirates
The imposture of the detective tale

The connective words between these names are all designed to maintain
the low emphasis and are more or less absorbed in the names. 'Has been
spent in' accomplishes a graceful identification of the reading 'I' with the
'I' who made company with swashbucklers and pirates. 'I have succumbed
deliberately and often to' accomplishes a stoically frank identification with
the 'I' who kept still less wholesome company.

Here, then, are three names set down as a statement of a difficulty:
(a) the time and energy given to reading by a man who, it is implied, has
more pressing obligations than reading, though he is a lover of books;
(b) his whole-hearted abandonment of himself to books of adventure;
(c) his less satisfactory abandonment of himself to the modern type of
adventure-story in the unfortunate absence of the old-fashioned type.
What are names for? They make a consolidation, a recognizable entity, to
associate with other entities with the object of discovering new entities,
new names. Language proceeds by names; and each new name embraces
the old names in a new entity which is at once more inclusive and more
concentrated.

In the three names distinguishable in the first sentence of the passage
quoted an unresolved situation is presented: three entities in need of relation. What relation do the succeeding sentences accomplish? But is there
an object of immediate relation? There is only, rather, a desire to state a
difficulty as impossible of immediate solution: there are no books being
written of the kind that give Lord Birkenhead pleasure. We might even
say that he has 'deliberately' chosen this situation as congenial to his
linguistic technique. There is a difficulty and a 'characteristically English'
treatment of the difficulty: he states it in its most unresolved form,
naming the factors of the difficulty and leaving them to stew in conversational low heat for a time – until little by little some relation between
them, some solution, is effected. And, however prosy the taste while the
process is going on, the 'I' is actually in the pot, and the pot is, for all the

prosiness and 'coldness', the poetic pot – stewing away at the lowest heat
at which it is possible to maintain the fire of language.

   'No prediction now', the fourth name, thus merely restates low heat; it
is the compromise-name for the conflicting impulses suspended in

>   I will attempt
>   Yet it seems not unlikely

'That our descendants will declare for' seems a fifth name, but it is really
only a critical elaboration of the fourth name: instead of 'no prediction
now', the possible declaration of our descendants. 'Pleasure rather than
pain in the realm of fiction' having been put in the mouths of our descendants as the name repressed in 'no prediction now' (i.e., this is the *desired*
fourth name of the passage), the courage of our descendants descends
upon the author, and 'no prediction now' is for the moment swept away:
naming, though temporarily restrained in criticism, is the ultimate object.
But critical caution prevails.

>   Those books
>   The secret of survival

'Those books', the fifth name and a more sensible, historical form of 'pleasure rather than pain', has a directly emphatic force, but only because the
critical accompaniment has been allowed to lag behind for the moment.
'The secret of survival' is the name of Lord Birkenhead's unwillingness to
commit himself further: the critical accompaniment has caught up again.
'Those books ... which are clear and kindling': the magnitude of this spec-
ification further sobers the emphasis. And they must, moreover, be out-
and-out story-books, *and* they must be emphatic ('without undue
circumlocution')! Here we have, that is, not so much a name, as a definition postponed in three concentric circles: the inner 'secret of survival',
the intermediate 'those books', and the critical circle of discouraging outer
atmosphere (books which must be 'clear and kindling', etc.). We cannot,
as it were, get out of the fifth name. So we are thrown back to the actual
fourth name, 'no prediction now': 'my advice to youth', and 'my advice to
novelists' – which is merely a cautious extension of the idea 'youth' to the
youngish idea 'novelists', the youth of his audience excusing the author
for somewhat modifying his intention of attempting no prediction now.
'My advice to youth, and to novelists much the same as youth, my much
the same advice': the fourth name seems about to leap across the too theoretical fifth name and urge in a sixth name. But as advice to so-and-so is
really a withdrawal of the authorial 'I' from the situation, diffidence leaks
through to the sixth name, and it is not a name at all but a gesture of
restrained encouragement to other more adventurous devotees of
language, from an arm-chair writer who is *not* a mere theorist: 'to set out
adventurously'.

some censure elsewhere
reminding adventurous youth
opportunities which await it

The 'some censure elsewhere' risked carries on the critical consciousness
of 'no prediction now'. 'Reminding adventurous youth' is the naming of
the censure in an acknowledgement and defence of the offence: he has
only *reminded*, and reminded only *youth*. So 'censure' and the further
naming cancel each other, and the cancellation is expressed in the third
name, 'opportunities which await it' – an acquittal on the ground that no
crime has yet been committed. In the next sentence a confession of honest
but cautious truth-telling substitutes for censure from outside an inner
conscience as the name of the critical consciousness indicated in 'no
prediction now'. The two sentences that follow endeavour to state this
consciousness as something different from *mere* criticism – criticism, that
is, with the mere object of discouraging results. Under his critical object is
hidden a poetic object. 'I do not naturally take to' mere criticism –
'perverted meekness or loose-thinking or the shirking of facts': here is a
denunciation by the critical 'I' of critical dissociation from the poetic 'I'.
The second sentence elaborates on the denunciation by repeating the
gesture of restrained encouragement to the poetic 'I' from the arm-chair
of the critical 'I'. And no inconsiderable portion of any success which he
may have achieved he allows to be possibly the result of such qualified
identifications with the poetic 'I' as his critical, older 'I' has permitted.
And so we are brought back to the original unresolved situation of a poetically inclined critical 'I' becalmed in an arm-chair by the uncertain results
accomplished by the poetic 'I', on whom rests the responsibility for
suggesting the results from which the critical 'I' must choose. We are
brought back to the original embarrassment of choice, after a very thorough demonstration of the critical force in English words as it constitutes
a temptation to a writer merely to play safe: a demonstration, in fact, of the
ponderous safeguards against dangerous poeticism in a poetic language.

5

The following passage from *Peter Abailard* by J. G. Sikes suggests a study
of the critical requirements which even so unambitious a process as narration must satisfy in English.

This action, evidently taken without consulting him, enraged
Fulbert. Entering Abailard's room one night, accompanied by some
companions, he attacked and robbed him of his manhood. Such a
dastardly act does not seem to have affected his physique, save natu-

rally during a necessary period of convalescence, for most, if not all, of his books were written at a later date. Afterwards, when reviewing the events of his early life, he came to see in their deed the working of the finger of God. The reprisal was indeed justified, and, since he was now freed from the lusts of the flesh and as he could henceforth devote both himself and his philosophy wholly to the service of God, Fulbert's action could not be regarded entirely as a misfortune.

Narration is the setting down of ideas in accidental juxtaposition – in conflict rather than in relation with one another: the setting down of as many unnamed entities as possible, in their numerical confusion. Such entities are blind entities. A blind entity is not a name but a title. In narration the concern is only with the competitive multiplication of titles. The test of good narration is one of titular thoroughness. How many different titles are presented in the passage quoted?

> Fulbert's Rage at this Action
> Abailard's Evident Failure to Consult Fulbert
> Fulbert's Consequent Rage at this Action

Something is wrong here; the writer has allowed himself to become so dominated by the narrative atmosphere that he offers false titles. Good narration must provide true titles; there must be no faking of numbers. What are the true titles here?

> Abailard's Evident Failure to Consult Fulbert
> Fulbert's Rage at Abailard's Failure to Consult him

The sentence should properly read, then: 'Abailard evidently failed to consult Fulbert about this action, and this enraged Fulbert.' If the author wishes to get in a true third title, he must add: 'as well as the action itself.' But better, in this case: 'Fulbert was enraged both by Abailard's action and by Abailard's evident failure to consult him about it.' The action itself is in either of these sentences a more distinct entity than in the author's sentence. But as it is clear that Fulbert would not have permitted the action at all if Abailard had consulted him about it, the impression that Fulbert was enraged at Abailard's failure to consult him is false and is only created for the benefit of a false third title. It is the action itself that enrages Fulbert; the expansive word 'evidently' softens the falseness. So we must revise our titles:

> Abailard's Evident Failure to Consult Fulbert
> Fulbert's Rage at Abailard's Action.

Our sentence should really be two sentences: 'Abailard evidently failed to consult Fulbert beforehand. His action enraged Fulbert.' Weakness or insincerity of narrative technique drags in poetic technique: the false title is really a poeticization, a relation between two titles rather than a new title. And whenever in English a poeticization creeps into writing that is not avowedly poetic, this is a sign that the writing has become false. The rule of a narrative sentence is: how many separate titles can one sentence maintain without stimulating false poetic relation between them? The narrative function is only to explore given material with the object of breaking it up into as many blind entities as possible.

> Fulbert's Entry into Abailard's Room
> Presence of Companions
> Fulbert's Attack on Abailard
> Robbery of Abailard's Manhood by Fulbert.

But the association of Fulbert's companions with the attack is an idle title by the narrative evidence that it was only Fulbert who attacked Abailard. Yet obviously Fulbert did not attack Abailard without the assistance of his companions, or at least he did not rob Abailard of his manhood without their assistance. There is, then, a poeticization in the use of 'he' to represent Fulbert *and* his companions, who may have identified themselves with Fulbert's rage, but not to the extent of magically willing their physical strength into his arm. So here we have impurity of narrative technique involving the writer in poeticization to the suppression of a title.

> Fulbert's Entry into Abailard's Room
> Presence of Companions
> Sympathetic Indignation of Companions against Abailard
> The attack on Abailard
> Robbery of Abailard's Manhood

But the last title here is only a poetic renaming of the attack – a criticism as it were of the narrative restriction that prevents the author from dwelling largely on the nature of the attack, its terrible significance for the victim. But the narrator must not criticize narration; he must accept the limitations, or else completely abandon narrative for poetic technique. Assuming that there is no serious desire here to abandon narrative technique, let us see what can be done within the limitations. Let us decide that there has been a preliminary attack, separate from the act which figures here only as the nature of the attack. Let us decide that 'attack' covers the wakening of Abailard and the overcoming of the resistance he would presumably offer. Then we are left not with a sentimental statement of the nature of the attack treated as a whole from Abailard's naturally very personal point of view, but with an act supplementary to the attack. Our true fifth title is, then, 'The Castration of Abailard'. So we may now rewrite the sentence, from the purified titles: 'Entering

Abailard's room one night, Fulbert, and some companions who shared in his indignation, made an attack on Abailard and castrated him.'

The next sentence carries over the false poetic sympathy of the fifth title in the adjective 'dastardly', and in the embarrassed confusion of intellectual with physical consequences. The true titles are:

> Period of Convalescence
> Complete recovery of Literary Energy
> Virility of his Literary Output After the Act (Representing Most
> of his Books)

'The necessary period of convalescence over, Abailard went to work again with his old vigour. Most of his books were written after his castration, but they show no traces of intellectual weakness.' In the next sentence there is a gratuitous title. 'Later he came to see in this act the working of the finger of God.' I do not know whether 'the working of the finger of God' is Abailard's phrase or not; but even if it is not, it may stand for some poeticization of Abailard's and can be left as such, though possibly his figure was a little more accurate. 'Deed', however, is an idle poeticization and spoils the narrative purity by the change from 'act' of the preceding sentence. And 'their' is a lazy reference going back two sentences; an illegitimate poetical tone is introduced by the failure to stipulate persons (only Fulbert has been stipulated, as a matter of fact). As for curtailing the sentence: 'came to see' is ample; unless the author means that there was a definite moment in which past events were reviewed – but then 'came to see' is wrong. In this case the sentence would have to read: 'Later, when he had reached a point where he could judge calmly of past events, he saw in this act the working of the finger of God.'

The last sentence continues the suggestion of quotation in 'the working of the finger of God'. The quotation-cast of the sentence is legitimate. But there is a confusion of religious submission to the act with the consolation he found in its effects, and the titular distinction should be insisted on even if Abailard (forgivably) tended to mix the points. Or else what Abailard said – if he did actually say something of the sort – should be quoted and the narrative take on the responsibility of making the distinction. But it would be best, on the whole, to abandon the suggestion of quotation. 'He now considered that the reprisal was justified and, further, that God had perhaps meant him to be maimed in this way so that he might serve Him better. And, as he was primarily interested in philosophy and theology, he could not regard this forced liberation from the distracting lusts of the flesh as an absolute misfortune.'

L.R.

6

The examination of some typical English names should demonstrate the equal 'goodness' of categorically concrete words like 'table', 'chair', 'house', and categorically abstract words like 'joy', 'comfort', 'security', as central meanings.

TABLE

'Table' is a flat, square, firm, raised object around which persons sit for the orderly disposal of what is laid on it. This central meaning loosens into such commonplaces as 'the pleasures of the table' and 'the agenda on the table'. In the material direction lie uses of the word which concern the squareness, flatness, stability, raisedness of the table rather than the formal activities of dining or deliberation connected with it. In the abstract direction lie the more poetic uses of the word: 'the table of his mind'. But 'his mind was steady as a table' is potentially poetic. From both directions there is a facing toward the central meaning: in the most concrete use of the word there is a tendency to abstract associations, and contrariwise. 'Tableland', meaning a flat raised piece of land, has an equivalent in 'plateau' and may be used interchangeably with 'plateau' in any text-book of physical geography; but it is a stronger word than 'plateau', carrying with it a greater awareness of raisedness and flatness and an attitude of expectant attention, amounting in certain contexts to a suggestion of invisible presences, or at least of some important business connected with the place.

'Table' in the meaning of an orderly disposal of material presented for such disposal – a clear example being 'logarithm-table' – has derivative associations of steadiness, square-cuttedness, flatness, raisedness. In 'a weathered rock-face carved with a fragmentary table of undecipherable hieroglyphics', the relatively concrete use of the word combines with the relatively abstract: the inscription is fragmentary and the hieroglyphics undecipherable, but they originally formed part of an intelligible literary arrangement, and 'table' is therefore justified by the ideal decipherability of the inscription as well as by the tabular treatment of the rock. It would not be straining the word 'table' too far to write: 'The schoolroom door, carved upon at random by succeeding generations of boys, had become a confused table of initials.' For though the initials were not carved as an ordered record of the boys who used the school-room, they were framed in the squareness of the door and the initial-cutting formality had been observed for a great number of years.

'Table' comes through the French from the Latin word *tabula*, meaning a board or plank – the rough mess-table of the Roman legionaries in Gaul. But *tabula* also had the varied concrete senses of 'tablet' and 'reckoning-table'. The 'liberal' Latin word for 'table', *mensa* (derived from the verb meaning to measure or mete out), had many of the same name-uses as the English 'table'. Thus, it could be used for a course of food, or the guests assembled at table; or for a money-changer's desk (a banker was *mensarius*). But *mensa is* not a true name in Latin, as 'table' is in English: it has various connotations, but these are figurative (by metonymy), not implicit. 'Table' has included in itself the senses of both *mensa* and *tabula*. It has such clumsy forms as 'entablature' and 'tabulation'; but as soon as the central meaning is completely disintegrated, 'table' yields to 'board', 'desk', 'plateau', 'index'. Being square-cut has been given as a characteristic of the table: this is due to the sense of 'table' as a thing composed of boards nailed regularly side by side – straightforward composition. A round table is an artificial treatment of the boards; and 'round-table' is a name in itself, connoting nervous conference and artificial unity.

'Board' is the twin-word to 'table'. As frequently happened at the time of the formation of English by the mixing of Teutonic and Romance dialects, where there was a pair of equivalent words the Teutonic word was adopted in the coarser uses, the Romance word in the finer. Hence 'board' took the sense of hearty eating rather than that of refined dining. One would speak, for instance, of 'the table of the Gods', but 'the board of the Giants'. 'Sideboard' is heavy with food; 'side-table' carries no more than a waterjug and some extra silver. 'Notice-board' is more vulgar than a table of laws or tides or even a timetable. 'Board', meaning a conference called to deal with some business, has a somewhat 'low' commercial connotation which it does not lose even when applied to such institutions as the Board of Agriculture and Fisheries. 'Table' is more parliamentary and covers principles of order rather than of enterprise.

JOY

In classical Latin, *gaudium,* from which the French *joie* is derived, is 'joy' used in a purely abstract sense; its use as 'enjoyment' is rare. By poetic licence it can be made to mean, in the plural, 'things which imitate the abstraction "joy"'. But it would not be possible in classical Latin, either in prose or in poems, to write, '*Lalage est gaudium meum*'. Only in very late Latin does the word come to be used of the object causing joy, such as a jewel; from which use comes the English word 'gaud'. The French *joie*, from which the English 'joy' is derived, is equally limited in its use. It is not French to say, '*La dame aux manches vertes est ma seule joie*', as it is English to say, 'Greensleeves is my only joy'. The French would naturally say, '*La seule qui me fait vraiment sentir de la joie, c'est la dame aux manches vertes*'; though the tendency would be to adjectivalize the declaration into:

'*La seule qui me rend vraiment joyeux, c'est la dame aux manches vertes.*' In German the emphasis would be verbal: '*Die mit den grünen Ärmeln ist die einzige, die mir Freude macht.*' In English 'joy' may be both the abstraction and the object that causes joy: a central personal consciousness of 'enjoyment' holds the opposite connotations together. Indeed, even when the word serves as a general abstract heading it carries with it concrete connotations of experience. It can be used with what would seem merely concrete force: 'Her breasts, her belly, and those hidden joys beneath', where 'joys' is apparently equivalent to 'genitals'; but the abstract force remains, as a rein on too physical a presentation. In French this use would be impossible. The Abbé de Grécourt would probably have written, dividing the concrete from the abstract by the use of two names instead of one:

> Those white breasts and that soft belly,
> And well hidden there beneath,
> That dainty region eloquent of joy.

The obsolete 'joyance' suggests concrete dallying in experience that has the quality of joy, to the diminution of the quality. Verbal rejoicing implies a momentary disregard of abstract senses. In compounds 'joy' readily unites itself with words of purely concrete force. When church bells are rung in jubilation for victories gained, or the birth, marriage, or coronation of royalty, they are distinguished as 'joy-bells'. Similarly, 'joy-ride'; and 'joy-stick', the gallant name given to the steering-lever of an aeroplane in the pioneer days of flying.[12]

CHAIR

The central meaning is a piece of furniture to which the body is confided for support, so that the person can enjoy freedom from physical embarrassment. 'Chair' is distinguished from 'seat' by being a detached personal sitting-place: seats being the places occupied by people in social session. There are cheaper and dearer seats, but a chair is always a chair, without thought of others. The detachment of 'chair' is expressed by 'Chairman', mere committee-men or debaters occupy benches or seats. The personal honour in which 'chair' is held is shown by the reluctance with which one would attempt to fill an empty chair, compared with the promptitude with which a vacant seat would be filled; and by the chairing of popular heroes. Yet 'chair' carries a guarantee of physical support; a chair is always endowed with means of subsistence.

'Stool' is 'chair' humbled (from the coarse German word *Stuhl*, as 'chair' is from the old French *chaire* which still survives in French in the elevated sense of 'pulpit' or 'professorial chair'). 'Throne' is supreme elevation of *position*. The person on the throne is not in himself a positive figure as is the person in the chair: the emphasis is on position, as with 'stool'.

'Musical-chairs', the 'Electric Chair', 'deck-chair' and 'rocking-chair' are vulgarizations; their appeal is in the liberty taken with a proud word. 'Arm-chair' in 'arm-chair theorists' indicates a critical deprecation of chair-vanity.

COMFORT

'Comfort', like 'joy', has a central meaning which lies between the abstract and the concrete. In the case of a decrepit mother and an industrious daughter who is 'the comfort of her old age', 'comfort' means both the daughterly ministrations and a modest state of bliss conferred by the daughter as an ideal beneficent figure. Like 'joys', 'comforts' can be used in what seems a purely concrete sense – 'a packing-case containing comforts for the troops'; but the abstract sense is present. If the packing-case were described merely as containing knitted scarves, socks, and Balaclava helmets, the beneficence of the volunteer knitters and the expected gratitude of the troops would remain unexpressed. In English one could say, 'The Rest-Easy chair is true comfort'. The French equivalent would be, *'S'asseoir dans le fauteuil Rest-Easy c'est vraiment comprendre ce que c'est que le confort'* or, *'comprendre ce que c'est que d'être confortable'*.

HOUSE

As 'chair' is to 'throne' and 'stool', so 'house' is to a large number of words such as 'palace', 'cottage', 'mansion', 'hovel', 'cathedral', 'cabin', 'castle', 'den', 'sty'. It does not consider the social condition or wealth of its occupants and so can be used indifferently in 'hen-house', 'poor-house', 'House of Parliament', or 'House of God'. It is not bound like 'home' by restrictions of conventional love – home is an apologetic word connoting personal partiality or bias – nor, like 'residence', by legal considerations. 'House' suggests *person* and the influence associable with the person. It is the name of entrenched identity, of the person increased by the material of his self-confidence, and hence also the name of independent authority. 'Dwelling', the verbal form of 'house', conveys no personal significance.

The central meaning of 'house' is a building with a corporate personality supported by its occupants. Thus: 'house of ill-fame', 'Famous House for Aged Gin', 'Royal House of Hohenzollern'. Christ Church College at Oxford expresses its own self-esteem by calling itself absolutely 'The House'. Actors, esteeming themselves the ruling family-occupants of the theatre where they are performing, even only for a night or two, speak of a 'full house' or an 'empty house'. 'House' in its astrological use similarly connotes the ruling authority of a householder. The twelve houses through which the Sun passes are more than mere 'stations'; the seven stations through which Jesus passed on his way to the Cross relate to events, not persons. Each astrological house has an occupant – Ram, Bull, Heavenly Twins, and so on – whose character is thought to affect the destinies of the person born when the Sun is visiting it.

The sense of privacy in 'house' is found in the proverb 'an Englishman's house is his castle' – often sentimentally misquoted as 'an Englishman's home is his castle'. The sense of security is most clearly shown where 'house' is qualified by another name to make a denial of security – 'a house of cards', or 'a house built on sand'.

SECURITY

'Security', like 'joy' and 'comfort', has a central meaning which lies between the abstract and the concrete: the idea of a state of security is combined with the concrete instruments of security. Like 'joy' and 'comfort', it can be applied to a person: one can offer oneself as security for a friend's debts. In the plural ('securities'), though seeming to have only concrete force as representing stocks or shares or other sure pledges for the repayment of money lent, the word has also the abstract force of stored riches, of a state of security created by the instruments.

In French, *sûreté is* security in an abstract sense, and in most of its concrete applications extremely freakish. Thus, a detective – 'detective' in English is a warning to the criminal that his doings are subject to discovery – is called *agent de sûreté*. To be put in custody – 'custody' in English is a warning to the criminal that once he is arrested he will be under the constant supervision of a gaoler – is to be put *en lieu de sûreté*. The French words *nantissement* and *cautionnement*, which mean security in the financial sense, merely characterize the unpleasantness of the borrower-lender situation. *Nantissement* means possession, from the point of view of the lender, of stock which he can convert to his own use or a mortgage which he can foreclose: it implies ultimate dispute between borrower and lender. *Cautionnement* conveys the impending forfeiture of the pledges if the debts which they cover are not punctually met: it has a threatening sense. A Frenchman does not have 'securities' at the bank: they are called *titres* or *effets*.

An old French word for 'sound security' was *caution bourgeoise, bour-geoise* meaning that the pact between borrower and lender was made according to the legal regulations in force in the bourg or borough where it was signed: an even more threatening sense, therefore, than *caution-nement*. The German word for 'security', *Bürge* (in the phrase 'stand security for'), is connected with this. 'Securities' in German are *Obligationen*.[14]

R.G.

7

In asserting the adequacy of English for the ideal purposes of language we do not mean by English a mode of conversation employed by many millions of human beings for many hundreds of years. We mean a technique of relation between human and non-human considerations that has gradually developed itself between the human and non-human. The exercise of English inevitably entails such relation; the niceties of English are the same as those to which we generally commit ourselves in EPILOGUE. Thus, the speech of Americans is not the English language, because it concerns itself with these niceties precisely to dismiss them.

Every sentence in EPILOGUE we regard as involving a problem of thought identical with a problem of language. We are aware that the dangers in the kind of statement we make may be summed up in the danger-word 'jargon'; our discipline against these dangers can only be a conscientious exercise of English. We are aware of the dangers of jargon in such words as 'truth', 'reality', 'spiritual', 'immediacy', which our object of comprehensive definition obliges us to use freely; our only security can be to use them within the limitations imposed by the exercise of English. We would rather attempt a just use of these words than invent snob-words in their place and thus invent jargon. Our object is not to invent; we prefer to accept the actualities of the English language and face the risks marked out by it, in the knowledge that these represent the final risks of statement. For example, we frequently use the very dangerous word 'spiritual', shudderingly aware of its associations with cheap psychic enterprise, as we are similarly aware of the associations of the word 'reality' with facile philosophical enterprise. We are, that is, ready to stand by our use of these words. If our use of them – so far – does not quite actualize them, we can only concentrate on the exercise of English more faithfully than we have yet succeeded in concentrating. For we have nothing to discover, nothing to record, outside the province of English.

M.V.

THE BULL-FIGHT

Laura Riding

I

THE BULL-FIGHT IS PERHAPS the only surviving ritual (in civilization) for the 'killing of the god'.[15] The execution of criminals is not such a ritual, because what is killed is, officially, only an illogical inhuman element in the human. The criminal has been possessed by some force which cannot be humanly explained, and it is this force which is being killed – or rather removed – in the execution; there is no attribution of personality to the illogical element, and even the personality of the human element is ignored in the sacrifice. War is another killing ritual that suggests some religious significance. Like the execution of the criminal, it is the destruction, or removal, of some outside force which, in so far as it is different, strange, outside, is regarded as inhuman – hostile to the particular humanity which is trying to establish itself, without critical interference from without, as a human stronghold. In official execution the inhuman force is really believed to have been present in the criminal, though it is not identified; the ritual is a serious one. War is a cynical ritual. The defence-side does not really believe that the enemy is really so possessed: its inhumanity is artificially, theatrically induced – it is devilish. War has thus an object of proving the humanity of the 'other' side, and assumes that when its humanity is so proved – when the devil is exorcized – a pact based on mutual humanity will result.

In the killing of the bull, the bull is a god. But, as in all cases where animals are deified, it is a lower god.[16] The object of all religious activity is to mingle the human and the non-human, and the lower gods represent that which is cast back to the human from the non-human – human gods merely, practice-gods who embody the errors which man makes in first conceiving the non-human They are sacred because they represent, though confusedly, a notion of divinity; they are doomed to be sacrificed to the true notion because as gods they are essentially grotesque. That which is sacrificed is the insane physical doggedness that follows man into his highest emotions – an insanity which the bull peculiarly typifies; most of all, the killing is a sacrifice of ignorance – the lamb as a sacred animal is the innocence-version of ignorance. This ignorance man is bound to cultivate because it permits of physical self-emphasis in religious activity; and he is bound to loathe it in proportion to the purity of his religious sense. The Spanish are the perfect bull-fighting people. Their religious sense is pure – without ambitious illusions of human identity with the non-human; it moves them to dramatize in the bull the irredeemable wilfulness of the phallic flesh and to deny, in killing the bull, the reality of physical force as a spiritual factor.

The bull, as a sacred animal, was the ritualistic key-note in the Mithraistic Legends. The Mithras-idea, though Persian in its cult-aspect, has a Vedic literary ancestry. Mithras himself was a lower god, merely the god of intelligence; while Ormazd was true being itself. Ormazd created the bull, as if in explanation of the difference between true being and opportunistic being. Mithras was forced to sacrifice the bull, against his will; for, though he overcame it, it had escaped him. It was the sun who persuaded him finally to kill it, the sun as representing the full course and measure of human happenings; and from the sacrifice came man himself, to be destroyed three times, the last time utterly. The bull stood for the physical crux of the religious problem that had to be passed through before solution came about in degrees of enlightenment; and such degrees characterize the ritual of the Mithraistic cults. Mithras, as intelligence, instinctively attacked the bull as ignorance. Then he would have left it; but it was itself a lower god – the lowest god – and as such carried in it a sense of destiny for the beings whose ominous sign it was.

The bull is the most incorrigibly male of animals, and as a sacred animal it embodies the uncritical maleness of physical life – the 'strong' qualities.[17] The horns, or feelers, of the bull, reverse the intellectual meaning of sensitiveness: through them the bull feels out and destroys that which stands in its way, is exclusively sensitive to that which obstructs its wild course. And so the bull figures symbolically in the spiritual activity of man when he has, in spite of a governing religious sense, an under-sense of intrepid physical committedness and phallic loyalty to himself that stands god-like between him and the true god – not a false god but merely a lower god, the god, of his wilfully blundering flesh. He admires in the bull his own stupid, insane obstinacy, even his own maleness. In baiting the bull he is making it state – for him – the intensity of this maleness, and at the same time he is punishing the bull in himself. In killing the bull he is sacrificing the mistaken god to the true god.

In bull-fights there is no sexual emotion as there is, say, in boxing, or in any close combat where the ability or nature of the opponent is relatively mysterious. The bull is the physical man in the bull-fighter – he knows all about it, it cannot possibly be something 'different'. And if it is the man who is killed rather than the bull, the initiated spectator does not feel differently about his death than about the death of the bull: the flesh which has been sacrificed is essentially the same as bull-flesh. The Mithraistic cults recognized that the symbolism centring in the bull-myth constituted a criticism of maleness; and women were rigorously excluded from membership. In Spain the presence of women at bull-fights is encouraged: there is no shame of the implications of the bull-myth. Spanish male pride rests firmly on stoic fidelity to the physical nature of man: there is no attempt to palliate it in spiritual quibbling.

The horse adds peculiar articulateness and literary emphasis to the bull-fight, otherwise a purely physical, dumb ritual. The horse is of all animals the most identifiable with man as a thinking being, that animal which is capable of being most at one with man; not, like the dog, a sentimental follower, but capable of translating itself perfectly, with an identical timing, into human terms. In riding a horse man's mind is as it were assisted by his flesh; the horse is his flesh in moving sympathy with his mind. The horse is the really superior animal; though domesticated and in close personal relation with man, it is not a pet. Man does not condescend to the horse; it is the horse which elevates itself to man. The horse in the bull-fight is, therefore, a reminder of the 'higher' man who is not of the same stuff as the bull. The picador does not really fight the bull; he deals it a strategical blow – a damaging but not vital blow. The picador is not supposed to receive any damage himself from the bull; if he does, this is a misadventure in a way that the goring of a matador is not. The almost certain goring of the horse does not matter; horse-flesh is the unimportant physical residue of man elevated above his flesh. From horseback man looks back on his physical past; the horse is history, which has carried man forward in time. It is supposed not to mind destruction; to enjoy assisting the progress of man. The horse is the flesh nobly, unobstinately ready to sacrifice itself, not having to be defeated; the 'strong', male qualities translated into strong-mindedness.

In the Bible the horse always has this character of intelligent strength; though generally there is a feeling that the horse gives a dangerous self-confidence. In Job it is described thus:

Hast thou given the horse strength? hast thou clothed his neck with
thunder?
Canst thou make him afraid as a grasshopper? the glory of his nostrils
is terrible.
He paweth in the valley, and rejoiceth in his strength: he goeth on to
meet the armed men.
He mocketh at fear and is not affrighted: neither turneth his back
from the sword.

The quiver rattleth against him, the glittering spear and the shield.
He swalloweth the ground with fierceness and rage: neither believeth
        he that it is the sound of the trumpet.
He saith among the trumpets, Ha, ha; and he smelleth the battle afar
        off, the thunder of the captains, and the shouting.

The English have translated the self-confidence associated with the horse into self-control. With the horse the fox is hunted, the animal which symbolizes physical rationalism, the self-protective cleverness of the flesh; the man on horseback means to be more than merely a rational being. In killing the fox, however, man is not killing a lower god with whom he feels physical identity. He is placing himself a careful degree above the mentality of the fox; making a nice distinction between brute intelligence and self-control. An interesting distinction is made with the dogs used in fox-hunting: in hunting circles it is a social misdemeanour to refer to the hounds as dogs. The dog, a mixture of man and beast, is reduced in the hound to a purely momentary but fantastically sharp identity with a momentary purpose of man. Hounds are not made pets of; not because, like horses, they are noble, but because they have only a momentary function in the fulfilment of which they have only a momentary identity with man.

The Portuguese, a horsier people than the Spanish, make more use of horses in bull-fights: there is a type of Portuguese bull-fight fought entirely on horseback; and the Portuguese tend, in general, to save the horse in bull-fights. This does not mean that they are a more noble people than the Spanish; on the contrary, the noble qualities associated with the Spanish undergo degeneration in the Portuguese. They are the cynically despondent Iberians; the Spanish are not cynical, merely without illusions that must inevitably bring shame. From their horses the Portuguese give death to the bull – with the mind rather than with the flesh. The death, whether from horseback or foot, is not a sacrifice but an act of vicious disappointment with the flesh; and what is left is only an ironic futility with which they masochistically spite themselves – there is no spiritual value extracted from the ritual. The French make bull-fighting into a theatrical pantomime centring in a strategical rosette: the bull, as their physical self, is no more serious to them than their sexuality. In the French philosophy of sensation, the physical senses titillate the spiritual senses; the spiritual senses titillate the physical in return. And the story rests at an intellectual emotion – a serious levity.

2

More complex than the bull-fight itself are the attitudes people adopt toward it. And the most curious thing about these attitudes is their peculiarly egotistical accent. The bull-fight, as a subject, somehow makes people enunciate opinions it touches with a personal arrogance they would not easily be tempted into by other subjects. And this must be because it is one of the few phenomena of modern life which stands outside the realm of opinion; the very right to have opinions seems to be challenged – and so out come the opinions. These opinions are generally anti-bull-fight; but not necessarily so. Ernest Hemingway's extravagant *Death in the Afternoon* is an example of pro-bull-fight opinionatedness. It is interesting as such; but also as an exposition of the American manner.

In his book Ernest Hemingway is interested in establishing, even more than the fact that bull-fights are a sound investment for American interest, the homely American manner as a literary style. Now, the only dignity possible to the American manner is as an open confession, by Americans to other human beings, that they are guided in what they do and say by one dominating resolve: to economize in mental energy. The American manner, therefore, in so far as it is a courtesy-index to other people of the kind of energy in which they must not expect co-operation from Americans, is capable of being a pleasant, disarming series of dumb-show signs representing the things that it would be best not to bother Americans about. So long as other people observe the taboos Americans impose on them, Americans treat them with the familiarity with which they treat one another. When the taboos are not observed, Americans go 'ugly': they treat other people as strangers. Familiarity is the highest compliment in the American scale of compliments.

When American homeliness of manner becomes a literary style it competes with the ways in which other human beings talk about the things that are tribally taboo to Americans: not to spend energy on them becomes a way of talking about them. The contradiction involved in talking about them at all is a reflection of the sentimental contradiction in the American attitude to reality. Americans do not believe that anything is to be gained by spending any more mental energy on existence than is demonstrably profitable – i.e., profitable in terms of immediate comfortableness. This standard of comfortableness Americans, on the whole, systematically apply to all considerations which present themselves to them; and, if it is not a consideration of the kind to which such a standard can be logically applied, their first instinct is not to be interested in it. Americans, however, are in a difficult position historically. Their tribal attitude represents a savage reaction against the tedious patience of civilized intellectuality with problems that do not seem so far to have yielded concrete results. But they do nevertheless exist synchronously with civilized communities and are themselves a civilized community in the sense that their standard of comfortableness is a by-product of civilized thought. And their jealousy of this standard becomes confused with a jealousy of their name as a civilized community: they do, and they do not, wish to be

involved in the niceties of civilized thought – even as they do, and they do
not, participate in European politics at Geneva. While they do not believe
that anything is to be gained by an expense of mental energy that does not
yield immediate comfortableness, they do not, on the other hand, like to
feel that they are losing anything that other people are gaining. They are
anxious to translate what other people think they have into American
terms: to prove whether or not it is an asset in the American sense, and, if
it can be so construed, to enjoy it as such.[18]

In this book of Ernest Hemingway's we see how the tribal manner is
used as a way with strangers as well: a way with Americans and all those
who are trained in, or at least willing to learn, American taboos.

> Valencia is hotter in temperature sometimes and hotter in fact when
> the wind blows from Africa, but there you can always go out on a
> bus or the tramway to the port of Grau at night and swim at the
> public beach or, when it is too hot to swim, float out with as little
> effort as you need and lie in the barely cool water and watch the
> lights and the dark of the boats and the rows of eating shacks and
> swimming cabins. At Valencia, too, when it is hottest, you can eat
> down at the beach for a peseta or two pesetas at one of the eating
> pavilions where they will serve you beer and shrimps and a paella of
> rice, tomato, sweet peppers, saffron and good seafood, snails, craw-
> fish, small fish, little eels, all cooked together in a saffron-coloured
> mound. You can get this with a bottle of local wine for two pesetas
> and the children will go by barelegged on the beach and there is a
> thatched roof over the pavilion, the sand cool under your feet, the
> sea with the fishermen sitting in the cool of the evening in the black
> felucca rigged boats that you can see, if you come to swim the next
> morning, being dragged up the beach by six yoke of oxen.

It is a way, in particular, with the stupid genteel Old Lady whom he uses
as a conversational convenience. She represents the kindly Old Europe of
Americans Abroad that is pathetically anxious to adapt herself to
American ways of thinking; for otherwise she is likely to be written about
as one Bob Brown has written about Old England – 'a mangy dog with its
tail between its legs'. By behaving nicely she learns the correct tone of
cheery self-protective brazenness with which to speak of homosexuality,
death, foreign authors and artists, and the native excellence of William
Faulkner's descriptions of whore-houses.

The tribal manner is here above all a way of taking possession of the
communal properties of other human beings and warding off interference
by demonstrating that Americans are not such fools of their own logic as
to deny themselves pleasures which other human beings enjoy, merely
because they are not American pleasures. When something abroad looks
good to Americans, the American manner, by its mere application to

something outside the strictly American field of interests, becomes a literary manner; although it is essentially a domestic instrument, designed for use at home to endow the American mind with an immunity from the temptation of not immediately profitable interests. This translation of a domestic manner into a literary manner, without any of the self-sacrificing mental processes and incidental physical waste that must accompany a real expansion of interests from the local to the general, cannot avoid the taints of 'ugliness'. The translation is only, indeed, an intensification of the domestic localising technique, with a strong warning to possible stranger-enemies that when Americans take the trouble to be interested in non-American subjects they are capable of supplying their own standards of authenticity of interest.

The blandly, loquaciously informed manner of Ernest Hemingway's treatment of bull-fights and bull-fighters past and present is not the product of a quixotic study by an American of an important item of general – not locally American – interest; it is proprietorship in a foreign sensation by an American mind conspicuously indifferent to the contrast in seriousness between the local and the general – so indifferent that he offers his indifference as an equivalent of seriousness. His knowledge of (proprietorship in) bull-fights is not derived from scholarly application, or cultural reconstruction of the kind in which Americans indeed frequently emulate the Germans – laborious naturalizing of the material of scholarship (ramified interests) in the domestic dialect; not really from the '2077 books and pamphlets in Spanish dealing with or touching on tauromaquia, to the authors of all of which the writer wishes to acknowledge his deep indebtedness'. Nor is it based on a poetic perception of the ritualistic significance of bull-fights or on a sympathetic intuition of the bull-fighting attitude of the Spanish. He knows bull-fights merely as a source of profitable (as regards returns in pleasure for expense in interest) theatrical experience or as a manifestation of a national idiosyncrasy that Americans can easily understand – that is, translate into facile literary-sounding localisms.

His analysis of the Spanish attitude to death is careless, disrespectful – a journalistic brief:

> There are two things that are necessary for a country to love bull-fights. One is that the bulls must be raised in that country and the other that the people must have an interest in death... Having this feeling they take an intelligent interest in death and when they can see it being given, avoided, refused and accepted in the afternoon for a nominal price of admission they pay their money and go to the bull-ring, continuing to go even when, for certain reasons that I have tried to show in this book, they are most often artistically disappointed and emotionally defrauded.

The Spanish are too ritualistically elaborate a people to confuse their most solemn private ritual with their most solemn public ritual. Bull-fights represent one set of emotions; death, another. And no one who made an unselfish study of the Spanish could possibly speak of their having 'an intelligent interest in death'; or read in the complicated chances of the bull-fight anything so emotionally crude as a play with death-chances. The bull-fighter and his audience are not thinking of death, but of beautifully impersonal standards of performance – so much so that when a bull-fighter is gored or killed everyone is for the moment surprised.

Ernest Hemingway's knowledge of bull-fights is clearly the result of a characteristic American procedure that we may call 'hanging about'. He has hung about in cafés frequented by bull-fighters, in bull-fighters' boarding-houses; he has not so much seen as hung about bull-fights. His information has been all picked up without any more derangement of mental ease than an economical spending of 'good' American money abroad involves (American money is always 'good'). And the result is a cheerful sense of security in the proved reality that bullfights are his. As an American he wants them if there is anything in them worth his money (his expenditure of energy, his 'time'). And they are worth his money because they seem to allow for a speedy exercise and freshening of normal emotions without any danger to self-complacency – without, that is, any severe mental obligation. The bull-fights are his; and not only the bull-fights – the bulls are his. He is in the bull-fighting know, as a man who has carefully invested some of his money in a mining venture in a foreign country identifies himself in a proprietary way with political events in that country.

The bull-fights are his, the bulls are his and the horses are also his – perhaps more so his because, as he makes his Old Lady say, it seems so sort of 'homey' when they are hit; and because, as she parrots in a further lesson, to see their lost organs temporarily replaced with sawdust is 'very cleanly, that is if the sawdust be pure and sweet'. It is all so local and intimate and provocative of simple emotions.

Being interested in bull-fights by his instinct of their emotional profitableness, not by an act of poetic comprehension, he is obliged only to be in the know, not to know. Some of the bull-fighters about whom he talks with such professional authority he cannot have seen at all. Faithfulness to the bull-fight actuality does not matter so long as he can talk freely, with sufficient air of proprietary interest not to have his proprietorship challenged. Therefore homely conversational exaggeration is not a serious offence; as people sitting round the family dinner table do not expect to be challenged on factual improbability or excessive eyewitness-ship. They have a proprietary right in what they are talking about.

A swaggering prejudice against a particular bull-fighter, picked up from irresponsible elbowing in bull-fighting circles, is conversationally legitimate – such freedom-taking is all by way of being in the know. 'I arrived in Spain immediately after the revolution and found him (Domingo Ortega) ranking with politics as a café topic. On the 30th May Sidney Franklin, who had just come to Madrid after a Mexican campaign, and I went out together to Aranjuez to see the great phenomenon. He was lousy. Marcial Lalanda made a fool of him as did Vicente Barrera.' The phenomenon Sidney Franklin (an American bull-fighter) sitting beside Ernest Hemingway may perhaps have been more directly responsible for Ortega's lousiness than café jargon. Yet:

> That day Ortega showed coolness and an ability to move the cape slowly and well, holding it low, provided the bull did the commanding. He showed an ability to cut the natural voyage of the bull and double him on himself with a two-handed pass with the muleta which was very effective in punishing and he made a good one-handed pass with his right. With the sword he killed quickly and trickily profiling with great style and then not keeping the promise of his very arrogant way of preparing to kill when he actually made the trip in.

But:

> All the rest of him was ignorance, awkwardness, inability to use his left hand, conceit and attitudes. He had, very obviously, been reading and believing his own newspaper propaganda.

Also:

> In appearance he had one of the ugliest faces you could find outside of a monkey house, a good, mature, but rather thick-jointed figure, and the self-satisfaction of a popular actor. Sidney, who knew that he himself was capable of putting up a much better fight, cursed him all the way home in the car.

And:

> At Pamplona he was so bad he was disgusting. He was being paid twenty-three thousand pesetas a fight and he did absolutely nothing that was not ignorant, vulgar and low.

Now, this prejudice against Ortega is a curious thing. I have questioned aficionados of various schools about Ortega; all regarded him with respect and complex interest. I have seen him fight, and sometimes along with Lalanda and Barrera, and to my mind unquestionably outrank them. Lalanda, the finished performer doing what everyone expects him to do and carrying off his honours with pretty, respectable pomp, and Barrera, the showman, getting as many stunts as possible out of the situations provided; to Lalanda the bull practically non-existent, to Barrera the strategical fool of the dialogue, to Ortega alone the bull. With Ortega the bull is something undeniably himself, a part of him that he must reject while admiring it because intellectually he loathes it. Ortega, in fact, is the critical modernist among contemporary bull-fighters: he both does his job and, while he is doing it, knows with analytic precision the meaning of what he is doing.

I must be forgiven this special interest in Ortega; it was acquired not from 'hanging about' in bull-fighting circles, but was excited spontaneously when I first saw him six years ago, and has been strengthened every time I have seen him since. Quite apart from his professional virtues, he is freer from theatrical mannerisms than any other bull-fighter I have ever seen. There are few books that have given me such a sense of learned simplicity as Ortega's work. In saying this I do not mean to mix metaphors, like the professional bull-fight critic, but only to indicate that the bull-fight is not a 'foreign' subject; indeed, there are few – if any – such subjects.

L.R.

LUCRETIUS AND JEANS

Robert Graves

LUCRETIUS STANDS FOR A PLATITUDINOUS excitement in the strangeness of the material universe: a state of consciousness above the brutally immediate consciousness of the body, below consciousness of reality itself. Man's comfortable range of thought reaches as far as the familiar strangeness of his own being – a going outside the body that still does not break the physical spell of the body over the mind. Such psychological exploration characterizes much of the behaviour centring in the figure of Rimbaud; Rimbaud himself indulged in it – there is a Lucretian touch in his colour-analysis of the vowels. Rimbaud, however, did not mean to indicate a happy scientific optimism. The physically locked internality of the human mind, and the fact that sensations seemed impossible to pursue truthfully beyond the limits of physical consciousness, he recorded as an assertion of the inadequacy of the human mind as a truth-defining instrument; he did not hide his despair in sentimental cosmogony.

Lucretius has a more direct connexion with the sentimental cosmogony of Sir James Jeans than with the psychological obscurities of poets who have turned aside from the straight path toward doom or resurrection, into an indeterminate cerebral pocket. Science, as has been pointed out in various contexts in EPILOGUE, is concerned with isolating a minimum incident of certain duration – duration so certain that it need not be thought of as future, merely as the inevitable extension (repetition) of the shortest, most instantaneous immediacy conceivable. Both Lucretius and Jeans (who demonstrates better than any other modern scientist the inevitable sentimentality of the scientific view) somehow manage to get happiness out of the notion that some time (not now) the universe must end. The outer immensity of space – the practical realm of sensation, within psychologically sober boundaries – is employed by both as the source of respectable scientific Corybanticism. And the littleness of earth, still more so the littleness of the individual, is for them the source of a more workaday optimism: terrestrialism represents the capacity to isolate the particular local incident, or reality, from the general way of things – to perpetuate it against the finality at the end of that way. A still more striking resemblance between Lucretius' Epicurean science and modern scientific thought is the impatience in both with causality, to the point of omitting the demonstration of cause, as something in itself bad, or fatally governing. Lucretius was only interested in causality as the technical source, and therefore stimulus, of effects; he did not care what causes he gave for things – how ostensibly fallacious they were – so long as in giving a cause he clarified (isolated) the effect that was somehow (perhaps as he said) precipitated.

A textual comparison of Lucretius' *De Rerum Natura* and Jeans' shortest and most poetical work *Eos: or the Wider Aspects of Cosmogony* strengthens this connexion. As a popular historian Jeans is as unreliable as Lucretius – their first similarity. He says, for instance, that only in the last ten generations has the earth ceased to be regarded as the centre of the universe. But Lucretius in the first century BC had explicitly asserted that there could be no centre of the universe, because it was infinite; and this was not his own peculiar view but an Epicurean commonplace. Jeans also speaks of the atomic theory as the property of 'our scientific ancestors of half-a-century ago': unaware that John Dalton only revived 'scientifically' another Epicurean commonplace familiar to every classically educated Englishman. Jeans is excited at meeting Newton's anticipations, in his *Opticks* (1704), of present-day scientific theory; yet equally close ones occur in Lucretius. For instance, Jeans' concept of space as being filled with wandering radiations from dead matter which contribute practically nothing to the sum of things is paralleled by Lucretius:

> Principio hoc dico, rerum simulacra vagari
> Multa modis multis in cunctas undique partis
> Tenvia ... multo magis haec sunt tenvia textu
> Quam quae percipient oculos visumque lacessunt
> ... simulacraque eorum
> Quorum morte obita tellus amplectitur ossa.

[In the first place I tell you that many images (reflections) of things wander about in many ways and in all directions, very thin ... they are much thinner in texture than the images which strike the eyes and assail the vision ... reflections also of those whose death is passed and whose bones are buried.]

And this is only one of several parallels. So we may conclude that Jeans has not read Lucretius. Yet there are numerous passages in *Eos* that would translate directly into Lucretian hexameters. For instance:

Under the action of great heat the outermost of the atomic electrons begin to break loose from the atom and fly off at a tangent, just as, when water is heated up, the outer molecules break loose and set off on independent journeys of their own. Finally the water is wholly evaporated; the heat has transformed it into a mass of gas (steam) in which each separate molecule flies along its own individual path like the bullets on a battle field. In precisely the same way, the application of heat to the atoms causes successive layers of electrons to break loose from their moorings, and the atoms become smaller and smaller until finally no coherent structure remains but merely a powdered *débris* of atomic constituents, each nucleus and electron going its own way regardless of the rest.

The resemblance lies in the humanistic way in which they both write about their atoms, or particles, or molecules, or 'first-beginnings', or 'seeds of things', or electrons, or whatever invisible tininesses they happen to be talking about. 'Set off on journeys of their own ... flies along its own individual path ... each nucleus and electron going its own way regardless of the rest.' So Lucretius, talking of certain of his tininesses:

> Multaque praeterea magnum per inane vagantur
> Conciliis rerum quae sunt rejecta nec usquam
> Consociare etiam motus potuere recepta.

[Many of them, too, go wandering through space: they are rejected from the councils of things and have nowhere been able to ally their motions together even when admitted.]

Both Lucretius and Jeans are philosophising in terms of infinitesimal units of matter or energy, or what–not – so insignificant that it is painfully head-achey, except for scientific adepts, to bring the mind to bear on them at all, but which exist more tangibly than difficult generalizations because they answer troublesome questions 'beautifully' (Jeans' word). For these infinitesimal units represent man in his most disorganised state of irresponsibility; as the beautiful answers in which they assist are the most irresponsible answers. Leucippus 'invented' them first, but they have been constantly recharacterized since his day in a variety of senses. To Leucippus they were infinitely small and indivisible. Later they had theoretically to be given 'parts', to distinguish one atom from another; but only qualitative parts, the atom being still admittedly indivisible – which is Lucretius' view. Dalton 'weighed' his atoms but still refused to allow anyone to divide them: 'thou knowest thou canst not cut an atom.' Rutherford and Bohr however, gave these qualitative parts separability, making a miniature solar system of each atom – which is Jeans' view. His 'atomic electrons' are infinitesimal parts of the atomic nucleus, of which the diameter is 'only a small fraction of the millionth of a millionth of an inch'. Yet Jeans writes about these *semina reram* as Lucretius did in the passage quoted (*Multaque praeterea* ...) – as if they were queer little idiosyncratic creatures of his personal acquaintance. Both writers are making every effort to be at home in a commonsense way in strange reality – to create an economical way of talking about universal problems, eliminating all the difficult aspects. So Jeans:

> The infinitely great is never very far from the infinitely small in science, but it would be hard to find a more sensational illustration of the unity of science than that just given [i.e. the resemblance between atomic structure and the structure of solar systems].

In discussing the stars Jeans speaks of 'groups of bright stars moving in orderly formation through a jumble of slighter stars, like a flight of swans through a confused crowd of rooks and starlings'. So also Lucretius:

> ... cum lucida signa ferantur ...
> flammea per caelum pascentis corpora passim

> [... bright constellations, with fiery bodies, go grazing here and there across the sky.]

Both are fundamentally more interested in analogy than in theory. So Jeans says, in writing of cosmogony, 'One could hardly be prosaic if one tried.' And Lucretius: 'It is pleasant to drink at virgin springs of song, and to seek an illustrious chaplet for my head from fields from which the Muses have crowned no poet before me.'

Yet Lucretius' commonsense is nonsense from the present-day scientific point of view. His wandering radiations or reflections, for instance, were offered as explanations of the fancies that men get in dreams about Centaurs and Chimæras. That the world was not the middle of things he used as a final argument against the existence of upside-down animal life at the antipodes. His erratic stars were represented as possibly going in search of food. The only real difference between him and Jeans, however, is that, though both are fancifully, and nonsensically, simplifying major universal problems, Jeans seems more respectably intricate in that he has a much greater accumulation of scientific hypotheses to deal with: the work of simplifying preceding simplifications. For, in its design of substituting simple for complicated formulæ of explanation, science was bound to become itself more complicated, the more ambitious it became of being a completely adequate substitute for truth. But Lucretius' task was intricate in another sense, even because he had no complicated scientific apparatus to work with. He had to be constantly making the change-over from abstruse into practical language, and fortifying his own system with abstruse explanations where it was incomplete. And Latin proved for him, at this stage of science, almost too good a scientific language – he frequently complained of the inadequacy of Latin, compared with Greek, for abstruse statement, though simple statement was his object. Thus, Jeans' swan-flock figure represents a complicated mechanistic nicety gracefully satisfying a whole tradition of scientific rhetoric; while Lucretius' 'stars grazing across the sky', though part of the plan which he shares with Jeans of fanciful simplification ('honey smeared round the medicinal cup of wormwood'), have behind them an irksome linguistic difficulty. For he really would have liked his figure to convey of itself the analytic notion of free-will on the part of the stars, as well as the merely descriptive notion of erratic movement; but Latin exacted more explicit precision. And so he felt obliged to complete the description with suggestions of purpose in movement that the strict, descriptive Latin use of the word 'grazing' could not possibly convey.

Yet Lucretius was more devoutly scientific than Jeans and other scientists who no longer think of themselves as fighting a lonely and difficult battle against superstition – the superstition of those who do not want too easy an explanation. For, as between science and religion, it is science that is the bigot – wanting to achieve mental peace by localized tricks of thought. Religion now indulges science in so far as by its charlatanism it keeps people in comfort and good humour while the higher business is going on, clothing its tricks in such pious language as 'in the service of mankind' and concealing the spiritually destructive nature of the service. The scientific battle is won and over-won. Scientists can make what conclusions they like in the name of science, and, so long as the public is convinced that 'people well up in science' treat their conclusions with respect, they will be accepted as pontiffs of practical truth – even where they are only improvising accounts of phenomena of which, by the nature of the analytical economies they practise, they can have none but the most arbitrary knowledge. Jeans speaks of the interior mechanism of the latest atom as confidently as if it were that of the latest aeroplane engine.

Lucretius, not so comfortably placed, always emphasizes the purely tentative nature of his cosmogonal doctrine. Having said that one of many causes may explain the motion of stars: either, that the whole sky may be driven by currents of air, or that the stars may, independently of the sky, be mechanically driven by internal force, or that they may be moved by tides in the ether, or that they may move consciously, in search of food – he ends by admitting that which one of these causes holds good in our universe it is difficult to say. For there are many various universes (as he has already proved by proving the infinity of matter in the total universe) and each of these theories must hold good somewhere: which one of them fits this universe, he will not rashly decide, for he must go step by step in a scientific spirit.

In present-day science such reservations have gradually dropped out because scientists are careful to express their suppositions in mathematical formulæ which, applied artistically to such problems as the structure of the atom or the inner temperatures of stars, give 'beautiful' results. They are, that is, only applied to sure, prepared cases – remaining unworkable in unstereotyped cases and therefore unassailable: there must be a sympathetic equivalence between formula and case.

> The mathematician need not hesitate to thrust his calculations right into the heart of the stars, and he can usually show, with something approaching very near to certainty, that at the centres of most of the stars nearly all, or perhaps quite all, of the electrons must have broken loose from their parent atoms leaving the stellar matter almost or quite pulverized into its constituent nucleii and electrons.

A beautiful result is as good as a demonstrable proof and can only be superseded by a still more beautiful result. 'Beauty is truth; truth, beauty,' writes Keats as a chemist-contemporary of Dalton's. Lucretius, too, likes beautiful results; but he has no mathematical bludgeon at his disposal – only a store of imposing phenomenal curiosities, such as the action of a magnet on iron rings, the hurly-burly of motes in a sunbeam, the origin of forest fires in the rubbing together of twigs. He uses these as far as they will go. Unbeautiful results irritate him and in the last event he is reduced to his general reservation about the tentativeness of his doctrine. Thus, at one point he has been led to state that men once used to employ wild beasts in battle, such as lions and wild boars, against their enemies. He remarks that this was an unbelievably foolish thing to do, because obviously the beasts would turn on their own masters with indiscriminate slaughter – but perhaps the men were reckless and did not care what happened to them, or perhaps the whole historical account which he has just given (with exciting detail) really belongs to the story of another universe altogether.

Lucretius is here doing what he always does when he stumbles against a piece of theory that seems humanly uncomfortable – discounts its immediate applicability: such as that men once had the habit of bringing lions into battle; or that men were once born (from wombs sprouting from the earth) whose limbs were all wrongly placed on the trunk, so that they could not fend for themselves or reproduce their kind; or that the earth originally brought forth enormous monsters. His object is to rid men of terror, not to substitute scientific terrors for religious ones. He points out that an infinite variety of happenings and creatures obviously occur somewhere in the total universe, but that the natural laws current in other universes do not apply to this. A Chimæra, he says, obviously cannot occur in this world because the fixed laws which, according to our practical experience, rule the natures of lion, goat and snake (the components of a Chimæra) would be set in contradiction by such a mixture – and the final impossibility of a Chimæra is that it is held to breathe out fire, which would burn the goat-stomach of the creature.

Lucretius is no more an 'original' scientist than Jeans, though both may claim to have added their quota of interpretation and suggestion to the scientific aggregate. They both ask authority for their work by citing previous scientists: to avoid the charge of idiosyncratic madness. What men have once thought – Democritus, Empedocles and Epicurus, Dr Hubble, Prof. McLennan and Prof. Millikan – it is not unnatural to think again. Jeans has a bigger body of authorities to cite and a more compact corpus of scientific facts: he is able to draw on these facts for the human comfort which it is his chief interest to give. Thus, Jeans would be unlikely to support a scientific argument, as Lucretius does, with the fact that a leaden bullet slung from a military catapult melts when sent a long distance; he would have a mathematical formula pigeon-holed somewhere proving that the friction of the air is not great enough to make the lead anything more than somewhat hot to the touch. But his historical inaccurateness, already referred to, suggests that, 'irreproachably scientific' though his work may be, this is only because he is writing when he is. Had he lived in Lucretius' time he would have been equally ready to believe, on Epicurus' authority, that clouds were bladders full of wind or water or fire, and that thunder probably came from their scraping their sides together, then bursting, discharging fire in the form of lightning and water in the form of rain: for it was a theory that fitted the known facts 'beautifully'. His own electrons and protons behave very much like Lucretius' clouds:

> They are pure bottled energy; the continuous breakage of these bottles in the sun sets free the radiation which warms and lights our earth, and enough unbroken bottles remain to provide light and heat for millions of years to come.

The optimism which is the chief link between these writers is founded on extreme fear of mortal extinction. But both treat this fear as troubling only other people; for themselves, they are secure in the serene retreats of science. Jeans can write unconcernedly:

> With an ardour equalled only by that of man's longing for personal immortality, many seem to desire that the universe itself should prove in some way to be immortal.

and Lucretius:

> Et quondam docui cunctarum exordia rerum
> Qualia sint et quam variis distantia formis ...
> Hasce secundum res animi nature videtur
> Atque animae claranda meis iam versibus esse

Et metus ille fores praeceps Acheruntis agendus,
Funditus humanam qui vitam turbat ab imo....

[And since I have explained the beginnings of things and how they
differ in their shapes ... I must next explain the nature of mind and
spirit, so as to cast that fear of Hell headlong out which affects man's
life so deeply.]

Both cast out the fear by concentrating on the relative littleness and isolation of man in the total scheme of things; also by saying that, granted that
some time human beings must face finality, mortal extinction will fall
equally on everything. Both admit that the universe is running down and
will come to an end one day. Lucretius insists that the end of this universe
does not matter: there are always other universes. Jeans' view is very much
the same; he does not speculate on other universes, because he makes this
one much more inclusive. Both comfort their readers by saying that it will
be so long a time before the universe ends that they need not worry about
the end. But both blow hot and cold according as they wish to affect their
readers emotionally one way or the other, alternately insisting on the
newness and on the oldness of the world for man.

In all probability the life in front of the human race must enormously exceed the short life behind it. *Jeans*.

Verum, ut opinor, habet novitatem summa recensque
Naturast mundi neque pridem exordia cepit.

[But my belief is that the universe is new and our world is new, and
that it is not long since the beginning.] *Lucretius*.

So far as we can judge, our part of the universe has lived the more
eventful part of its life already; what we are witnessing is less the
rising of the curtain before the play than the burning out of candle-
ends on an empty stage on which the drama is already over. *Jeans*.

Sed quia finem aliquam pariendi debet habere,
Destitit, ut mulier spatio defessa vetusto.

[But because she [Mother Earth] must have some limit to her
bearing, she ceased, like a woman worn-out by old age.] *Lucretius*.

Similarly they blow alternately hot and cold in the matter of fixed laws
and arbitrary phenomena. Jeans disposes of the idea that an original fortu-
itous combination of atoms made the universe, by a mathematical
pronouncement that the chances for its fortuitousness are precisely one in
$10^{420000000}$ (this last figure being short for a sum starting with 10 and ending
in four hundred and twenty thousand million zeros); yet he concedes that
how the universe was originally set going is shrouded in impenetrable

mystery. When he comes to speak of the earth itself he says that it is quite an unusual phenomenon, an astronomical freak, and that there are 'millions of millions' of chances to one (he does not give the precise figure) against the surface of any planet being in the same bio-chemical condition as ours today. So too Lucretius. He insists on the fixed laws, the decrees of fate, which govern everything. Yet he holds that the original atomic beginnings of things broke these eternal fixities by an accident: which resulted in the present universe, a compromise between fate (the fixed unalterable properties of things) and accident (things that come and go without prejudice to these properties).

Lucretius declares that space is infinite, but that this universe (meaning as much of physical totality as people of his time could have knowledge of) is comfortably finite. Lucretius' 'this universe' was a much more modest one than Jeans' 'this universe', because it did not include all matter, the infinitely greater part of which he held to lie outside in other universes. Jeans, while agreeing with Lucretius that space has no limit, and even with his contention that space and matter are co-extensive, makes 'his universe' include all the universes outside the visible one – and still declares it to be finite. How does he evade this paradox of finite limit-lessness? By a word he has learned from Einstein, which curiously enough is the very word that Lucretius learned from Epicurus; a word that Epicurus used in evading the paradox of how his originally fate-bound atoms started the hurly-burly of creation – namely, clinamen, or swerve. Lucretius writes:

> Quare etiam atque etiam paulum inclinare necessest
> Corpora; nec plus quam minimum, ne fingers motus
> Obliquos videamur et id res vera refuter.

[So I insist that the atoms must make a slight swerve; and not more than the least possible, or we shall seem to be assuming oblique movements – which is an untenable hypothesis.]

And Jeans writes that 'a general guiding principle, that of generalized relativity, fixes a limit to space'. Light does not travel straight, but with a swerve so slight as to have been hitherto unsuspected. The mathematicians found it out only the other day. This swerve denotes a curvature of space. So, if we go far enough, we only 'come back on ourselves'; travelling as fast as light, we would come back on ourselves in one hundred thousand million years. Lucretius uses *clinamen* to account for human free-will, too. (The swerve is, of course, the very nature of scientific thought, as well as the carefully irresponsible, disobedient nature of matter itself; and it allows of infinity, or continuous duration, so long as people think at individual random, even as it provides the comfort of finity, or individual peculiarity of being.)

Both Jeans and Lucretius feel the same embarrassment in talking about divine being: and yet neither can resist mention of divinity. There is no room for divinity in their self-like universe, yet they cannot help bringing it in emotionally. For they both let it be understood that Gods or God (Lucretius preaches with missionary zeal what by Jeans' time has become a scientific assumption) have nothing whatever to do with things as they are; while indulging the sentimentality of themselves and of their readers in poetical references to the divine. So Lucretius:

> Hunc tu, diva, tuo recubantem corpore sancto
> Circumfusa super, suavis ex ore loquellas
> Funde petens placidam Romanis, incluta, pacem.

[Goddess Venus, as you and Mars lie twined together in a divine embrace, please beg him charmingly to give us Romans peace.]

And Jeans:

> And we cannot say how long the stellar matter may have been in the nebular state before it formed stars. Nothing in astronomy fixes with any precision the time since 'the great morning of the world, when first God dawned on chaos.'

The strongest note that both Jeans and Lucretius strike is optimism as the counter-weight to fear – optimism derived from the admission and exploration of fear:

> ... we are standing at the first flush of the dawn of civilization. Each instant the vision before us changes as the rosy-fingered goddess paints a new and ever more wonderful picture in the sky ... *Jeans.*

> Diffugiunt animi terrores, moenia mundi
> Discedunt, totum video per inane geri res.

[Terrors of the mind flee away now, the walls of the universe open out, I see action going on throughout the whole of space.] *Lucretius.*

But this lyricism necessarily brings reaction. Lucretius, for example, in spite of his serene philosophy, comes in the course of his argument upon several uncomfortable fatalities from which he swerves away, recovering his balance with difficulty. Eventually he gets into what motor-cyclists call a 'roll' – a slight skid or swerve inducing a greater and greater swerve from which there is no recovery. He is discussing the plague at Athens. Hitherto he has been able to limit his digressions on uncomfortable topics to a few lines, though the account of the wild-beasts in battle lasted for fifty lines before he could extricate himself. But in talking about the plague he goes on and on, trying to find some way of discounting this fatal horror, or of alleviating it; but can think of none. He is fascinated against his free-will by the ulcers, the retchings, the salty yellow spittle, the black bowel-discharge, the nose-bleeding, the desperate self-castration; and after a hundred and sixty lines he collapses at a point where the terrified survivors are brawling over the stinking and loathsome corpses of their relations. There the poem breaks off.

Jeans ends in nightmare too:

> In any case, our three-days-old infant cannot be very confident of any interpretation it puts on a universe which it only discovered a minute or two ago.... And ever the old question obtrudes itself as to whether the infant has any means of knowing that it is not dreaming all the time. The picture it sees may be merely a creation of its own mind, in which nothing really exists except itself; the universe which we study with such care may be a dream, and we brain-cells in the mind of the dreamer.

R.G.

THE LITERARY INTELLIGENCE

Laura Riding

I

PEOPLE WHO DEVOTE THEMSELVES to literature fall into three classes: those to whom it is a field of activity like any other, rich in opportunities of personal success and in pleasures of craft-exercise – those who 'know how to write', as it is put; those to whom literature is the region of reality, where all the disjoined problems of time become one all-immediate Problem; and those to whom it is, again, a profession – but the exercise not so much of craft faculties as of 'the intelligence'. It is these last that interest here.

Intelligence is for these a compromise between a wilful position of failure-in-Problem (described in 'The Cult of Failure', EPILOGUE, Volume I) and the worldly vantage of literary success. Their activity is a dignified journalism and halved intensity of interest – a stand between spiritual defeat and worldly triumph, and equally between absolute disregard of and absolute concern with Problem.

Because Poe aimed at this kind of intelligence he did not properly belong in the failure category – he did not mean to figure in the records as an apostle of failure. Poe had the characteristic American disregard of Problem; but he saw the possibility of qualifying this disregard and figuring seriously in the inner records of literature without figuring profoundly. His first step was to translate the disregard into terms of failure. Then failure becomes the sentimental source of intelligent lies about concern with Problem – lies which cannot be attacked as lies because the half-heartedness toward Problem that inspires them seems to derive from a sense of failure rather than from fundamental disregard. Later intelligents do not resort to this technique of lying; not because they are necessarily more scrupulous than Poe, but because they realize that, if they are to figure in the records at all, they must show solid clerical talent.

They realize, in fact, that it is the Problem which judges of their pertinence, not their own sensations of pleased vanity in being able to work
themselves into the records without identifying their personal fate with
the fate of literature. And so, from Poe's first crude gestures of lying
preoccupation, the literary intelligence stabilized itself into a modest clerical competence with very high standards of 'disinterested' preoccupation. There is no intelligent in France or England or America who does
not feel vaguely grateful to Poe for having established the precedent for
literary intelligence in its modern form of important official connexion
with the Most Important Department.

T.S. Eliot, in an essay on Dante, asserts that Dante's picturings had the
quality of surprise 'which Poe declared to be essential to poetry'. Poe's
surprise is precisely this pleasurable sensation of being connected with
'Things' without the responsibility of fundamental connexion. And while
T.S. Eliot is a more complicated case of literary intelligence than Poe, his
connexion with literature has a quality of restrained excitement in being
so connected in spite of fundamental disinterest. When we read of a
quality of surprise as essential to poetry, we are immediately made aware
that what is being talked about is not poetry itself but people who are
connected with poetry from without.

Poe was irascibly sensitive about the dignity of the clerical type of
which he was a pioneer, and 'intelligent' criticism has appropriately enno-
bled him into a pioneer-martyr. In his immediate literary world he was
recognized by conventionally serious writers as someone who was creating
a peculiar kind of literary office for which he was demanding a dignity of
an assured degree. Ordinary writers were prepared to run the risks of free-
lance adventuring in the unknown chances of literature; they resented a
fellow writer who was busily establishing for himself a chance-proof position based not so much on what he wrote as the sophistication with which
he wrote it. A typical intelligent defender of Poe, in an article published
some years ago, wrote:

> Poe later became estranged from Hirst when that worthy parodied
> two lines of 'The Haunted Palace' thus:
>
> > Never nigger shook a shin-bone
> > In a dance-house half so fair.

Poe was particularly sensitive to such breaches of good taste. The lines
parodied will be found to read:

> Never seraph spread a pinion
> Over fabric half so fair!

They are, that is, essentially foolish lines saved from foolishness by the
intelligence with which they were written. And the writer of the article

referred to is not defending the lines themselves but the dignity of this intelligence; and Poe's irascibility must have had the same ground. The same writer excuses 'poor Poe's' general irascibility thus:

> A reviewer of current books could not escape reading what came from the press, and the literary output of that day was in most cases unconscionable trash…. Poe must have gasped at such figures as

> > My love, goodnight! let slumbers steep
> > In poppy juice those melting eyes.

But Poe himself was capable of writing:

> The very roses' odours
> Died in the arms of the adoring airs.

The difference between Poe and his trashy contemporaries is the technical one of a certain opportunistic intelligence. He attacked his contemporaries with sarcasm, not criticism: for failures in intelligence, not in conception. Neal, Pinkney, Willis and Longfellow were fools because they did not specialize as consciously as himself in professional literary intelligence.

Professional intelligence had in Poe's mind a great deal to do with 'popular taste' (a favourite slogan of his): it was the means of keeping alive in the public mind the fact of authors, above the fact of literature. And later intelligents are no less jealous of their authorial reality in the public mind. For always they are more wedded to the public mind than to literature, which they officially serve. The intelligents wish to figure in the records, but they wish also not to be dissociated from the human world; it is to this world that they go back after several hours of official service each day, and in which they enjoy the recognition that they are 'doing something'. Their being above all things 'intelligent' teaches them to expect from literature itself recognition of only a very theoretical kind; it is human recognition that keeps them going. Poe translated this desire for recognition into a justification of intelligent literary procedure as more pleasing to the public mind than haphazard inspirational procedure; whereas T.S. Eliot, say, would translate the desire for recognition into a self-mortifying assertion of the ways in which intelligence is conditioned by, and ever returns to, unintelligence.

But all intelligents are in one way or another preoccupied with their human importance and in one way or another sensitive to public opinion. They are anxious that the human world should understand their connexion with literature as no fantastic attachment destroying their humanity. The connexion is, on the contrary, a most business-like, human arrangement, in which they are civic clerks standing realistically between the human world and the State of Literature (a State being a vague, incommunicable entity). Though Poe was famous in his lifetime, and became increasingly famous after his death, and has now reached the legendary degree of fame, intelligents cannot get over the feeling that he never had sufficient recognition, and has not now – not the kind of special recognition to which an intelligent is entitled. Yet we find him fully and favourably represented in the major anthologies of his own time, such as Griswold's *Poets and Poetry of America*; in Dana's *Household Book of Poetry*, published eight years after his death; in Bryant's *Library of Poetry and Song* (1870); and in Stedman's *American Anthology* (1900), in which the editor says, 'He gave a saving grace of melody and illusion to French classicism, to English didactics, to the romance of Europe from Italy to Scandinavia.' As a schoolroom classic he is almost outworn. He was recognized, indeed, as an intelligent in his own time, though with hostility – even by the not altogether unintelligent Lowell, who was, along with Poe, sensitive to the British attitude to American writers as vulgarians. Lowell wrote of Poe:

> Here comes Poe with his Raven, like Barnaby Rudge –
> Three fifths of him genius, and two fifths sheer fudge;
> Who talks like a book of iambs and pentameters
> In a way to make all men of common sense damn meters;
> Who has written some things of the best of their kind;
> But somehow the heart seems squeezed out by the mind.

Yet it is only with an inside knowledge that Poe had the journalistic object of 'slaughter of banality' (as it has been called) that his poems can be read as intelligently designed for their effect rather than as inadvertently banal:

> For alas! alas! with me
>   The light of Life is o'er!
>   'No more – no more – no more – '
> (Such language holds the solemn sea
>   To the sands upon the shore)
> Shall bloom the thunder-blasted tree
>   Or the stricken eagle soar!

It is not an infrequent occurrence that one has to rely on some such inside knowledge to prevent one from finding certain passages in Eliot's poems inadvertently banal.

> Because I know that time is always time
> And place is always and only place
> And what is actual is actual only for one time
> And only for one place
> I rejoice that things are as they are and

Poe's poems were intelligent puppet poems, his stories exercises in puppet effectiveness – full of puppet criminals and puppet police. This puppet atmosphere is the magazine atmosphere, in which the quasi-intense has an advantage over the pseudo-intense, the hysterical-intense and the true-intense, in seeming to have found an unquestionable alternative of competence to intensity: official but not personal identity with Problem. Poe always wrote as for a magazine; whatever Eliot writes, whatever any intelligent writes, has a magazine half-intensity – it is an official but not a personal act. Literary intelligence, as a standard of authorship, saves the person. Poe, by his own confession, conveyed the grotesque merely by heightening the ludicrous; the horrible, merely by colouring the unpleasant; the strange and mystical, merely by exaggerating the different. His object was to avoid simplicity of any kind, and equally to avoid the essentially difficult. 'There is nothing easier than to be extremely simple,' he wrote in the same letter in which he analysed this quasi-intensity. Byron was an earlier intelligent than Poe, but too imperious to assume the competent clerk pose. He pursued 'the slaughter of banality' more recklessly than Poe did, wasting the energy of his intelligence in this, so that his puppet poems had to be eked out with emotional substance and were thus more vivid than puppet poems usually are.

2

For the intelligents, Problem resolves itself into the problems of the literary job; which means, really, the development of a technique of comment. Literature itself is seen as coming perpetually later – as in a State the sense of intrinsic community comes after political, economic and social community, meanwhile serving as rhetorical background to these other communal senses. As T.S. Eliot says, 'When it appears that the existence and concept of literature depend upon our answer to other problems, the distinction between the "critic" and the "creator" is not a very useful one.'

Literature has become the Archive of Literature – an official edifice rather than the State of Literature. In older days it was no more than an official edifice, either; but it had, nevertheless, the character of an open forum to which everyone periodically resorted and felt for a little while at least that he belonged to something. Now no one comes (other problems), and there is only a sense of improbable personalities closeted like ghosts with the improbable State itself: the State is deserted, there is a danger of losing touch with it altogether. The intelligents, it is true, 'work' there, and the public feels them to be real – they are not of the improbable personalities behind the secret doors. And there are documents. But they do not, somehow, seem real – the public, naïvely, would say 'original'. They consist of no more than clerical observations and comments – they are intelligent: made by 'critics with international learning and standards' (another phrase of Eliot's).

Thus Poe's first shrewd instinct toward stabilizing the literary job – without selling the soul to literature – resolves itself into a desire for a 'moral hierarchy' or principle of commentary: a ready professional formula freeing the clerk from too intimate connexion with the State. Poe did not get so far as the idea of a moral hierarchy, but he did see that the security of the literary job depended on reliance on the rules of the game – on there being such rules. The emphasis has shifted; it is not literature, but the literary mind which is the concern of the literary mind. It becomes unnecessary to think of literature-in-itself, to discover special terms for the nature of literature and sensitiveness to its realities. Eliot has said, simply and aptly: 'For anyone who has devoted even a little attention to St. Thomas, or to Aristotle, the term "intelligence" is adequate.' These are, indeed, two model ancestor-clerks.

Eliot uses as a motto to his essay on Dante an observation of Charles Maurras': '*La sensibilité, sauvée d'elle-même et conduite dans l'ordre, est devenue un principe de perfection.*' This statement nicely establishes the limits of the literary intelligence: sensibility restrained from its consequences – static sensibility. Sensibility is converted into the clerk-mind, which trains itself to recognize Problem without being personally affected by or involved in what it recognizes.

Dante is a model clerk-mind because he did a full literary job without stepping into the crucial poetic region that lies outside the comfortable boundaries of the intelligence. He made the middle way seem the whole way. He had the advantage of mediæval universality (Eliot calls him the most universal of poets in the modern languages) as a philosophical background, and therefore was not so sharply personal as Shakespeare – who, nevertheless, overreached the narrow limits of mediæval universality, which was really the muddled centrality of human fear. Shakespeare, we are told, is more 'local' – now in this, now in that place outside the limits, not in one place so humanly centralized that it is 'universal'. And so 'more can be learned about how to write poetry from Dante than from any English poet': he was a fixed poet, and yet fixed with an air of being everywhere. Dante, Eliot means, is the safest master of professional self-assurance; there is 'no poet in any tongue ... who stands so firmly as a model for all poets'. Eliot can delight in Dante's use of allegory as a poetic method because allegory makes incomplete poetic activity seem fuller and more finished than it really is; it makes artificial centrality convey an impression of universality; it enables the literary job to be done well, yet not exhaustively well.

And so Shakespeare sets only an example of width and variousness; while Dante is far more finished – because the *Divine Comedy* provides 'a complete scale of the depths and heights of human emotion', a centralized range which gives the satisfaction of intelligent completeness. The standard of the scale is the high dream of static sensibility. All degrees of human feeling 'fit together according to the logic of sensibility'. And the language of this scale of intelligent sensibility has 'a peculiar lucidity' – 'the thought may be obscure, but the word is lucid'. Shakespeare is textually too complex to be a good model of intelligent clerkship. 'It is a work of years to venture even one individual interpretation of the pattern in Shakespeare's carpet. It is not certain that Shakespeare himself knew what it was. It is perhaps a larger pattern than Dante's, but the pattern is less distinct... Furthermore, we can make a distinction between what Dante believes as a poet and what he believes as a man.' So he finds Dante a purer poet than Goethe because he had a more efficient sense of the literary job; he did not sink his personal meanings in the job, but made an intelligent construction of meaning adequate to the job-purpose – meaning which may be accepted morally, without the sentimental commitment that Goethe demands. It is not the quality of this commitment that inspires Eliot with lack of confidence in Goethe, but that Goethe should have demanded personal commitment at all: to an intelligent all intensity, whether natural or forced, is abhorrent.

It is amusing to see, toward the end of this essay, the pains Eliot takes to be at difference with I.A. Richards on a point of intelligence-dogma. He is in agreement with Richards in the view that poetry may be accepted, in the professional sense, without being believed in personally. Eliot's argument on this problem of commitment hangs by his own admission on the 'short word *full*': that full professional acceptance does not necessarily imply full personal acceptance (his own words are 'understanding' and 'belief'). What he fears most is falling into a heresy – a heresy being any digression from a safe middle path of intelligent non-committal activity. Yet he has a high sense of professional integrity – hence his wistful preoccupation with the implications of *full*. And hence his dissatisfaction with the quality of I.A. Richards' principle of acceptance, as meaning perhaps little more than vulgar office-efficiency and thus giving a touch of cynicism to the literary job.

Eliot's position, we must all agree, is a difficult one; and he himself keeps us frankly in mind of this. Its difficulty, in fact, is the ground of contemporary patience with him. As E.M. Forster has put it in a recent essay, he is one of those who keeps returning to his sufferings. The only question is: are the private psychological difficulties of a writer a proper subject of criticism, especially when his actual writing is quantitatively trivial in comparison? ... It is not as if T.S. Eliot had produced a few really beautiful poems by which to endear every aspect of him to us, however irrelevant critically. Yet somehow we all keep noticing him, apparently. Perhaps because of the fascination of watching a literary mind at work within a trepanned skull – closed with watch-glass. That the operation of thus making his private mind a public show has distracted his intellectual energy from the poetic task which he originally set himself – this has not interfered with his literary repute. People like watching inside works; and his is undeniably a literary mind. As Mrs Oliphant, in all kindness, wrote of Keats: 'No poet who has done so little bears a higher fame.'

L.R.

NEO-GEORGIAN ETERNITY

Robert Graves

THERE CAME A TIME towards the end of the nineteenth century when it seemed clear that civilized man, after a struggle of hundreds of thousands of years, was now bound to triumph finally over material circumstances. He would never have to worry again about famines or pestilences or wild beasts or barbarian hordes or floods or hard winters: he had perfected, or as good as perfected, mechanical means of combating material restraint. The sea, the old ground of struggle and adventure, had been tamed by the steam-ships. Certain birth-control was in sight. Twenty years had been added to the expected span of life, and twenty very comfortable years. And all this had come about by patient co-ordination and individual self-sacrifice.

In England the immediate political reactions to this realization were cheers of 'Press on, press on' from the liberal elements and 'Not quite so fast, if you please' from the conservatives. The immediate artistic and literary reactions were either political in these senses, or decadent-æsthetic: 'Now that we have achieved this material victory, let us relax and take a pleasant holiday in the contemplation of the non-essentials, the apparent frivolities which have been so long disregarded.'

By the time of the first aeroplanes the triumph was more assured than ever: the machines of prosperity were running very nicely (and of litera-ture, too), only going amiss occasionally when there was a small war or industrial disaster or when the politically unrepresented classes found a champion to interrupt both the 'Press on, press on' and 'Not quite so fast, if you please' with a screaming 'A damned sight faster'. Aesthetic deca-dence had ended because the production of apparent non-essentials became a recognized part of the machine itself; valuable recreative by-products.

So what were members of the new generation to do about it? They were born at a time when the battle had been already won, bar the shouting; and they did not want to shout, to celebrate the triumph of their progressive parents, whom they either hated or despised. There has perhaps never been such hatred between ages as between the neo-Georgian and Victorian-Edwardian age. It was far more bitter than that between the pious Puritan age and the ungodly Carolean age that went before it, or between the free-living Restoration age and the canting Puritan age; for neo-Georgians had no rational grounds of complaint, their predecessors had done only too well. It was no fun to be merely greasers of a perpetual-progress machine for the invention and setting up of which they had to thank the priggish great men of the past; and yet it was difficult to do without the machine altogether.

The neo-Georgian malcontents were in a quandary. They refused to be perverse like the decadents; they wanted to be virtuous, infinitely more virtuous than the Victorians. But it seemed that they were bound by this abominable legacy to keep along a prescribed path. Somewhere there must be a weak spot in the machine, by pointing out which their self-respect would be restored, even if they were not strong enough to get the machine scrapped. The two chief prophets the neo-Georgians acknowledged as prematurely born into the Victorian age were Samuel Butler, first declared enemy of the machine, and A.E. Housman, who had passionately expressed the conviction in his *Shropshire Lad* (written in the Jubilee year) that Heaven and Earth ailed from their prime foundation and that the only possible course was to endure awhile and see injustice done. A.E. Housman had been careful not to characterize either the ailment or the injustice: he had merely glorified the defeat which came at the moment when human aspiration was at its prime, and congratulated the athlete who died in the middle of his victories as more fortunate than 'Runners whom their fame outran, And the name died before the man'.

The most paralysed of all these neo-Georgians was E.M. Forster. A single book of his, *The Eternal Moment*, is perhaps the frankest statement extant of neo-Georgian paralysis. It was written during the pre-war moral crisis, though not published until some years after the War; when the following foreword was written:

> Much has happened since; transport has been disorganised, frontiers rectified on the map and in the spirit, and under the mass-shock of facts Fantasy has tended to retreat or at all events dig herself in. She can be caught in the open here by those who care to catch her.

So he stands by his book as an expression of the spiritual longings of his age, an expression he thinks no longer easily made because the War and its after-effects have subordinated spiritual discontent to questions of practical immediacy. Yet spiritual discontent remains along with the machine-legacy. What was spent of this legacy in the War was only its supercharged ebullience; it is still the same soul-destroyer. And it will not be long before Fantasy, the fairy-sister of spiritual discontent, comes into the open again: meanwhile these preliminary conclusions can be republished. So it is dedicated 'to T.E.' (T.E. Lawrence), whose solution of the neo–Georgian problem was to revert spiritually to mediævalism, first as a scholar, then as a warrior, finally as a flying monk – 'in the absence of anything else'.

There are six stories in the book. The first, 'The Machine Stops', is a story of the remote future in which the mechanical age has reached a *reductio ad absurdum*. Everyone lives underground in ideally lit and warmed rooms in telephonic and televisual connection with everyone else; but there is no actual contact except, as an occasional disagreeable social duty, for mating purposes. All personal needs, including food, medical attention and euthanasia, are supplied by pressing a knob. People do not visit the upper air except for necessary airship journeys when rooms have to be changed, and even then they are not exposed to its rigours or forced to walk on the actual surface of the earth. Ideas dry up. Muscles are flabby. Everyone worships the machine. At last a single young man becomes discontented, hardens his muscles by walking about in his quarters and, against all the rules of the machine, climbs out for a visit to the upper air; where Nature gives him spiritual ecstasy among the ferns of Wessex. His only tie down below is his mother, a typical machine-devotee whom he nevertheless loves in that human way which the machine-devotees think disgusting. When he tells her of his experiences she is horrified by his blasphemy in wanting to revert to Nature in defiance of civilized practices. Then, though not through any act of his, the machine starts to run down. The bath-water begins to smell, the music to be distorted, the food to taste queer. The Central Committee promises that the Mending Apparatus will put things in order again; but even that proves in need of mending. There is no initiative left anywhere, because everyone has been accustomed merely to press knobs; so finally the machine stops, communication fails, the lights go out and everything crashes. The son does not do what one expects him to do: escape and mate with one of the uncivilized people (descendants of exiles) who still live above the surface, with one of whom he has had a love passage. He is involved in the crash and dies, yet with the satisfaction of having loved his mother and knowing that the human race will continue its natural way above ground: that humanity has learned its lesson, nobody will ever start the machine again.

The tirade is illogical in postulating thousands of generations of perfection for the machine before its own perfection can defeat it, while denying the machine the most elementary efficiency in keeping the bodies and minds of its devotees in athletic health. But it is clear that this is a dramatic statement of present emotional conflict, rather than an idly robust Wellsian forecast of the end of civilization.

They were dying by hundreds in the dark. She burst into tears. Tears answered her. They could not bear that this should be the end. Ere silence was completed their hearts were opened, and they knew what had been important on the earth. Man the flower of all flesh, the noblest of all creatures visible, man who had once made God in his image and had mirrored his strength on the constellations, beautiful naked man was dying, strangled in the garments that he had worn. The sin against the body – it was for that they wept in chief; the centuries of wrong against the muscles and the nerves and those five portals by which we can alone apprehend – glozing it over with talk of evolution, until the body was white pap, the home of ideas as colourless, last sloshy stirrings of a spirit that had grasped the stars.

The real discontent of the author is not with modern civilisation as ruining the bodies and minds of its victims, for the early stage of industrialism had already passed and the late nineteenth century had worked very hard to improve the health and imaginations of the workers; but as making life too easy. The author is saying: 'Scientific perfectionism was admissible so long as it made man run his steeple-chase against all natural obstacles; but now that he is in sight of the winning-post, over the last ditch and running down the straight, what is he to do? Once he breasts the tape, all will be over – what waste then of a pair of beautiful athletic legs! It would be absurd for him to turn round and run all the way back. Oh, for a good thunderstorm or earthquake or something to interpose providentially between him and the tape! So that he could die like Housman's hero!'

Well, the prayer was answered, almost immediately after the story was written, with the War; and one or two of the neo-Georgians, such as Rupert Brooke and Charles Sorley, were satisfied with the answer and died like Housman's hero. Others, who either did not or could not identify themselves with the War experience, did not know what to think; until later the War itself took a grossly mechanical turn, when they said that it was a wasteful and cruel performance and should be stopped at once – that it was the logical outcome of quantitative material activity. At last there was a good case against Victorianism. But E.M. Forster, although he was among those who did not have direct experience of the War and could see it in perspective as a manifestation of the machine's viciousness, did not blame the machine for the War; rather, the War did not supply a permanent enough athletic mood. He recognized that it was only a temporary ardour and that another Victorian reign of spiritual facility would follow. The protest that he had made against the machine before the War, that is, still held good. The very disadvantage of the War to the machine would make it suppress war altogether, and with it all athletic occasions. The machine had learned its lesson. And man's spiritual muscles would become flabbier.

The next story is called 'The Point of It'. Two young men, Micky and Harold, are in a row-boat. Harold has a bad heart, but in an athlete's rapture, encouraged by Micky, he rows against the tide which has unexpectedly risen. Micky, who is steering, says, 'That's right – one, two – plug it in harder … Oh, I say, this is a bit stiff though. Let's give it up, old man, perhaps.' But Harold plugged it in harder, 'he was approaching the mystic state that is the athlete's true though unacknowledged goal: he was beginning to be.' Micky then definitely dissuaded him: 'Look here, Harold, you oughtn't to – I oughtn't to have let you – I – I don't see the point of it.' To which Harold answered: 'Don't you? Well, you will some day,' and collapsed, dying half in the boat and half out of it.

The rest of the story concerns Micky's old age. He had for a moment shared Harold's ecstasy, but this ecstasy had been wiped out by the death and all memory of it gradually faded in his last fifty years of life. He had proved a success in the worldly sense, a grand old man of science and letters, who made no enemies because of the perfection of his conciliatory technique; and 'merged his feeble personal note in the great voice of tradition'. His only trouble was with a son who was like the son in the previous story, discontented without apparent reason. When the old man's wife died, the son, after a brutal scene, ran away from home to the Argentine: it was only for his mother's sake that he had stayed so long.

'I don't see the point of it,' quavered Sir Michael. 'I have given him freedom all his life, what more does he want?' It was explained to him by his other son and a daughter, who remained loyal, that there were some people who felt that freedom cannot be given. Perhaps their brother was like that: unless he took freedom for himself he might not feel free. (The neo-Georgian position exactly).

But Sir Michael thought this ridiculous. In extreme old age he had an accident which left him feeble-minded for the last two years of his life; until a final lucid interval, just before death, when he overheard his loyal family's real opinion of his futility. They called him played-out. His rage was only changed to laughter when he further overheard his grand-children making the same remarks about their parents. Then he died, and in a spongy-sandy Hell suddenly saw the point of it. After suffering torments of banality, he had a vision of Harold rowing against the tide and was sympathetically conveyed by him across the deep gulf to Paradise. He does not actually reach Paradise in the story, but has a foretaste of it in the 'crack of angelic muscles' and the 'one, two – plug it in harder!' of his own heart.

The argument is carried on in the next story, 'Mr Andrews', where two men reached Heaven together. One was Mr Andrews of Winchester, Oxford and the Board of Trade; the other was a Turkish bandit. Each pleaded for the other's admittance and both were admitted. Mr Andrews went off on a tour of inspection and found that everyone was rewarded according to his expectations but not beyond them; and that one experienced no great happiness or mystic union with good. Heaven was a sham. 'There was nothing to compare with that moment outside the gate when he prayed that the Turk might enter and heard the Turk uttering the same prayer for him.' So, meeting each other again by chance, he and the Turk decided to get out of it; and 'as soon as they passed the gate, they felt again the pressure of the world soul and suffered it to break in upon them, and they and all the experience that they had gained and all the love and wisdom they had generated, passed into it and made it better'.

To recapitulate. In the first story the point was that perfect social co-ordination was a false goal, as leaving the battling human will and human imagination out of account. In the second the point was that the only human experience of value was the moment of struggle against odds, a foretaste of Heaven; Hell being the punishment for identifying oneself with the machine, or the theory of progress. Charles Sorley called it the 'grind-stone'.

> The false Delilah of our brains
>> Has set us round the grind-stone going.
> O lust of roving, lust of pain!
>> Our hair will not be long in growing.
> Like blinded Samsons round we go,
>> We hear the grind-stone groan and cry,
> Yet we are kings, we know, we know!
>> What shall we do? how shall we die?
>
> Take but our paupers' gift of birth
>> And set us from the grind-stone free
> To tread the maddening gladdening earth
>> In strength close-braced with purity …
> Up unexploréd mountains move,
>> Track tireless through great wastes afar
> Nor slumber in the arms of love
>> Nor tremble on the brink of War.

In the third story the point is that Heaven is never any more than a foretaste, the realization being a blank; we are to understand this foretaste to have lain in the moment of love for each other that Mr Andrews and the Turk experienced, in spite of traditional prejudices, at the gate – love in the sense of athletic eccentricity, not banal co-ordination. As for co-ordination, the next story is one which has the word for a title, about a girls' school where the headmistress, to impress the Board of Education, has decided to co-ordinate all the lessons of the curriculum to a single subject – Napoleon.

Thus – not to mention French and History – the repetition class was learning Wordsworth's political poems, the literature class was reading extracts from *War and Peace*, the drawing class copied something of David's, the needlework class designed Empire gowns, and the music pupils – they, of course, were practising Beethoven's 'Eroica' Symphony, which had been begun (though not finished) in honour of the Emperor.

Here the author introduces a figure that occurred in the previous story – of gods and great men sitting up in Heaven drinking in the incense of adoration. Beethoven and Napoleon, gratified, ordered the school to be rewarded with a perfect performance of the A minor Quartette, and with a participation in the victory of Austerlitz. But the co-ordination was so imperfect that the school interpreted the rewards confusedly and thus gave the Devil a case against the human power to co-ordinate, particularly as regards co-ordination with dead genius. For the Headmistress had happened to hold a shell to her ear and hear in it murmurs as of a forest, which so softened her soul that she decreed a whole holiday the next day; and the girls had heard a military band which so thrilled them that nothing but a whole holiday would satisfy them. And in the holiday happy disorganized games were played – 'everyone hid and nobody sought, everyone batted and nobody fielded and no girl knew on what side she was and no mistress tried to tell her'. The Headmistress, the mistresses and the girls all repudiated co-ordination.

But the Angel Raphael explained that this was true co-ordination: 'These people, Mephistopheles, have co-ordinated through the central sources of Melody and Victory!'

So the true co-ordination, as opposed to the false co-ordination of the machine and tradition, is happy individualistic disorganisation without care for results, a feast of animal spirits, with reason and the Board of Education banished: this is the source of the love and wisdom which shall pass into the world soul and make it better.

The fifth story is 'The Story of the Siren'. The story of the Siren is told to a flabby man of letters by a beautiful naked Sicilian boatman who has just dived into the water to recover the man-of-letters' fellowship-dissertation on the Deist Controversy, which has accidentally dropped overboard. It is a story of the Siren whom the priests hate and whom few people see, and then only the good; when they do see her they go mad with unhappiness because then they know everything, especially about Death. Their only hope is to find someone else who has also seen the Siren. The boatman's brother had seen her once, having forgotten to cross himself before diving, and gone mad with unhappiness; but he had found a girl who had also seen the Siren, and married her. There was a prophecy that of such a union would be born a child who would fetch the Siren out of the sea and marry her, and take the spell of silence off her, so that she could save the world with melody. But the priests had murdered the woman before her child could be born because they said that it would be Anti-Christ; and the brother had died of grief and consumption. 'But silence and loneliness cannot last for ever. It may be a thousand years, but the sea lasts longer, and she shall come out of it and sing.'

The Siren is Ecstasy, known only by accident, not to be sought purposely. She lives in the sea, symbol of endless chance, and when she emerges finally the world will be saved: there will be sustained ecstasy. Her singing represents the tune which is constantly being postponed by the priests, who presumably represent the false-perfectionists, the false co-ordinators, the great voice of tradition, everything that is hostile to the eternal moment of Melody and Exaltation and Youth. But that time is not yet. At present the only result of knowing ecstasy is death by consumption (the fate of at least two of these neo-Georgians) or murder by the priests, and all one can do is to go on crossing oneself in the patience of suppressed excitement and preparing dissertations on the Deist Controversy for fellowships at Cambridge. But is there no immediate way out of the quandary? Are Heaven and Hell to continue ailing from their prime foundations? Is there no way but endurance for those who have not been able to rush out and get killed in battle or to strain their hearts in rowing?

The last story is 'The Eternal Moment': about Miss Raby, a woman-novelist who, after a twenty-year absence, returns to the village in the Maritime Alps which she has made famous by an early novel, and finds it completely spoilt with huge hotels. The concierge at the biggest hotel, a fat, greasy fellow, turns out to be a man who, when only a luggage-porter (but a fine-looking fellow), had once made violent love to her among the mountain flowers. She had repulsed him 'as a young lady should' and cried out that he had insulted her. Now in her shrewd middle-age she suddenly realizes that this was the one real moment in her life, and she insists on recalling it in the hotel lounge (full of guests and hotel servants) in spite of the scandalized bewilderment of the concierge himself, who has forgotten all about her and cares for nothing now but tips and commissions and keeping his job:

> ...the most enduring moment: she had drawn unacknowledged power and inspiration from it, just as trees draw vigour from a subterranean spring. A presumptuous boy had taken her to the gates of heaven; and, though she would not enter with him, the eternal remembrance of the vision had made life seem endurable and good.

So she continues talking about the incident, until the hotel manager has to be fetched. The concierge is in danger of losing his job, but the respectable English colonel, whom she is about to marry for a comfortable old age, smooths things over by making it seem that Miss Raby is mentally irresponsible. But Miss Raby has slipped away to look at the mountains from the verandah and is congratulating herself that she has lived worthily. 'In that moment of final failure she was conscious of a triumph over experience and earthly facts, a triumph cold, hardly human, whose existence no one but herself would ever surmise.'

'The Eternal Moment' is a romantic resistance to the brutal onrush of time toward finality. E.M. Forster put this prayer in the withered mouths of the neo-Georgians: this longing for an experience of finality in a thrillingly immature atmosphere. The final moment is to be brought back into time by the athletic clinging of each obstructionist to his moment; the problem is, how to compress the final moment into one's own. For the final moment is from the romantic point of view dull and destructive – that is, it lasts; while the individual moment is truly momentary and fascinating, lasting only in the sense that it is a perpetually passing moment, perpetually caught at and perpetually lost. This is the only book in which E.M. Forster has really let himself go, really given away the secret of what to him constitutes happiness. All his other writing is about unhappiness, how the spiritually frail person is driven from one shadowy post of conscience to the other. The difference, apparently, is in the courage to tell white lies to yourself: you stick to one post and call it your eternal moment. And it is remarkable how much neo-Georgian eternity has lasted over into these forthright neo-Edwardian days.

R.G.

GEORGE SAND

Madeleine Vara

GEORGE SAND THOUGHT OF HERSELF as functionally connected with suffering: not in the theatrical male sense of her time, as being a 'great' sufferer, but in the impersonal sense that it was her function to be sensitive to suffering. Her writing thus records not only her sensitivity but the suffering to which she applied herself. Her sensitivity was strong, wide and real; but the illness that she came to nurse was the petulance of men who grandly pitied themselves for being no better than they were. Her energy was wholesome, but her material was execrable; and her writing is weighted with this execrableness, as her life was. She was an agent of truth judging of the genuineness of this epoch of sorrow, and it was inevitable that she should technically identify herself with the sorrow in all its grotesqueness and execrableness.

Her writing is therefore a more faithful historical record of what her time thought it suffered than any of the elaborate confessions of sorrow left by any of its pseudo-tragic pygmies of egoism. But it also contains an almost invisible elixir of bucolic calm, a cruel poetic essence of indifference to the suffering to which she functionally applied herself. Her inner judgement upon her century's sorrow is that it was not sorrow at all, but petulant affectation; and while following it through, as a mother follows through a child's trouble which is fundamentally petulant affectation, she was all the time reserving a smile of repose, the bucolic smile which is poetic relief to the trivial anguish of mortal death. This smile was ignored by the time that evoked it, and so she kept returning more and more intensely to the subjects of sorrow until her critical sympathy was exhausted. It might be said that her writing consists of two halves: her feeling, or recording, of sorrow, which seems the more attractive half, and her exhaustion with feeling – the tedious philosophizing necessary to her patience with her material. These two halves compose the public whole of her writing – the secret essence being publicly incommunicable.

In her private journal she created a Doctor Piffoël as a serene, remote other self with whom her emotional self debates. Doctor Piffoël is calm and smiling; she, however, knows how the world behaves, what it expects – to have its illusions indulged. Piffoël's wisdom is: '*Sainte fatigue, mère du repos, descends sur nous pauvres rêveurs, maintenant à l'heure de notre mort.*' But her answer is: '*Non. Non. Piffoël! Docteur en psychologie, tu n'es qu'un sot. Ce n'est pas là le langage que l'homme vent entendre. Il méprise parfaitement le dévouement, car il croit que le dénouement lui est naturellement acquis, par le seul fait d'être sorti du ventre de madame sa mère.*'

Men, as she was fated to deal with them, were concerned only with romantic self-dramatization and the connivance of women in their illusions. And so her smiling wisdom was not acceptable: it represented something in herself, not in them. The bucolic smile was undoubtedly the clue to the situation, but they did not want a clue. Like Joan of Arc, with whom she strongly identified herself, it hurt her to lay the clue by. Joan of Arc, too, had this quiet, smiling bucolic persistence. Her ruling hope was to help men who were entangled in uneasy diplomatic shifts of conscience to simple ease of conscience. 'Come,' she said, 'you are not really troubled: leave the great problems to God – let Time take care of them and of you. That is what you mean to do; the diplomatic quibbling is unnecessary and nonsensical.' Joan tried to give them bucolic ease instead of diplomatic ease, but their vanity in their unsimple manners made them ashamed to take her clue. If they had, they would have admitted that they had no real troubles of conscience. If George Sand's French had taken her clue they would have admitted that their suffering was only a diplomatic mortification of the soul, out of which they made only elegant tragical effects: that they had little native sorrow. Joan was a saint because she let her clue be destroyed rather than lay it by. George Sand had saintly fancies, too, but she did not throw her clue into the historical fire. She laid it by privately.

Contes D'Une Grand'mère, written in private isolation from the violent discrepancies of her emotional life, is an unexcited, smiling record of bucolic humour. Four are given here. In *The Talking Oak* personal misery is submerged in leisureliness of being – a gentle movement through difficulties toward a cheerful, self-respecting death. The oak is a symbol of the keying-down of extravagant self-pity to sensible mortal ease. Emmi in running away from the swine is as if running away from unclean pathos. In *What the Flowers Say* Zephyr is the smiling patron of temperate emotions. In *The Red-Hammer* the story of the survival of a piece of cornelian through long ages of time is a lesson in the law of survival: how time wears away the self-important forms of things and saves only the honest residue, only the ingenuous and unpretentious and natural part. *The Dust-Fairy* is superficially corrupted with notions of historical progress: but the emphasis is again on the pleasant, untragic living and dying of forms to which deceptive historical importance is attached. The vision of a future in which 'Reason, Science and Goodness will reign' is merely a smiling answer to the child's prudish complaint that animals should be 'destined to enrich the earth as manure': an assurance that it is really all right, ultimately. Hans Andersen's 'all right, ultimately' was prayerful; he longed for a redemption of the mortal little in the immortal large, and his method was an artless exhortation of the large on behalf of the little, rather than a stern lessoning of the little in littleness. In so far as it is possible to compare him with George Sand he is a religionist preoccupied with universal happiness, she a moralist dwelling on the homely happiness within individual control. It may seem strange to think of George Sand like this; but her children's tales force us to recognize the private accent of sobriety behind her work.

THE TALKING OAK

Emmi was a poor little swineherd who lived with a mean old aunt and kept swine, which he hated, for a farmer living on the edge of a forest. In the forest was a talking oak which had been struck by lightning and which warned all who approached to keep out of its shadow. One day Emmi beat one of the swine, who had made a fuss; and all the swine chased him until he had to take refuge in the oak, which sheltered him for the night. He was missed and the oak was thereafter avoided by the peasants. Returning to the village unseen he overheard a conversation which showed him that he would be unwise to return. So he took a little pot and some skins and returned to the forest, where he managed to live on nuts and fruit, and on the rabbits and birds which he caught. He also learned to spin and knit wool caught on the bushes.

Sometimes an old idiot beggar-woman would come and rest under his tree, and he would exchange his meat for some of her bread. She told him that she was no longer an idiot, though she had once been one; and how, having discovered the advantages of begging over working, she now pretended to be an idiot and earned a good living thereby. She invited him to go to live with her in her house in a village of beggars. He spent one luxurious, uncomfortable night in her house. But at a fair the next day she tried to sell him to a circus-proprietor. With the help of a good-natured peasant he escaped. The peasant invited Emmi to work under him (he was in charge of some men clearing the forest) and Emmi accepted and proved to be the cleverest of the workers, so much had he learnt by living alone in the forest – he who had been such an extremely unsuccessful swineherd. He worked thus for a year, going every week to see his aunt, with whom he had become reconciled. Every Saturday and Sunday night he slept in his oak tree. He grew more and more intimate with the forest and its inhabitants.

Then he left that forest to work in another. On the way he went to see the old beggar-woman, for whom he still felt an affection because she had been his only link with humanity in the forest. She had become paralysed and was overjoyed to see him because she wished to leave him all her money, grateful that he had refrained from giving her up to the police at the fair as he might have done. She died soon after and the peasant kept the money for him while he went on working. He became one of the chief woodmen on the forest-estate and married the peasant's granddaughter. Even then he did not forget the oak, but left on it a plaque bearing his name and the date of his stay. The oak ceased to talk, but became, even after his death, revered for his sake; for he had been everywhere well loved.

WHAT THE FLOWERS SAY

I heard the flowers talking one evening in the garden. The plain poppy was protesting that all flowers were equally noble and that the rose had no claim to royalty. She was supported by the daisy and the larkspur. Perfume was held to be no advantage, in spite of the protest of the scented poppy. The roses had just been pruned and so could not reply, and all the flowers combined to criticize them. I cried out against their petty jealousy in their own language and went to the wild flowers, hoping to find there better dispositions. I paused under a wild rose and heard it ask Zephyr the origin of the garden rose, queen of flowers. 'Once,' said Zephyr, 'I was the eldest son of the god of storms, and I raged over the earth where no life was. When life began, in tiny multitudes, in plants, in trees, I obeyed my father and did my best to destroy it all. Once, pouncing down to destroy, I smelt a delicious scent and found a lovely rose from which it emanated. The rose begged me to spare it and I, overcome by its beauty and perfume, did so and took it in my breast to my father. Angry at my pity, he tore it to pieces and wrenched my wings from me. I fell to earth, where I found the rose, revived and blooming. The spirit of life pitied me because I had pitied one of its creatures, and made me into a pretty boy with butterfly wings. The rose was his symbol to men of the sovereign power – not of material wealth, but of charm, beauty, gentleness. He proclaimed her queen of flowers. Since then I have lived with earth's creatures, loved by them all, the lover of the rose, friend of the wild rose.' I told this story to my botany master, who thought me ill, but my grandmother knew that it was childhood's privilege to understand the language of flowers.

THE RED HAMMER

The fairy Hydrocharis (Beauty of the Waters) was much distressed because the streams were swollen with rain and overflowed their banks where grew the flowers she tended. Her flowers were spoilt and she feared that her enemy the Queen of the Glaciers was plotting to expel her from her territory, as she had before, farther north. She could not understand the confused babbling of the water, so, finding a piece of cornelian, she threw it into the stream, broke it into first four, then eight pieces, until the water spoke round and through it intelligibly enough for her to understand that her enemy was indeed intending to drive her away. So she took her plants with her and went away.

In course of time only one piece of the stone remained, a piece as large as a head. One day the son of an armourer who lived near a stream found it and brought it home to play with. The father saw it, took it and showed it to all to be admired for its unusual beauty. One day a man painted all blue came for a weapon he had ordered, and, seeing the stone, asked for an axe to be made of it for him; he gave in exchange fourteen doe-skins. He lived (for this was in the stone age) in a house built in a watery hollow whose rim was level with the ground, and ruled over his neighbours, who were protected by his strong hand. He showed them the axe and allowed them to believe that some god had given it to him. Then, when the enemy came, he gained a great victory, killing many with it, and from the talisman he and his descendants gained the name of Red-hammer.

When he died the hammer was buried with him, and only disinterred many years later by a superstitious descendant; and hidden by him to be discovered again when the tribe had been driven to other homes. Then (it was in the bronze-age) an old woman found it and used it for digging roots; then again it was lost and, when the iron-age came, lay neglected. Then a hunter found it, but threw it into a garden. Later it was found by a gardener who took it to his master, an antiquarian enthusiast. Geologists got excited, said that it could not have been made in the country, which had no cornelian (forgetting the transporting power of a stream), nor made in the stone age, since the design was too good (forgetting the genius of the individual in advance of his time). The axe was placed on a velvet cushion in the master's collection. When he died his wife had it cut up to make a buckle. Then, finding it ugly, she gave it to her niece for her doll. The child found it too heavy as an ornament but excellent to crush into powder to make soup for her doll. One piece escaped and was sold to a lapidary, who made rings of it, one of which was carefully kept by a little girl. So ended the cornelian. Inanimate things have value only by our whim. But of all of them life makes use. And the fairy Nature lets none of them perish utterly, but makes and remakes them into ever new forms.

THE DUST-FAIRY

The grown-ups always chased from the house the grey dust-fairy and reproached me because I was sorry for her and let her come near me and stay in my garden.

One day she spoke to me and said that if I wanted to know why she was as she was I must call her when I went to sleep. Though sceptical, I did so, and immediately found myself in a beautiful garden, with a little lake in a marble basin and every kind of flower. 'I make all these things,' said the fairy, 'and with the help of wind, water, fire and electricity I make rocks and precious stones.' Suddenly she sank below the earth and I with her, and we were in a roaring furnace with flames of all colours all around, her laboratory. From there we went to what she called her kitchen, where from dust she made granite, saying that with infinite patience she did all this herself, broke in pieces to build up again and built up to break. Then I slept for a while (she said for some centuries).

After that she went to a bowl of water and, saying, 'See what dust produces when it goes to the bottom of the sea,' she brought out first plants, then strange half-plants, half-animals, then fish.

Then I saw a layer of dust on some rock, a forest with strange animals growing rapidly. The animals, she said, were destined to enrich the earth as manure, and when I cried out at the waste of creatures being produced to serve no better purpose and wished that everything could have been perfect from the beginning and that only angels, beings all spirit and no body, should ever have existed, she replied that there is no production without destruction, and that Nature could not endure a state of rest, she is eternal, ceaseless activity; that the world will be different in the future from what it is in the present, that the present is different from the past; that Reason, Science and Goodness will reign. And every use Life or Nature makes of Matter or Dust is wonderful; the eyes of the ichthyosaurus are more perfect than ours. It is no waste that they belong to a creature who thinks of nothing but eating to live, for the Universe has no need of beings to admire the wonder of its laws. If Nature is destined to create a being who may understand those laws, still everything must be subject to slow time.

Then she showed me the procession of the earth's inhabitants, each one more admirable than the last and less selfish. When the reign of the ape was over, I slept from fatigue and wakened to find myself at a modern ball, and the fairy pointed out to me how all their robes and jewels were made of infinitesimal particles of matter, and the flowers were born of dust. Again she said, life is an eternal cycle of coming into being and passing out of it, and left me for remembrance a piece of her lovely gown, which when I awoke I found to be a heap of dust but in which I could see the germ of diamond, flower and wood, of all the matter of life.

M.V.

FROM A PRIVATE CORRESPONDENCE ON REALITY

Laura Riding and Robert Graves

L.R.

THE EXISTENCE OF 'REALITY' is suggested by a faint but undeniable flavour of permanence in things known to be impermanent. There is nothing in experience altogether without this flavour; it is impossible for anything to be, no matter how short its life or unsubstantial its structure, unless it is in some respect 'real'. There has been something real about everyone who ever lived, about everything which ever held together and was – an object with a name, and this faint but undeniable flavour by which it convinced that it was.

Everything, everyone, suggests reality. What is reality? We become aware of it through things, people; but it is not merely an attribute of things, people, to be experienced only through things, people. Things, people, suggest it, 'reveal' it, but are not it in their separate existence. Reality exercises an influence, and according as things are sensitive to its influence they are real; but it is more real than that which it influences. Reality is the finally real existence by which the existence of comparatively real things or beings is conditioned; it is the originally real existence from which the existence of comparatively real things or beings derives. Everything which is suggests the existence of reality by a flavour of permanence, no matter how impermanent it be: everything which is has a relative permanence. Reality has an absolute permanence.

What is the nature of permanence? That which has a flavour of permanence must have, necessarily, a certain sufficiency, and a certain resemblance to the universal identity which pervades all existence. Its sufficiency is its effort to be – the strength of its desire to 'belong'; its resemblance is the grace with which it accepts its own relativeness in the totality to which it desires to belong.

All things, all people, then, as they are this blend of strength and grace, suggest reality. But to have experience of the conglomeration of things and people which is called the world is not to have experience of reality. And yet reality is to be experienced. I do not mean that it is understandable by logical induction from the suggestions which present themselves to the human mind at every turn of consciousness. I mean that those faint, undeniable flavours by which things and people are to you somewhat real can be superseded by a more crucial flavour – the entire flavour of the all-real. But to have this experience one must, step by step, put behind one the comparatively real as the less real. One must deny oneself that philosophical future by which the human mind has made the progress to more and more real a progress conditional upon the survival of the lesser human realities. One must risk this test of the realities: for to him who dispenses with a greater there can be no lesser.

And I say this now as an immediate injunction: meaning that the lesser realities have now been articulated in their possible numbers, and that the human mind is on the verge of the greater reality. If reality itself is not now experienced, experience itself will vanish: for it always implied such an ultimate experience. This is the time of all dangers and all securities. Men have often prophesied that on such and such a day the world would end. And the world has said, 'By what signs do you know this, by what right do you ask our belief in your reading of them?' My signs are no phenomena, but all phenomena, that I see them arrested between disintegration and integration; and my right is that, from being outside of them, so to see them, I have gone among them and suffered their paralysis.

R.G.

I accept your statement of the crucialness of the present moment, not only because it appeals to me emotionally and then seems a historically inevitable conclusion, but also because it is your statement. That is to say: I concede that you have the right to speak with such certainty because I am aware that you do indeed perceive human history with eyes trained on it from some point outside. I am aware that your consciousness is of a final quality and that you are yet someone immediate and actual. How do I know this? By a process of elimination, I should say: I have always had a blind but obstinate will to discover a consciousness of this quality and a realist's conviction that it was to be found in my time, and a painful frankness with myself that it was not my consciousness, and a physical intuition that it would be a woman's. And the process of elimination points to you, with a fantastic kind of logic. But there is nothing fantastic in my conviction that you think finally: because the recognition your thought invokes in me is not blind, but becomes clearer at every step.

The inadequacy which I have progressively felt in what you call the lesser realities, and with philosophy (in spite of a palate appreciative of 'faint, but undeniable flavours' and a mind attracted by optimistic generalizations) has corresponded with an increasing antipathy toward the philosophical nihilism in which the mind would be sunk if a rejection of the lesser realities were the only alternative. To envisage their rejection is, indeed, to flirt with death; and I have always feared death more than anything. My rejection of them, in fact, has always been conditional on some kind of survival. I have come to understand that the reality you speak of is not merely a negation, nor yet a matter of belief or speculation. And so I have looked to you for the way out: mere negation, or belief, or speculation, I could have accomplished myself.

But I do not regard myself as an intellectual or mystical freak outside the human ruck, only as a peculiarly forward-minded inquirer after reality among other inquirers of varying degrees of forward-mindedness. Nor are you an erratic being whose utterances are of merely esoteric interest. You speak a language intelligible to anyone who is ready to follow the varied implications of language through to their inevitable meanings. I know that you do this, because the intelligence that understanding of you requires of me is essentially no different in kind from the understanding it takes to live any normal day through in an observant and considered way.

But there does remain, if not for me, at least for others, the question of practical authority: how is one to be sure that what you say is so? For myself this problem does not arise, because my personal experience of you satisfies me that you have no motive outside that of saying what you say, that there is no discrepancy between what you say and what you do, and that what you say in general you apply to every major and minor particular of daily existence, and that the result is not an arbitrary compost of private fancies but an immediate interrelation. Yet the fact must be faced that the problem does arise for people habituated to more formal titles of authority.

But to go from this question, which is only a technical one, really, to the active matter of this correspondence. When you say that reality is to be more closely experienced than through intimations, my response is a recognition in myself of a desire so to experience it. But at the same time I am, as I have said, haunted in this desire by a fear of death. I know that I will not accept anything that involves self-extinction. And yet 'death' can be used as a positive as well as a negative word: you have constantly used it as such in your poems, and I myself feel its duality. What is death in terms of experience of reality: what aspect of reality is death, and what is the reconciliation between positive and negative death?

L.R.
The question of authority, and of the limits of authority, is like any ques-

tion of personal capacity or virtue. People take a composite view of
capacity and virtue because they live in a composite world; and of
authority as well – the public credit with which individual capacity or
virtue can be endowed. Thus, to a government is granted the authority to
determine what is politically right; but not the authority to pronounce
upon literature or art or science. The mathematician may be an authority
in his field; and even the philosopher may be an authority, since he does
not claim for his activity, which is speculation, any more positive recognition than the credit of being reasonable. The human mind's first impulse
is to doubt anything that seems to claim general authority – or general
goodness. People like to think along specialistic lines, and are indeed most
generous in acknowledging specialized talents or virtues. But there exists
a strong self-protective instinct against admitting more than a single
specific capacity in any one person, or more than a single set of virtues.
Capacity and virtue are the common pot from which everyone draws his
share; and the person who seems too widely capable is hated as a tyrant
who deprives others of the liberty to have capacity, and the person who
seems too good is mocked as a hypocrite. People love their friends, but
because they are no better than they are rather than because they are so
good; and they admire this or that work as it keeps strictly within its
conventional 'field'.

A carpenter is called to the house to mend a door. The door, in
responding to variations of weather, has sprung cracks, and these must be
filled in; it scrapes the floor on being opened or closed – it must come off
its hinges and be planed down a little. The carpenter is received with a
certain stipulated respect: he is a carpenter – no more, no less. The people
of the house feel a security in his presence; not merely because he is a good
carpenter, but because he is no more than a carpenter. His activity does
not sum other activities, but it is in itself only a minor cipher in the
lengthy column which adds up to the human grand total. A doctor
inspires much the same sort of feeling, though on a larger scale. He may
be, as well, a family friend and adviser, but his status as such is unofficial
and whimsical; and what he says in this capacity is qualified in the minds
of others by the thought that his primary emphasis is on physical well-
being. A gunman is granted a certain respect for his professional efficiency; he is more respectable, in fact, than a clergyman who sets up, also,
as a playwright – since he confines himself, with modest fanaticism, to a
single exclusive profession. Einstein is an authority as a scientist; that he
is also a musician is a whimsical fact of his private life. If it happened that
his musical performance entitled him to as much authority as his scientific
performance, the public would be irritated and suspicious. Authority is
divided up into fields; and every field is a minor one in relation to all the
others. A person may be a major force within his field, but if his activity
unites several fields, he is regarded either as not serious or as dangerous.

And yet this is so: that there are people so intensely active within their own field that they seem to rise out of it and drop off specialism and assume universal force. The person whose excellence operates scrupulously within his special field is called an 'artist' – a small, brilliant, self-satisfied word uttered with little enough sentiment. The person whose excellence overleaps professional boundaries, difficult to describe because critical language is so specialistic, is called a 'poet' – a large, opaque, nervous word uttered with all too much sentiment. Of contemporary bull-fighters, for example, Vicente Barrera is of the type to be called an artist, Domingo Ortega of the type to be called a poet. Yet one would hesitate to use the word 'poet' of Ortega not because it is too good a word but because, by its sentimental associations, it is suggestive of all that is pretentious and untenable in human activity. One is torn between recognition of his more-than-specialistic excellence and a desire not to outrage the clear breadth of his performance by a nebulous word.

There is capacity that transcends the specialised field and is present, with other capacities which have similarly transcended their particular boundaries, in a final generality: there is, that is to say, such a generality to be present in. And it is not the result of a synthesis of fields, but indeed an essential nucleus against which the fields have been individualized and to which some saving impulse may relate them again. As we call the specialist who transcends his field a 'poet', so this generality is to be called 'poetry'.

But we cannot easily forget the sentimental abuses from which these words have suffered. 'Artist' and 'art' have suffered far less, retaining a certain dignity in the public mind because of the implications of special technical talents they carry. Neither 'poet' nor 'poetry' has sound professional standing, because a poet cannot be defined as a specialist nor poetry as a speciality; and thus the person is suspect and the field open to vulgar exploitation. What happens, therefore, when a poet wishes public respectability, is that he presents himself as an artist in words. Or as a philosopher. Or as a moralist. Shakespeare's breadth is countenanced because his work is loose and disintegrated enough for him to be seen as a specialist in these three fields; and the effect of the combination is acceptable because none of these fields is regarded as very authoritative in itself, and their sum is presented not as authority but, disarmingly, as a sturdy confession of indeterminateness. It is this that makes Shakespeare so universally attractive.

Religion, like poetry, presumes a wide generality of field. But religious authority has suffered rather less contempt than poetic authority, because it is always experimental, offering itself in terms of advice to people whose habitual reliance on social authority has bred in them a greed of being taken care of in every department of life. Religion consists of nursery truths which, like proverbs, are authoritative and effective only if no one contradicts them, and only in those situations where almost any decisive statement is valuable because it relieves emotional hesitancy and tension. All religious wisdom, I mean, has this quality of being invented for the benefit of ambiguous occasions and temperaments. And it may be added to any special field of human activity without embracing it and colouring its authority with its own: religion is always a detachable supplement – a ready-made extension beyond the local reality with which to fill up, temporarily, the unexplored vacancy (vacant because unknown) beyond it. It is true that numbers of people devote themselves to religion as to an all-embracing reality; but they do, in fact, rather withdraw into vacancy, and there keep alive and renew those myths of extension which many people depend on for their sense of universality. The person who specializes in religion is no more universal-minded, fundamentally, than the people to whom he ministers. He is someone whom they have chosen from among themselves to inflate their localism into an illusion of size by which to feel that their world is the world-at-large in miniature; religion is, as it were, more air let in – not really more air, but as a fan creates air. When the fan is laid aside the air is as stifling as before.

Poetry is not an extension from other fields: it expresses no beyond, but entirety itself. And its truths therefore are not practically applicable, as religious truths are – they are not moral truths. If religious authority is, in the very elasticity of its application, merely experimental, poetic authority is indeed no authority at all; it rests on truth rather than on moral shrewdness, and is thus comprehensive rather than elastic, final rather than positive. With poetry, that is, the question of authority disappears; it becomes, instead, a question of scope. One must ask, not, 'What is your authority?' but, 'What is your scope?'

If the scope assumed is an absolute scope, then the truths are spoken in a poetic sense; which means that behind whatever is said is a consciousness of what is left unsaid, and an implication of ideal completeness, by the discontent with which the single statement is uttered. A characteristic quality of the poetic statement is this dissatisfaction with itself: it is the most that can be said in such and such a context, or in such and such circumstances, but it is not sufficient to all contexts and to all circumstances. There is a striking and unexpected rhetorical difference between the religious and the poetic statement – an odour of self-sufficiency in one, a glow of relativeness in the other through which can be felt a burning insistence on more.

It is a sensitiveness to the existence of the perfect more (or 'the greater reality') that differentiates the poetic mind from other minds. All poetic minds are alike in this sensitiveness. They differ in the quantity of 'moreness' they can make explicit, but all indicate moreness; they differ only in energy. You ask me a question about my 'authority', and my answer is that the term is not appropriate here: because the kind of statement I am making – and you are making – is poetic.

I hope I have shown what I mean by 'poetic', as a term of classification: not that which is to be understood 'figuratively', but that which is to be understood in the fullest possible sense, in the largest possible scheme of contexts and circumstances. Poets do, certainly, employ figures: but in saying, for example, that X is like B they are reducing the import of X to the import of B because they feel that X is too large a notion to be conveyed in one stroke of definition. B is a simplification of X, but at the same time less than X. And so to speak figuratively is to mean, for the moment, less than one means. It is against the common assumption that a poetic statement is necessarily figurative that I say that I mean what I say literally; and that in this literalness, this non-figurativeness, my statements are more rather than less poetic.

Your question about authority really turns into a question about energy: given a common sensitiveness between minds of poetic quality to 'moreness', there is in me, you feel, an unusually concentrated energy of moreness. And I accept the description in these terms. The question of modesty cannot arise, because the terms are not competitive: energy is not an achievement but the factual basis of personal distinction – that by which two characters of the same quality of mind are two different characters. My energy is not so diffused by humanistic considerations as most energies are – I should call such considerations 'peculiar interests'. But that I am like this is not a result of my having disregarded, designedly, the variety of interests by which this is a world of divided forces and differentiable characters. My energy is not a wilful abstraction, but myself.

That I say, for instance, that reality itself is to be experienced, and with the meaning that I can, through my energy of presentation, assist toward experience of it, is no idiosyncratic precipitation of myself against a world where experience is envisaged largely in terms of this or that peculiar interest. That I speak as I do is not from any will to challenge, tease or confound the world of common experience. I speak so in answer to a cumulative appeal to an energy, energies, like my own.

The genuineness of the appeal will appear in the generosity with which the response is accepted: the degree to which room is made for the response. As for the genuineness of the response, I can only say – speaking for all of us joined in this energy – that it can be attended by no self-interested design to ensure its acceptance. We must be concerned with its successful delivery, to whatever fate with others; we cannot be concerned with personal success. I am – speaking for myself – as prepared for acceptance as for non-acceptance. If what I say is not accepted as a response, it is nevertheless not uttered, on my side, in a spirit of arbitrary self-isolation and irrelevance. For it is, besides being my own response, part of something that is happening of itself: a self-assertion of reality at a certain point in time which, however temporal it may seem, automatically evokes a sane finality of statement – a moment in which, indeed, it is the unfinal, irresolute statement that has a tinge of insanity to it.

But how is it for other people? How final do they feel the time, how finally do they gesticulate and speak? In what condition is the world? It still 'moves', and scientists are busy calculating how many millions of years are still left to it. Children are still born in great numbers, male and female, and each with the traditional apparatus for reproduction. And every year sees new promise in scientific development. Nevertheless, there is an acute difference taking place now in the nature of life, in the nature of time: because an acute difference is taking place in the human mind. The human mind has reached the end of temporal progress: the future is not what it used to be, and people talk with less and less progenitive self-precipitation into the future, and behave with more and more fatally decisive immediacy. The future, that is, contains nothing but scientific development. It is an involuntary spending and manipulation of physical forces, empty of consciousness: it no longer matters. It may be reckoned in terms of millions of years; but it is rather these millions of years which are being foreshortened toward the compelling immediacy of this day, than this day which is assuming perspective in the temporal extension represented by those millions of years.

There is now, if not – in so many describable scenes – an end of the world, a describable end of change. In respect to physical achievement, the world is largely engaged in activities which repeat intensively all the physical conventions that have survived the modern elimination of physical realities. For example: the physical convention 'travel', which has nearly lost reality through aeroplanes, is maintained with less and less variety of event. And similarly: production contains few real new events – new products are increasingly the result of derived processes rather than of spontaneous creation. Science, which has replaced the old notion of natural physical progress, is the muse of this repetitive temperament. In respect to intellectual achievement, there are no further stages in view – no new temporal stage of thought in which to exercise effort. All is summary (and more and more definitive, more and more detailed): definition of past varieties and stages of consciousness. As for the plotting of future action, there is only violence plotted. The only future event the world can prefigure is a new war – in its helplessness to inspire the future with movement. The future contains nothing but scientific development; and scientific endeavour converges, inevitably, toward war. Its life-saving and life-easing and life-analysing aspects are incidental to its major direction of violence: that violence which is an uncritical reassertion of physical reality, and which can have no physical manifestation but war.

Although the world still seems to 'move', its apparent movement has no temporal validity: the world has reached spiritual stasis. And this stasis is a deadlock until a movement is found which shall replace the lost power of temporal progression with a power that I can only call, in this context, the power of attention. For while the stasis represents the reaching of an utmost degree of activity of consciousness, the conclusions of the human mind at this point are contradictory and indecisive – more contradictory and indecisive than ever before; and because, while they are the results of mental activity in its most profuse condition, they do not compose a unique, a finally integrated result. The effective sum of the world's experience, as recorded by this static moment, is profusion of experience, but not reality: the sum can only be stated negatively, as something short of reality. And yet reality is 'there'; at a distance, however, not to be traversed by the dynamics of the will – namely, by time. The old habit of continuance creates the scientific future; but this is a self-induced, mechanical illusion. The possible continuance now is not by the will, only by a power of attention: what 'more' there is to be experienced – the more-ness which is just fallen short of – can only be experienced by a deliberate receptivity toward the inevitable whole. For the whole is incompletely accessible if the human mind depends on volition alone. Of what use has this long life of time been if it has not at least taught the final limitations of the will that instigated and furthered it?

Such is the impression that the world makes on me in its immediate state. And I can only defend the correctness of this impression by saying, first, that it is an impression irrespective of any notion I may have of my own functions or nature, and, second, that it is one which has been renewed and strengthened by a constant retraining of my senses on the world before me, in pursuit of the complete immediate perception. My defence, in other words, is that I could as well say all this in the form of a prophecy to take effect at some indefinitely later time. A will to make what I say true for this time as against that would amount to a desire to destroy a potential future; and my way of thought is certainly not destructive. The compulsion behind my pursuit of the complete immediate perception is no more than the compulsion of my senses to measure the time in which I say what I say against the finalistic accent of my thought. And the result is an ever-decreasing space between the time of my mind and the time of my senses: there is practically no space between them except that which I create, constantly, to satisfy myself that I am not in conspiracy with myself. My mind and my senses are as it were accidentally alive in the same time; my actual perception of the world and my evaluations in thought tally immediately, without private connivance.

So much then for this question of authority in its more personal aspects – a question, here, of 'integrity': whether or not my reader can feel assured that I am concealing no psychological bias. I must accept the risk of whatever psychoanalytic suspicion 'my' kind of statement may arouse. And I have already said that in characterizing this kind of statement as poetic I did not mean that I wanted to be understood in a merely figurative sense.

And, if understood literally, I am subject both to the test of reasonableness – the plausibility of the particular statement – and to the test of poetic consistency – the relevance of the particular statements to the general statements and the correspondence of these with one another.

But who is to be the judge, whether I have reasonableness, and such consistency? In discussing the question of authority I observed that while a mathematician is easily granted authority of performance, authority is grudged the poet, or the person engaged in poetic statement, because his field is too universal – he would, it is felt, if granted authority, have a power of persuasion hostile to the desire of every human mind to form its own individual notion of the nature of reality. And so the poet is seen merely as someone with a faculty for expressing his private notion of the nature of reality more expertly than others; and the satisfaction of reading poems is merely in the wistful illusion they stimulate in the reader that, if he could express himself with such verbal felicity, he too would be a poet. Yet for every activity there must be authorities: these save the public from too much preoccupation with one activity as against another. The poet himself is never granted authority – for the reasons I have explained; and so there are critics – people who specialize in comparing one poet with another in verbal felicity. Even artists, who are concerned only with rendering minute, disconnected sensations of reality, cannot be granted authority: for these too there must be critics – people who specialize in comparing one artist with another in technical felicity.

The content of poems remains itself untested. Poets themselves are tempted not to test the consistency of their notion of the nature of reality – the basic content of any poem; and the atmosphere of irresponsibility with which poets are perforce surrounded encourages many people who are not poets to write poems. Yet it is the chief responsibility of the poet to be the critic of himself: he is not truly a poet unless what he says is, by the tests to which he has submitted it, uncriticizable. To profess that reality is to be experienced, as I am doing here, is not to be writing poems, but it is nevertheless to insist on the existence of that final and absolute setting which poems point to from the various settings in which they are written. And the responsibility of self-criticism which rests upon me in such a position is so strong that what I say is critical rather than poetic. I do not, that is, so much assert as restrain myself from assertion that would not satisfy the tests of others – since the notion that reality exists is an extremely primitive one demanding an emotional equivalence of myself with others.

The question of authority disappears in the fact that we are here being more actively severe with our subject than others might be – because we are elaborately sensible of the extent of its implications and of all the potential suspicion of and resistance to it. This would be a truly private correspondence, indeed, if we did not identify ourselves with such suspicion and resistance, besides assuming the responsibility of envisaging all the implications of our subject. We make the difficulties our own by the fact that, with a difference from each other in which you are predominantly loyal to human, personal values (in spite of the attraction that the notion of final reality has for you) and I predominantly loyal to final, impersonal values (in spite of the attraction 'humanity' has for me), we deliberate together unconditionally, facing the contingency that we may find no ready formula of reconciliation. We are prepared to dwell in the difficulties.

I shall not immediately answer your question about the relation of death to reality, in case you have something more to say about authority and the various incidental questions it has raised.

R.G.

It was as a poet in search of an integration of reality that you first knew me. The problem for me was at that time the same technical one that faced all my fellow-poets: what to do when the world of thought had grown unmanageable? We could look back enviously to a period like the Homeric one when a single gifted mind could cover the world-field in an easy sweep. To a lesser degree Chaucer and Shakespeare could epitomize their periods in this epical way. (But Shakespeare, as you say, in a loose discursive way; and Chaucer only by emotional simplification.) We felt that in the *Iliad* little had been left out that was included in the thought of that time; that in the *Canterbury Tales* much was symbolically represented; that in Shakespeare's plays much was present, by sensitive implication. But in the poetic material of the last three centuries, we felt, a gradual decrease in universality had taken place; so that more and more of our thought (poets' thought) had become private, and hence speculative rather than poetic.

The strong sensation of an apocalyptic end of things that expressed itself in England towards the end of the seventeenth century was not unjustified. If one looked for a precise date to mark the beginning of the end of the ramshackle world of Christendom, as one chooses 1453, the date of the conquest of Constantinople by the Turks, to mark the beginning of the Renaissance, one would naturally choose 1662, the date of the foundation of the Royal Society. After this, Science began organizing its exploration of time and space – each new expedition under the command of a specialist – and mapping out an abstract mental region, most of it barren mathematical or astronomical desert, far too extensive for any single mind to cover. Poets were impressed by the vastness of the new empire of the mind, and, when the philosophers claimed to be able to provide a guide to it, some of them tried to turn philosophers; as to-day, when philosophy has obviously broken down, and nothing seems worth considering but social security and the avoidance of an economic world-collapse, many of them try to turn economists. Then, of course, there are the poets who try to discipline their range of thought by subjecting their minds to such repressive authorities as the Catholic Church, the Communist Party, or the poetic practice of the past.

Our problem (to speak on behalf of the poets of my then period) was how much of the world of knowledge to acquaint ourselves with, how much we could manage to be poets of, without making the name of poetry cheap or ambiguous, or settling down in country which was definitely anti-poetic. We remembered the ludicrous example given by Tennyson when he was appointed Poet Laureate: he conscientiously set himself to school again with a weekly curriculum covering modern languages, physics, mathematics and philosophy.

To you the problem of poetic scope presents no difficulties. You are able, by orderly definition, to reduce to the status of idiosyncrasies large fields of specialist activity which earn popular respect, and with the same assurance and obvious common sense with which I, for instance, would declare that it was not necessary to memorize all the names and numbers in the London Telephone Directory. Could you give me a simple clue to your method of gradation?.

You define the trend towards war as a reassertion of physical reality against a background of scientific futurism. That agrees with my experience of the last war. The effect of war is temporarily to shrink the universe to manageable proportions. Only a very few things matter in war-time, and those are exactly the old-fashioned physical realities which science sublimates into intellectual realities – things like food, drink, warmth, songs, sex and surgery. There is room for God as fate, and for old-fashioned poems conveying the moment's poignancy. But thought as such ceases; international learned societies are torn by schisms and collapse; the universities become military training-centres. The nostalgia for war is a nostalgia for a common small purpose, even if it is only a foolish one, and for a common small universe, even if it must be dedicated to self-destruction. The madness of Armistice Day marked the sudden end of the common purpose, a wilful return to the individualistic irrelevancy and diffuseness of peace-time.

The respect that science has won for itself seems to me largely due to its self-sufficiency and its air of impartiality. It does not claim to be a universal authority, or even a centrally governed kingdom. It is a collection of -ologies, joined by a loose federal authority – a sort of United States; and tolerates the arts and religion as a sort of old-fashioned Europe with which it exchanges diplomatic ambassadors. Science is easily the most reputable power in the world to-day. Nevertheless, science has to admit the greater strength of war, because war provides an authority with which it cannot compete in realism – death. The false fascination that death had for poets in the War is best seen in Charles Sorley's poems, especially the one starting:

> Saints have adored the lofty soul of you,
>   Scholars have whitened at your high renown.
>
> We stand among the countless thousands who
>   Must hourly wait to tread your pathway down.

Sorley saw death as 'a slate washed clean, a merciful putting away of what has been', and as giving 'the bright promise' of the poet a mystical flowering in a world altogether the opposite of the living world. He felt the task of being a poet impossible in this world. He had tried the philosophical way of integration, but this had failed him; so he gave up, and was killed, preferring to stand by his bright promise, rather than continue as a poet in a poetry-impossible world.

This is why I asked you about death. The world has come of itself to a point where it can, as you say, get no further by the same methods of progress – except further in contradiction. It has a respect for death, which in war-time it makes the supreme reality; yet the sort of death that war brings is not the reality it means. So it is now behaving exactly as people behave when they cannot quite make up their minds to suicide. They keep a store of poisons in the medicine cupboard in the hope that one day they'll take one by mistake; or walk about on the edge of a cliff in the hope that the cliff top will break away; or carry a loaded revolver in the pocket in the hope that the trigger will catch and shoot them.

If death could be seen by poets – and by everyone anxious to see along with the poets – as the finis of a long, violent and unpleasant story, after which, given the power of attention of which you speak, a purified experience of reality could follow, there would be no further need for perplexed effort, perplexed renewal, confused provisional solutions. People are aware, even in war-time, that the sort of death to which they pay tribute is not a final death, but only a physical analogy of a true death. My question therefore is: by what principle can one learn to think and live poetically, seeing all the varied fields of activity in a just proportion of importance, so that one can contemplate the universe again with no less serenity (though with greater understanding) than that with which in pre-astronomical days people contemplated the moon and the stars?

L.R.

Death is a simple thing to think about – as is anything in which people instinctively believe. The word evokes instantaneous recognition: one does not need to identify death in talking about it – everyone knows what one means by it. People can construe death intelligently, yet be mystified by such a notion as reality and easily led into abstraction or disbelief. To construe reality one must have passed through many preliminary stages of thought. For the recognition of death are required only those initial physical sensibilities with which one recognizes life – the temporal face of life. By these one can know – without needing to define – what death is: by what life is not.

Death is the great negative supplement to life. Reality, we might say, is divided into life and death. Where there is no integral perception of reality, there is at least this divided perception: life, death. Life is an ever-changing synthesis of particulars; death is the dissolution of the experimental, tentative appearance of totality which life involuntarily acquires. Life takes us toward reality; death takes us away from the deceptive appearances of reality into which life forms itself. Death is a cancellation of the fallacies to which life tempts us to adhere.

The recognition of this simple, primitive distinction between life and death is our original and essential equipment for knowledge. The succession of life by death is in itself an act of knowledge: the power of denial exercised against that power of assertion which is life. We might call this succession the rhythm of reality. But reality itself is something more than a rhythm: the rhythm is only the rhythm of human acquaintance with reality. It is this given acquaintance which constitutes the equipment for knowing reality – for being oneself 'real'.

The more we think – which is to say the less we rely on the loose, instinctive life-and-death rhythm to redeem us from error and chaos – the more do the life-power and the death-power approach simultaneity. Our assertions become more and more qualified by the death-negative; and it is as this immediacy of thought, this cancellation of temporal delay, that death figures so insistently in poems. The simultaneous combination of the death-accent with the life-accent makes the voice of the mind something besides an instrument of personal utterance: it becomes capable of carrying extra-personal inflections, of expressing general as well as personal truths. Life is the exercise of consciousness in individual contexts; death is the critical phase of consciousness – the nullification of the merely individualistic meanings. To know that the truth of any act or utterance is qualified by the degree to which it is entailed in the peculiar circumstances giving rise to it, that its application is limited by the nature of the field to which it is designed to apply: this is death. Criticism is death.

It is not, that is, necessary to 'die' in order to experience death. And the more actively death is experienced in life – the more precisely co-incident its accent with the life-accent – the less significance it has as a physical event. Death cancels the over-positiveness of the assertions that make up life; and, in so far as it is an element of our consciousness, it also cancels itself as a historical incident. A consciousness tempered with death – a

critically purified consciousness – is already beyond contradictory physical existence; it has drained the self from the temporal material by which
it asserted itself against other selves. The self now stands neither in life
nor in death, but in reality. In life it exists by a strength of opposition to
other selves. In death all that is contradictory passes into non-existence. In
reality the self emerges with infallible accuracy as a demonstration of the
existence not of itself but of reality.

For this is how reality is to be experienced: by letting reality be oneself.
And this is what I meant by the power of attention: the lending of one's
consciousness – one's minutely sensitive apparatus of perception – to the
absolute generality in which we are more deeply entailed than in our local
circumstances. When we think, we are refining our consciousness to this
end. But few of us dare to pursue the process to its consequence: suppose
the consequence is not reality, but nothingness? Yet how can we speak
with awe of nothingness, if by somethingness we mean only self-exis-
tence? There is no one who whimpers at the notion of nothingness who
means more by it than the disappearance of his local, vital self.
Fundamental somethingness is not proved or disproved by what becomes
of each of us, personally. It is the implicit source from which our individual existence derives; and indeed we disappear, and to petty nothingness, if we do not belabour ourselves, without mercy to our individualistic
obduracies, until we are the passionately flexible instruments by which
fundamental somethingness is transformed from an implicit into an
explicit reality.

We may each have a private purpose in being, and by this purpose have
succeeded in being. But the right to exist at all depends on a primary act
of acknowledgement: on the articulation of reality, above the articulation
of self. If we fail to achieve this primary act, because our private purpose
steals our primary energy, our right to exist becomes corrupted with vital
fallacies, with temporal delusions. Certainly: people die. They are reab-
sorbed into undefined somethingness – mother somethingness; or, if you
like, father nothingness. But if we give ourselves death – if we think death
– then we acquire a self-redeeming aptitude for reality.

At the beginning I spoke of a flavour of reality which everything has.
This flavour is the result of the admixture of death with life. There is
nothing which does not contain death as well as life – either by thought, or
by having died already, as with inert matter or what are called 'things', or
by living in acquiescent anticipation of death, as with flowers, plants,
trees, or by living anonymously, evading self-assertion, as with animals.
Everything which is, everything which has not gone into disappearance,
must of necessity evoke reality: a scope of existence in which it is included
along with all other possible existences. The confirmation of existence is
not by what a thing is, but by what it can co-exist with – by the energy
with which, in its particularity, it evokes generality. The flavour of mere

existence is caused by a strength of self-assertion. But the flavour of reality rises from the question about reality which existence becomes when its emphasis is modulated by a death-emphasis.

And, if we think death, we make ourselves an instrument for the answering of the question about reality we personally constitute. We experience reality to the degree to which we are at once a question about reality and its answer; to the degree, further, to which the question that we constitute supplements, confirms or intensifies other questions, and the answer that we constitute supplements, confirms or intensifies other answers.

But discussion ought not to go much beyond this point; for the rest is something to happen rather than to write about: to write about, I mean, as something happening rather than as a critical prospect of experience.

And the clue to the relative importance of this branch of knowledge and that? What is knowledge? Knowledge is, first, the extension of consciousness by someone to something else or someone else, and as such it implies a scope of extension limited only by the accessibility of the material to consciousness. I do regard knowledge as limited by capacity of consciousness, because I do not regard consciousness as a quantitative attribute, of which some people have more, some less. All people have an equal capacity of consciousness, in the quantitative sense – as one lives in the same large world in which everyone else lives, no matter where one is particularly stationed or how small one's particular community of interests. Difference in consciousness can only be expressed in terms of difference in experience: what, specifically, we have conscious experience of as compared with what, specifically, others have conscious experience of. This brings me to my second stipulation about knowledge: that knowledge implies, besides the extension of consciousness to something, a response of consciousness in that to which it is applied. Knowledge is mere fancy unless it is in some way a communication, with all the checks on false assumptions which communication provides.

We may be so absorbed in our experience of a particular set of things that our consciousness remains applied to them, and to them alone. But there may be two reasons for such a specialized divagation of consciousness. It may be due to the nature of the material – which by its triviality provokes a tenderness in us, so that we linger with it in communication against the aggressive appeal to our consciousness of more impressive entities. Or it may be due to a deliberate refusal to communicate in the large. And it is this permanent specialisation which is typified in the myriad name of Science: consciousness used against consciousness. In science the energy of knowledge is being constantly returned to itself; which is why the reality of science must be typified in the myriad name of Psychology – so-called 'self-knowledge', or idiosyncratic personal reality.

Consider the specialist in astronomy. What communication do you think goes on between him and his material? The result is, precisely, a record of what communication does not go on. Very good: this is interesting, and even valuable, for it saves the consciousness of us others from wasteful experience – should we not already know to what degree astronomical entities are weakly charged with the flavour of reality by which one entity has communicable co-existence with others. The dishonesty of the scientific method lies in its offering itself as a method of knowledge – rather than as a method of economy in the application of consciousness. In offering itself as a method of knowledge it tempts us not to think, to stand arrested in our life-assertion: instead of communication, there is assertion against assertion, with all entities in mutual antithesis and no standard of entity but that of counter-existence. Science, indeed, is life without the critical admixture of death; existence without the coherent effort of reality.

The clue I have to offer to the question of the relative importance of this branch of knowledge or that is indicated in this view of science. The first duty of the consciousness, if one does not mean it to abandon its responsibilities to others, is not to squander itself on material which yields no response – which, according to its incommunicativeness, lies outside the borders of explicit reality. Do not overlinger with what throws your mind into private silence: beware of destructive scientific patience – unless, of course, you really wish to abandon the advantages and responsibilities of consciousness to others. The test of the importance of anything as knowledge is the degree of communication it represents: whether it is an occasion in which our consciousness can participate with some expectation of a companion response. And this is not a mystical test. We soon know, sitting opposite a stranger in a railway carriage, whether or not a gesture of friendliness would meet with a response; we know this by the degree to which we feel alone. If, with your consciousness fully applied to some confronting material, you nevertheless feel yourself alone – hurry from the spot: you are in danger of becoming a scientist, and enjoying it.

```
┌─────────────────────────────────────────────┐
│                   NOTES                        │
└─────────────────────────────────────────────┘
```

The Idea of God

1   Virginia Woolf's sensitiveness to the modernistic mood results, in her work,
    in an atmosphere of hermaphroditic ambiguity in which sexual distinction is
    blurred with pious artistry. She not only dilates on the historically cultivated
    vagueness of women about their identity, but enriches traditional femininity
    with the sexual vagueness of modernistic man. It is as if final clarity might be
    in this way perpetually futurized – spiritual adolescence being more inter-
    esting, less exacting. Various other 'sensitive' writers, both women and men
    (E.M. Forster, for example), have contributed to the thickening of this
    atmosphere. Frequently the male contributors are homosexual in temper-
    ament: the blurring of sexual distinction is characteristic of sexual as well as
    spiritual adolescence, and male homosexuality is a characteristically adoles-
    cent state of mind. This is not, however, an identifiably Lesbian atmosphere.
    Lesbian women generally display a commonplace maturity of mind; they
    oppose a curiously puppet-like ordinariness to the romantic oddness that
    women have in heterosexual relations, and advertise respectability and
    normal competence of behaviour – while homosexual men advertise the
    contrary. The peculiarly Lesbian atmosphere is produced by an abrogation of
    finalities, a perverse denial of the existence of problems of final importance;
    hence the preoccupation with so-called 'normal' problems – the boring
    vigour, the superficial alertness of the Lesbian temperament. Like the other,
    it is an atmosphere which resists the ultimate significance of sexual distinc-
    tion. But it is as the interpolation into history of some static, time-insulated
    atmosphere which makes the mind numb to futuristic shocks of truth; while
    the first atmosphere is as a nebulous dwelling on the borders of truth, which
    is tamed by sensuous manipulation – a taming in which, perhaps, homosexual
    men play the part of emissaries, or broken elephants, sent to tame the wild
    elephants of truth, as in the *Thesmaphoriazusae* of Aristophanes. – M.V.

2   The first two chapters of the Book of Job are considered post-Exilic exactly
    because Satan occurs in them, the larger part of the book being considered to
    date from 900-800 BC. Similarly, the two other references to Satan in the Old
    Testament – I Chronicles xxi and Psalm 109 – are post-Exilic. – M. V

3   St. Matthew, who wrote his gospel for the Jews, thought it necessary, never-

theless, to provide Jesus with a historical genealogy through Joseph, though he expressly states that Joseph was not his father. St. Matthew was clumsily trying to satisfy the Jews' realistic sense of human sequence: male genealogy represented to them the substantiated immediacy of generation on generation. – R.G.

4   These distinctions are not merely a freak of the Authorised Version, but three distinct figures specified in the Hebrew text. Horeb (Sinai) is always called 'the mountain of *the* God' in this passage and in the Ten Commandments passage; in this strictly local appearance God is a strictly local deity. –M.V.

5   The scientific view is, then, that the world ('–') has a constant immediacy and exists in a series of coincident dynamic moments: '–' bounces on 'O' (nothingness), the world repeatedly touches death, but the contact with death creates the energy for the bounce. Life is the material expression of the energy created by the impingement of something on nothing. There is a sympathetic connexion between this view and the religious view of survival: the same to–day, yesterday and forever – death and resurrection. The scientist's observation that matter continues to defy nothingness is not unlike the priest's axiom that life survives death. Religious truth confines itself to the historical, and in effect scientific, observation that man has not yet come to an end; it is from this observation that all religious confidence in the eternity of man derives. The following diagram suggests itself:

Historically: ⊥̸̧   (historical heaven)
                            (historical time)
                            (nothingness)

Scientifically: ⊤̧   (scientific immediacy)
                            (nothingness) – M.V.

6   To the two roots *the-*, meaning 'run' and 'put', as possible sources of 'theos', may be added another root *the-*, meaning 'see, witness or contemplate'. The following is a table of further sympathetic associations phonetically centred in *theos*.

   Theos: a god, God.
   Theā: a goddess.
   Theā: 1. a seeing. 2. a thing seen, a sight.
   Theaomai: I see, or behold.
   Theatron: a theatre, or place of religious spectacles.
   Theoreo: 1. I behold or am a spectator of. 2. I contemplate in the mind.
   Theōros: 1. a spectator. 2. an ambassador sent by the state to consult an oracle or perform religious rite at a public spectacle. 3. a magistrate. Ancient grammarians derived *theoros* in its third sense from *theos* and *orā* (a concern or care), i.e., a man who looks after divine concerns.
   Theōriā: 1. a beholding. 2. mental contemplation. 3. theory as opposed to practice. 4. science in general. 5. the being a spectator at religious spectacles. 6. the being an ambassador. 7. an embassy. 8. the office of magistrate.
   Theōrizo: I theorize
   Theōristes: a theorist

These last two forms, constructed on the classical models of *sophizo* (practise philosophy) and *sophistes* (a professional philosopher or sophist), are not classical words, and in their modern sense have taken over from *sophizo* and *sophistes* the invidious secondary sense of intellectual futility which practical people attached to the irrelevant philosophizing of the sophists. They did not exist in classical times, and even in late Greek did not have the invidious sense: contemplation of the divine, or the abstruse, was a deliberate but not frivolous act of the mind. The theatrical spectacle was intended to be witnessed both by the human audience and the god in whose honour it was performed; indeed, the characters often included the god in person. It dramatized the relations of men with the divine: represented the actuality that their thought on the most difficult subject of thought had for them. There was none of the humanistic realism that the Romans introduced on their stage to the exclusion of the *theoretic* (god-apprehending) element. – R.G.

Joyce's punnings are not exercises in phonetic sympathy; they are phonetic conceits, wilful misspellings. 'Sanscreed' (without creed) caricatures the dignified 'Sanskrit'. The object of such clowning is, in fact, to undermine the integrity of language. Joyce selects, significantly, just those phonetic approximations whose differing senses confound – rather than illuminate – one another. Language thus becomes a facetious, irresponsible brogue in which meaning, syntactic coherence and phonetic precision are vulgar grist to the wit's mill. Words represent, merely, opportunities for disruption of sense; and the more violent the disruption of sense, the greater the intellectual triumph. Misspelling is a common psychological phenomenon among the Irish. I have known an educated Irishman to write 'teature' for 'teacher'. – L.R.

Poems and Poets

7   Coleridge's new interest in metaphysics was a defiance of the witch of poetic unreality with whom he was obsessed: a defiance with which he naturally became infected in Germany. The Germans defy poetic unreality – 'abstract' reality – as a region to be mastered and freely manipulated. So in this metaphysical adventure Coleridge attempted to show strength against the reality that was unreal to him – to plunge into it and yet survive, be humanly real; which explains the artificial energy derived from metaphysics. But Coleridge was not naturally energetic, and he was, moreover, honest; he could not pretend the cold-bloodedness which metaphysical adventure required and soon relaxed into his usual uncertainty. – L.R.

8   'Man's absolute self' – Coleridge has introduced here some artificial thunder out of metaphysics. Wordsworth's station of spiritual security was a homely country cottage. 'Dread watch-tower' is a figure borrowed from Coleridge's haunted poetic life and presented to the tame philosophical Wordsworth. 'Man's absolute self' is purely metaphysical; it is Coleridge's metaphysical caricature of Wordsworth's self-sufficient, arrogant humanism. – L.R.

9   He thought of poets, that is, as possessing attributes conventionally attributed to women: passivity of mind and an emotional organisation adapted to the enjoyment of loss of identity in another identity. This was a natural consequence of his failure to make a strong distinction between the poet and

poetry. And since it was a failure resulting from intellectual laziness, he expressed his sense of identity with poetry (a non-male figure) in indiscriminate behaviour. So women, in confusedly identifying themselves with man-nature, become 'feminine': feminine behaviour is indiscriminate behaviour. – L.R.

10   A misreading of Shakespeare's intelligent resignation to the limitations of the human mind when confronted by spiritual difficulties which become, without such resignation, treacherous 'uncertainties, mysteries, doubts'. In the same letter Keats writes: 'Coleridge, for instance, would let go by a fine isolated verisimilitude caught from the Penetralium of mystery from being incapable of remaining content with half knowledge. This pursued through volumes would perhaps take us no further than this, that with a great poet the sense of Beauty overcomes every consideration, or rather obliterates all consideration.' Keats rightly felt that Coleridge had a poetic conscience which would not let him be content with random ecstasies. He wrote, further: 'As to the poetic character itself (I mean that sort of which, if I am anything, I am a member: that sort distinguished from the Wordsworthian or egotistic Sublime: which is a thing per se, and stands alone) it is not itself – it has no self, it is everything and nothing – it has no character.' Keats was here making a just distinction between Wordsworth's self-protective insensitivity to the pleasures of poetry and his own cultivation of poetry as the science of hedonics. – L.R.

11   Shelley's hermaphroditic millenium was a philosophical postponement of judgement, in the hope that a more virtuous humanity might meanwhile be evolved. Non-human Spirit was to co-operate in this evolution by lending itself as a standard; and the human part of the bargain was Promethean striving to equality with the superior Spirit. Both sides were to be bound by a sense of justice: the sentiment that superior Spirit did humanity an injustice in being superior and that humanity did the superior Spirit an injustice in being inferior. But Shelley was not really satisfied with his philosophical solutions of poetic problems. His object in formulating them was as if to keep up the flagging patience of man with poetry, and of poetry with man, a little longer – to ward off premature fatalities. And this much he perhaps did. – L.R.

12   Spenser created a ritual of emotional elegance by the practice of which the poets of the Romantic tradition could flatter themselves that their extravagances were poetically worthy, in being magnificently expressed. Much of the vocabularistic magnificence of the Romantic poets derives from Spenser; and he is also responsible for the ease with which the romantic habit was assumed by poets as an intellectual feat – by such essentially non-romantic poets for example, as Darley, and Tennyson. Spenser was concerned to fix a mode of irresponsibility that would not damage poetic prestige, and he did this by dressing irresponsible energies in brilliant costume and thus making a poetic pantomime of them – even as his pastoral fairyland was, by its demonic vividness, a satiric equivalent of poetic reality. – L.R.

The Exercise of English

13   'Joy' in English is the name of *conscious* satisfaction: of intellectual satisfaction

physically immediate. 'Pleasure' is the name of purely physical satisfaction followed by an intellectualisation: 'pleasure' carries the sense of memory. 'It was a joy' states the immediate consciousness that existed *then*. 'It was a pleasure' states the subsequent memory. 'It is a pleasure to know you' does not mean 'I have joy in knowing you,' but rather 'I know that meeting you now will be a pleasant memory to-morrow.' 'Happiness' is the 'biggest' word: it is the name of looking forward to an indefinitely prolonged consciousness of satisfaction (indiscriminately physical and intellectual) – even the separation of the consciousness from the occasion of satisfaction. It combines and extends, that is, both 'pleasure' and 'joy.' And so it is the most dangerous, most vulgarisable of the three, the most crudely poetical. *Bonheur,* the French word for 'happiness', is used for the prospect of solid, material continuity of satisfaction. *Plaisir is* not merely reminiscent, as it is in English; it is capable of ironic expansion, and is thus the stock courtesy-word in French. *Joie is* a perplexing word to the French, exactly because it invites the immediate combination of physical with intellectual satisfaction. What in English is an extremely vivid word is in French an extremely blank word: either rhetorically awkward or, if stylized, swallowed up impudently in the word to which it is attached, as in *joie de vivre* or *fille de joie. –* L.R.

14 'Security' in English, like any English name, has a tested amplitude of meaning. It enlarges the concrete conception 'taking care' with an associated condition of goodness. The associated condition of goodness is the notion that it is good for things to remain unchanged. 'A sense of security' is a conviction that to be locked in fixed circumstances is good. The stronger an English word is as a name, the stronger is the moral commitment to the idea inherent in the name. A name exists like an internal law of the mind, not merely to be obeyed in its concrete applications (in the 'letter'), or formally acquiesced in as a statutory abstraction (obeyed in the 'spirit'). – M.V.

Marginal Themes

15 Many of the gods in pre-Greek and Greek mythology were represented sometimes, if not always, in bull-form. Parjanya, the old Indian thunder-god, and Apis, an Egyptian god, were bulls. The Cretans called the sun a bull, and there was a legend that every year Athenian youths and girls were sent to Crete to be eaten by the Minotaur – that is, sacrificed to the bull-god. The Hittites sacrificed rams to a bull, and a bull was the emblem of their Father-god. Dionysus was often worshipped and imagined in the form of a bull, and river-gods in Greece and Rome were represented with bull's horns. Prophetic inspiration was thought in Greece to be possession by the god, the presence of the god in the prophet; Pausanias mentions an instance of the drinking of bull's blood to obtain this prophetic inspiration.

In Greece bulls were used as well as other animals for sacrifice to the gods (Zeus and Poseidon for instance), the heroes and the dead, and in such cases there is no direct suggestion that the sacrifice was the killing of the god. But in Crete in the Minoan age, the killing of the bull was not merely one among many possible sacrifices, it was an unique and elaborate ceremony; men and girls of high rank took part in it, everyone went to watch it, and it was a subject which painters and goldsmiths used again and again. According to Sir

Arthur Evans, the object of the bull-fighters was rather to display their acrobatic skill than to kill the bull, and they were more often killed themselves. In that case, they would be sacrifices to the bull-god, or to the supreme Mother-god. But after the fight, the bull himself was sacrificed to the goddess by the priest: the bull-god was killed.

In Greece the god Dionysus was ritually killed when a bull was sacrificed to him; his worshippers acted again the killing of Dionysus-Zagreus in bull-shape by the Titans. After the sacrifice, they drank the blood of the bull – that is, of the killed god – and ate its flesh.

The bull-fight was unknown in the more progressive parts of Greece, and only continued in Thessaly, from where it passed to Rome. The ritualistic killing of the bull is again important in the Mithraic cult. There Mithras kills the sacred bull whose soul is then placed in Heaven to watch over flocks and herds, to be their guardian deity.

16   In Crete the supreme deity was the Mother-goddess, the bull-god was an inferior deity. Minoan art is full of her images, her priestesses, her cult; while the bull, disproportionately large and over-carefully worked in comparison with the human figures, manifestly a god, is nevertheless represented only in bull-fights, and occurs in legend only in the story of the Minotaur. It is possible that he stood in the same relation to the Mother-god as did Attis in later times. So in Egypt Apis was an inferior god; and the goat-god Pan and the Centaurs were as much below the Olympians as the Greek river-gods were. And in Mithraic legend, when the soul of the sacred bull rose to Heaven, he was identified merely with Silvanus, the Roman version of Pan.

17   According to Sir James Frazer, the bull has always been considered the type of virility. Parjanya, the Indian thunder-god, who was a bull, made plants, animals, and women conceive, as in a Vedic hymn which begins by addressing him as a bull: 'Parjanya is the god who forms in kine, in mares, in plants of earth, / In woman, the germ of life.' In Crete the bull-god was the symbol of maleness, sacrificed to the female. And in Mithraism, the sacred bull was the origin of all plant and animal life, the earth was made fertile by his blood and corn grew from the wound in his tail. – M.V.

18   That the American manner is not necessarily, when converted to writing, an aggressive literary assault on the properties of other human communities, is happily demonstrated by E. E. Cummings – perhaps with sophisticated content in the manner by him alone. For he is only interested in clarifying the instantaneous sensation of local self implicit in the manner. He is not interested in self-protective justification or safe emotional expansion, but only in rendering the manner with technical accuracy. This is how he deals with Afrique, a fellow-prisoner in *The Enormous Room*, without proprietary knowingness, merely in the honest course of possessing his own – strictly his own – sensations:

> You did not know Afrique suddenly. You became cognizant of Afrique gradually. You were in the *cour*, staring at ooze and dead trees, when a figure came striding.... Or again, it's a lithe pausing poise, intensely intelligent, certainly sensitive, delivering daily a series of sure and rapid hints that penetrate the fabric of stupidity accurately and whisperingly; dealing one after another brief and poignant instupidities, distinct and uncompro-

mising, crisp and altogether arrow-like. The poise has a cigarette in its hand, which cigarette it has just pausingly rolled from material furnished by a number of carefully saved butts (whereof Afrique's pockets are invariably full). Its neither old nor young but rather keen face hoards a pair of greyish-blue witty eyes, which face and eyes are directed upon us through the open door of a little room....

The same scrupulous self-possession, more emphatic because the experience is less personal, more publicly abroad, is recorded in *Eimi*. He is waiting in line to see the tomb of Lenin:

> ... as when a man inhabits, for stars and moons, freely himself (breathing always round air; living deeply the colour of darkness and utterly enjoying the sound of the great sun; tasting very slowly a proud silence of mountains; touched by, touching, what never to be comprehended miracles; conversing with trees fearlessly and fire and rain and all creatures and each strong faithful thing) as when the man comes to a where tremulous with despair and a when luminous with dissolution – into all fearfulness comes, out of omnipotence – as when he enters a city (and solemnly his soul descends: every wish covers its beauty in tomorrow) so I descended and so I disguised myself; so (toward death's deification moving) I did not move ... another futile aspect of 'materialistic dialectic' ... merely again (again false noun, another fake 'reality') the strict immeasurable Verb neglected, the illimitable keen Dream denied –

For the 'immeasurable domain of the Verb' is only the private reality 'Is' – the sentimentally independent enactment of all the dream meanings in which the selfish but unpretentious 'I' has chosen to lose itself. – L.R.

APPENDIX

Full contents lists of EPILOGUE I–III

Compiled from the original volumes by Alan J. Clark, authorized bibliographer of Laura (Riding) Jackson. (A.J.C.'s full checklist of L.(R.)J.'s published work 1923–2001 appears in *Chelsea 69*, December 2000, pp. 147–179.)

{**bold** = included in the present selection; *italic* = revised (in whole or in part) by R.G. for his *The Common Asphodel* (1949)}

EPILOGUE: A Critical Summary; volume I – Autumn 1935
Editor: Laura Riding / Assistant-Editor: Robert Graves
Contributors to this issue:
Madeleine Vara / Laura Riding / James Reeves / Robert Graves /
Thomas Matthews / Honor Wyatt / John Cullen / John Aldridge / Len
Lye / Ward Hutchinson

1–5	Preliminaries	Laura Riding
6–54	**The Idea of God** [1–5]	Thomas Matthews and Laura Riding

[40–42: 6 endnotes: numbers 1–2, 4–5 by M.V. no. 3 by R.G., no. 6 half by R.G., half by L.R.; 42–54: Supplementary Argument by T.M. and L.R.]

55–59	Poems [four]	Thomas Matthews
60–86	The Cult of Failure	Laura Riding and Madeleine Vara

[60–66: The Rimbaud, by L.R.; 66–86: Critical Detail 1–3, by M.V., note by L.R.]

87–92	A Poem-Sequence (To the Sovereign Muse)	Robert Graves
93–129	Germany [1–4]	Laura Riding, John Cullen, Madeleine Vara

[111–112: 3 endnotes by M.V., J.C., L.R.; 113–125: *Nietzsche*, by M.V.; 126–129: Germans as a Social Problem, by L.R.]

130–133 Poems [three]   John Cullen
134–143 An Address to an International Audience   Madeleine Vara
144–156 **Poems and Poets** (Conversation on the Criticism of Poems)
        Laura Riding [questions by R.G.]
157–174 *Coleridge and Wordsworth; Keats and Shelley* Robert Graves
175–199 The Romantic Habit in English Poets [1–2]   James Reeves
        [14 footnotes by L.R.; 2 by J.R.; 1 by R.G.]
200–207 *A Note on the Pastoral*   Robert Graves
        [footnote by L.R.]
208–212 Poems [two]   James Reeves
213–219 Picture-Making   Laura Riding
        [4 John Aldridge plates]
220–227 Poems [five]   Laura Riding
228–230 Poems [three]   Honor Wyatt
231–235 Film-Making (Movement as Language;
        Movement As A Medium)   Len Lye and Laura Riding
236–245 Photography   Ward Hutchinson
        [1 plate] [243–245: 4 endnotes by L.R.]

EPILOGUE: A Critical Summary; volume II – Summer 1936
Editor: Laura Riding / Associate Editor: Robert Graves
Contributors to this issue:
Alan Hodge / Honor Wyatt / James Reeves / Kenneth Allott /
Madeleine Vara / Laura Riding / Ward Hutchinson / Robert Graves /
Katherine Burdekin / Gordon Glover

1–7   In Apology   Laura Riding
8–56   Crime [1–5]   Laura Riding
        [52–56: 11 endnotes, 2 signed L.R., 3 signed M.V.]
57–61   *Official and Unofficial Literature*   Robert Graves
        [footnote by L.R.]
62   A Poem   Kenneth Allott
63–64   **Homiletic Studies: [Introduction]**   Laura Riding
65–75   **Stealing**   Robert Graves
76–83   Laziness   Ward Hutchinson
84–89   Enthusiasm   Gordon Glover
        [endnote by R.G.]
90–107 **In Defence of Anger**   Laura Riding
108–109 Poems [four]   James Reeves
110–136 **The Exercise of English** [1–7]
                             Laura Riding and Robert Graves
        [section 5 signed L.R.; 6 signed R.G.; 7 signed M.V.]
        [2 endnotes, signed respectively L.R. & M.V.]

137–138 Poems [two]   Honor Wyatt
139–144 A Story (Poor Adam)   Katherine Burdekin
145–147 Poems [three]   Robert Graves
161   A Poem   Ward Hutchinson
162–189 A Film Scenario (Fantasia of Life) [1–11]   Laura Riding
190–191 Poems [three]   Alan Hodge
        Marginal Themes
193–207 **The Bull Fight** [1–2]   Laura Riding
        [4 endnotes: no. 3 signed M.V., no. 4 signed L.R.]
208–220 *Lucretius and Jeans*   Robert Graves
221–230 **The Literary Intelligence** [1–2] Laura Riding
231–242 **Neo-Georgian Eternity**   Robert Graves
243–249 **George Sand**   Madeleine Vara
        [incl. transl. of 4 tales from *Contes D'Une Grand'mere*]
250–252 Poems [three]   Laura Riding

EPILOGUE: A Critical Summary; volume III – Spring 1937
Editor: Laura Riding / Associate Editor: Robert Graves
Contributors to this issue:
Madeleine Vara / Alan Hodge / Norman Cameron / Honor Wyatt /
Sally Graves / Karl Goldschmidt / Basil Taylor / Robin Hale / Lucie
Brown / John Aldridge / William Archer / Harry Kemp / Laura
Riding / Robert Graves / Ward Hutchinson / Thomas Matthews /
James Reeves

1–5   The End of the World, and After   Laura Riding
6–53   *Politics and Poetry*   Laura Riding, Robert Graves,
                                Harry Kemp, Alan Hodge, Madeleine Vara
        [44–51: 14 endnotes (9 A.H.; 4 H.K.; 1 R.G.);
        51–53: Note on German Poets and Politics, M.V.]
        Homiletic Studies:
54–62   On Praise   Thomas Matthews
63–65   On Generosity   Norman Cameron
66–74   On Courage   Alan Hodge
75–99   The Theme of Fame   Madeleine Vara
100–106 A Story (To Die in a Story)   Honor Wyatt
107–130 **From A Private Correspondence on Reality**
                                Laura Riding and Robert Graves
131–137 Poems [ten]   Harry Kemp
138–139 Poems [two]   Norman Cameron
140–148 Poems [four]   Laura Riding
149–150 Poems [two]   James Reeves

151	Poems [two]	Sally Graves
152–157	Poems [six]	Alan Hodge
158–160	Poems [four]	Ward Hutchinson
161–163	Poems [three]	Robin Hale
164–169	Poems [six]	Robert Graves
170–172	Poems (From India) [three]	William Archer
173–190	Humour and Poetry as Related Themes [1–3]	
		James Reeves and Laura Riding
191–192	The Memory of Basil Taylor	Lucie Brown and John Aldridge
	[4 Taylor plates]	
193–226	*Drama* [1–3]	Laura Riding, Alan Hodge, Robert Graves
227–229	A Letter from England to Majorca	Laura Riding
230–239	Advertising: 1. National Characteristics	Karl Goldschmidt
239–246	2. Book-Advertising	Robert Graves
246–255	3. The Justifications of Advertising	Laura Riding
255–258	4. The Fairy-Tale Element in Advertising	Norman Cameron

INDEX OF NAMES

Andersen, Hans, 159
Aristophanes, 181 n.1
Aristotle, 47, 95

Bach, Johann Sebastian, 43
Bacon, Francis, 70
Baptista Mantuanus, 75
Barclay, Alexander, 73, 74, 75
Barrera, Vicente, 127, 167,
Birkenhead, Lord Frederick, 106–8
Bohr, Niels, 131
Bottomley, Horatio, 81
Brawne, Fanny, 67
Brooke, Rupert, 151
Bryant, William Cullen, 143
Buddha, 15, 34
Butler, Samuel, 149
Byron, George, 61, 68, 144

Chaucer, Geoffrey, 77, 173
Clare, John, 75
Coleridge, Revd George, 61–2
Coleridge, Hartley, 65
Coleridge, Samuel Taylor, 53, 56–7,
    58–65, 183 nn.7–10
Corneille, Pierre, 44
Cummings, E.E., 186 n.18

Dalton, John, 130, 131, 134
Dana, Richard Henry, 143
Dante Alighieri, 70, 141, 145, 146
Democritus, 135
Dillinger, John, 81
Donne, John, 53

Einstein, Albert, 26, 35, 166
Eliot, T.S., 141, 142, 144–6

Empedocles, 135
Epicurus, 135, 137
Evans, Sir Arthur, 186 n.15

Faulkner, William, 124
Forster, E.M., 146, 149–56, 181 n.1
Franklin, Sidney, 127
Frazer, Sir James, 186 n.17
Fuller, Thomas, 95

Gandhi, Mahatma, 41
Godwin, William, 59
Goethe, Johann Wolfgang von, 43, 45,
    146
Googe, Barnabe, 75
Greene, Robert, 76

Händel, George, 43
Hegel, Georg, 45
Heine, Heinrich, 43
Hemingway, Ernest, 123–7
Herodotus, 28
Hiero [n], 72
Homer, 28, 173
Housman, A.E., 149, 151
Hubble, Edwin, 135
Hunt, Leigh, 66

Jacob, 20
Jeans, Sir James, 129–39,
Jesus Christ, 15, 16, 32, 33–4, 55–6,
    87, 117
Joan of Arc, 158
Job, 121–2, 181 n.2,
Joseph, 32
Joshua, 20,

Joyce, James, 17, 21–2, 26, 35, 36, 183, n.6

Keats, John, 56, 66–71, 75, 134, 147, 184 n.10
Kotzebue, August von, 45
Krishnamurti, Jiddu, 41

Lalanda, Marcial, 127
Langland, William, 74, 77
Lawrence, D.H., 17
Lawrence, T.E., 150
Leucippus, 131
Levy, Oscar, 44
Lodge, Thomas, 76
Longfellow, Henry Wadsworth, 142
Lowell, James, 143
Lucretius, 129–39

McLennan, Sir John, 135
Mary, 33-4
Matthew, St, 181 n.3
Maurras, Charles, 145
Millikan, Robert, 135
Milton, John, 70
Molière, 44
Morris, William, 65
Moses, 18–20, 26

Newton, Isaac, 130
Nietzsche, Friedrich, 38–47

Oliphant, 'Mrs' Margaret, 146
Ortega, Domingo, 127–8, 167

Parker, Bonnie, 81
Patrick, St, 23
Peele, George, 76
Poe, Edgar Allan, 140–4, 145
Plato, 28
Ptolemy Philadelphus, 72

Quarles, Francis, 78, 98–9

Racine, Jean, 44
Ranke, Leopold von, 43
Richards, I.A., 52, 146
Rimbaud, Arthur, 129
Rossetti, Dante Gabriel, 65
Rutherford, Arthur, 131

Sand, George, 157–62
Schopenhauer, Arthur, 43
Schütz, Heinrich, 43
Shakespeare, William, 44, 49, 70, 75, 145, 146, 167, 173
Shaw, George Bernard, 20–1, 45
Shelley, Mary, 71
Shelley, Percy Bysshe, 53, 56, 61, 66–71, 184 n.11
Sidney, Philip, 77
Sikes, J.G., 109–12
Skelton, John, 75, 77
Socrates, 36
Sorley, Charles, 151, 153, 175
Southey, Robert, 58, 59, 62–3, 65
Spenser, Edmund, 56, 77, 184 n.12
Stedman, Edmund, 143
Stein, Gertrude, 7, 26
Stephens, James, 23

Tacitus, 38, 40, 41, 46, 47
Tagore, Rabindranath, 41
Tennyson, Alfred, 174
Theocritus, 72, 75

Vallon, Annette, 58, 63
Virgil, 72–3, 75

Wagner, Richard, 43
Woodhouse, Richard, 70
Woolf, Virginia, 181 n.1
Wordsworth, Dorothy, 61, 63
Wordsworth, William, 56–7, 58–65, 183 n.8, 184 n.10

Yeats, William Butler, 53